Pioneering Ascents

Pioneering Ascents

The Origins of Climbing in America, 1642–1873

David Mazel, Editor

STACKPOLE
BOOKS

Published by
STACKPOLE BOOKS
Cameron and Kelker Streets
P.O. Box 1831
Harrisburg, PA 17105

Printed in the United States of America
10 9 8 7 6 5 4 3 2 1
First Edition

Cover illustration: Crawford Notch in the White Mountains, by Harry Fenn
Cover design by Caroline Miller
Interior design by Marcia Lee Dobbs

The chapter on Charles Preuss was excerpted from *Exploring with Frémont:
The Private Diaries of Charles Preuss, Cartographer for John C. Frémont on His First, Second,
and Fourth Expeditions to the Far West,* translated and edited by Erwin G. and Elisabeth
K. Gudda. Copyright © 1958, 1986 by the University of Oklahoma Press.

The chapter on William Brewer was excerpted from *Up and Down in California in
1860–1864,* edited by Francis Farquhar. Reprinted by permission of the University of
California Press.

The chapter on John Muir in the Minarets and on Matterhorn Peak was excerpted
from *John of the Mountains: The Unpublished Journals of John Muir,* edited by Linnie
Marsh Wolfe. Copyright © 1938 by Wanda Muir Hanna. Copyright renewed 1966
by John Muir Hanna and Ralph Eugene Wolfe. Reprinted by permission of
Houghton Mifflin Company.

Library of Congress Cataloging-in-Publication Data

Pioneering ascents : the origins of climbing in America, 1642–1873 /
    David Mazel, editor. — 1st ed.
        p.   cm.
    Accounts reprinted from various old sources.
    Includes bibliographical references.
    ISBN 0-8117-3045-X
    1. Mountaineering — United States — History.   2. Mountaineers —
United States — Biography.   I. Mazel, David.
GV199.4.P56 1991
796.5'22 — dc20   90-48443
                                                                                                      CIP

Dedicated to Annie Troncoso-Mazel,
who made it all worthwhile.

Contents

Preface   1

Introduction   3

Prelude: From William Bradford's *History of Plymouth Plantation,* 1620   10

Darby Field Climbs Mount Washington, 1642   12

John Josselyn Climbs Mount Washington, between 1663 and 1671   16

John Lederer Reaches "the Top of the Apalataean Mountains," 1669 and 1670   18

Robert Fallam Crosses the Blue Ridge, 1671   21

Mark Catesby in the Southern Appalachians, 1714   23

Alexander Spotswood Climbs "Mount George," 1716   26

William Byrd in the Blue Ridge Mountains, 1728   37

John Brickell Visits the "Charokee Mountains," 1730   44

William Bartram Climbs Oconee Mountain and Mount Magnolia, 1776   49

Jeremy Belknap on Mount Washington, 1784   54

André Michaux Climbs Roan Mountain in the Unaka Mountains, 1795   61

Charles Turner Climbs Katahdin, 1804   65

Zebulon Pike Attempts Pikes Peak, 1806   69

Edwin James Climbs Pikes Peak, 1820   73

An Anonymous Ascent of Mount Washington, 1825   81

Benjamin Bonneville in the Wind River Range, 1833   88

Zenas Leonard Crosses the Sierra Nevada, 1833   94

Elisha Mitchell Climbs Mount Mitchell, 1835   101

William Redfield Climbs Mount Marcy, 1837   105

John Charles Frémont Climbs Frémont Peak, 1842   113

Charles Preuss on Frémont Peak, 1842   125

Henry David Thoreau Climbs Wachusett, 1842   136

Thoreau Climbs Greylock, 1844   142

Thoreau Attempts Katahdin, 1846   148

Sidney Ford Attempts Mount Rainier, 1852   156

T. J. Dryer Climbs Mount Saint Helens, 1853   159

T. J. Dryer Attempts Mount Hood, 1854   165

A. C. Isaacs Attempts Mount Shasta, 1856   175

Julia Archibald Holmes Climbs Pikes Peak, 1858   179

William Brewer Climbs Lassen Peak and Mount
Brewer, and Attempts Mount Goddard, 1863–64   184

Clarence King and Richard Cotter Climb Mount
Tyndall, 1864   192

George Davidson Climbs Makushin, 1867   221

William N. Byers Climbs Longs Peak, 1868   227

John Muir Climbs Mount Ritter, 1871   232

John Muir in the Minarets and on Matterhorn
Peak, 1873   248

Selected Bibliography   255

Key to Illustrations   261

Preface

EVERY SPORT HAS a history and literature of its own. Certainly mountaineering is no exception; most climbers I know spend as much time reading about mountains as they do climbing them, and their concern with who was the first to make a particular ascent leads naturally to an interest in the history of the sport. My own interest in the subject began in precisely this way, and intensified when I took a job with Norlin Library at the University of Colorado – a library that just happens to have one of the finest collections of mountaineering books in the world. My interest deepened further when I left that job to become editor of a modest journal devoted to the history and literature of the sport.

Like others before me, I was aware of what seemed to be an almost total lack of climbing in America before the late 1800s. As a library assistant and editor, however, I found scattered references to long-forgotten mountain ascents and began to suspect that American mountaineering had deeper roots than had been thought. I began to collect the accounts I found, and tried to learn something about their authors, our earliest recorded mountaineers. The result is this anthology, which contains many – by no means all – of the mountaineering stories that turned up in my search for the origins of American climbing.

With perhaps a few exceptions, none of the early mountain explorers in this book were "alpinists," as that term has come to be understood. They did not make their ascents primarily for the sport of it. Of course, alpinists are not the only ones who climb mountains, or who enjoy them and write about them. The mountaineers whose writings make up this anthology were botanists, explorers, traders, writers, surveyors, and geologists, and their stories are as varied as their reasons for being in the mountains. Often, in fact, their writing is more vivid and original than that of the genuine alpinists who succeeded them – many of whom wrote, and still write, about their ascents using the sort of jargon and clichés that plague every specialized activity.

Because the authors of these accounts were not primarily mountaineers, assembling this collection involved more than simply looking under "mountaineering" at the local library. In fact, locating these accounts involved a fair amount of detective work, and I was glad for the assistance of a number of librarians. For the loan of text material and period illustrations, as well as for other assistance, I would particularly like to thank the following: Nora Quinlan, Carol Klemme, Virginia Boucher, Phyllis Hunt, and the late Wally Carson of the Special Collections Department of the University of Colorado, Boulder, Libraries; James Hemesath, Betty Dorney, Christine Moeny, Shannon Patterson, Gwen Gregory, Lynn Layton and Judy Carlson of the Adams State College Library; Rick J. Ashton, Lisa Backman and Eleanor M. Gehres of the Denver Public Library; Nicholas Noyes of the Maine Historical Society; Alden Moberg of the Oregon State Library; Joseph G. Swinyer of the Special Collections Department at the State University of New York, College at Plattsburgh; and Jerold Pepper of the Museum Library of the Adirondack Historical Association.

Many others had a hand in preparing this book. Peter Green photographed period artwork from a variety of sources for use as illustrations. Willie Montoya made it possible for me to use the computer resources of Adams State College. Samantha Cortés and Brett Howard helped transcribe and type material, some of it in the form of nearly illegible photocopies. The University of California Press, Houghton Mifflin Company, Denver Public Library, and University of Oklahoma Press allowed me to reprint copyrighted material. Sanford and Jeannine Mazel lent encouragement throughout, as did Cole Foster, Sue Ann Betsinger, Richard Joyce, and Barry Greer. My wife, Annette Troncoso-Mazel, not only supported me financially but emotionally as well, and made the whole effort worthwhile.

I am also indebted to numerous authors and historians whom space did not always permit me to acknowledge in the text. The writings and bibliographies of Laura and Guy Waterman, William Howarth, Phillip G. Terrie, Thomas L. Connelly, James Henry McIntosh, Aubrey Haines, Roderick Peattie, Lito Tejada-Flores, Michael Frome, Russell M. L. Carson, Paul Schullery, and Chris Jones pointed to many of the accounts excerpted herein, as did the work of one of their predecessors, the late Allen H. Bent. Finally, the late Francis Farquhar, whose ashes were scattered from the summit of a 14,040-foot Sierra peak called the Middle Palisade and whose lively *History of the Sierra Nevada* I read repeatedly as a teenager, is probably as responsible as anyone for my undertaking this project.

David Mazel
Alamosa, Colorado
June 1990

Introduction

FROM THE VERY BEGINNING, mountains loomed on the horizon of the American pioneer. Mount Washington, visible from miles out at sea, was known to Europeans before they settled here at all, the mariners John and Sebastian Cabot having sighted its snow-covered crest as early as the winter of 1497. Verrazano, exploring the New England coast in 1508 and again in 1524, wrote in his log of "high mountains within the land," and a century later Champlain sighted the Green Mountains and placed them prominently on his map of New France. For many who came afterward across the Atlantic, these high outliers of the Appalachians must have been the first glimpse of the New World. For a time they were the outer boundary of the world those early settlers created there, a barrier at first, but not too much later a challenge to be transcended. When the Appalachians had been crossed, the Rockies bulked in their stead, as did the Sierra Nevada and the Cascades in turn. When the latter had been breached there was only the Pacific Ocean, and a chapter in the nation's history closed forever.

The mountains were there from the beginning, in consciousness as well as in fact, yet America never developed a mountain-climbing tradition to rival that of Europe. In the century after the birth of alpinism – generally given as 1786, the year of the first ascent of Mont Blanc – European climbers had ascended not only Mont Blanc but also Monte Rosa, the Matterhorn, and scores of less famous peaks. They had also, in the course of chronicling their exploits, produced a rich and varied literature. But in America no such tradition was evident. A visiting Englishman, E. T. Coleman, writing in 1877 to his fellows in the Alpine Club, observed little enthusiasm here for mountains, a circumstance he attributed to hard-headed Yankee practicality:

> The absorbing pursuit of money, the strangely practical character of the American mind, so averse to anything merely visionary, are quite sufficient to account for the absence of that *passion des montagnes* which is so often to be met with in older communities . . . Those who come out to the Western States do so either to make money, or to build up a home for themselves and families; conse-

3

quently they have neither the time nor the money to spend in what is generally considered to be a visionary, if not a foolhardy, pursuit.

It would not be long before Americans *did* have the time and money for leisure pursuits, and something like European-style mountaineering gradually grew in popularity. By the early twentieth century there were mountain clubs headquartered in New York, Boston, Denver, San Francisco, and Seattle. But even so another Englishman, Chris Jones, arriving in this country a full century after Coleman, could still remark on the absence of any sense of history or tradition in American climbing. America's mountains to him "were superb, but they seemed strangely empty," largely because he had no idea who had climbed there before him. By then the history of British and Alpine climbing had been set down in scores of volumes, but that of America in none – an inequity Jones hoped to correct with his own book, *Climbing in North America*.

Jones's work was the first, and is still the only, attempt at a comprehensive history of American climbing. Unfortunately, though it admirably chronicles the development of the sport in the twentieth century, it devotes just a few pages to its earlier history. Both Coleman and Jones were among the leading climbers of their day, and they naturally took an insider's view of what constitutes "mountaineering" – a sport engaged in for its own sake and involving a substantial amount of challenge and technical difficulty. If one accepts that rather narrow definition of climbing, then there were indeed few American mountaineers before the late 1800s. For the purposes of this book, however, I have taken a layman's view, and am willing to call a "mountain climber" anyone who climbs up a mountain, regardless of the difficulty of the feat or the motivations underlying it. What I discovered, after reading the accounts of dozens of mountain-climbing explorers, scientists, surveyors, and others, was that a uniquely American mountaineering tradition did in fact exist, though it was so different from the Alpine version that Coleman would not have recognized it as such. It was not, as in Europe, a highly specialized sport practiced by a close-knit fraternity hewing to a complex set of rules. Instead it was a quintessentially American activity, a natural offshoot of the exploration of a new and strikingly beautiful continent. This early American climbing was never as technically advanced as its European cousin, but it was much older, having begun, as this anthology demonstrates, more than a century before the first ascent of Mont Blanc.

This collection, I hope, will serve as a window into both the history and the literature of American mountaineering. As literature, it includes the earliest examples of a genre that in modern times has grown vigorous enough to support a number of specialized periodicals and anthologies. As history, it charts one aspect of American discovery and western movement, of a people coming to know its land and itself. It is also a record of an evolving attitude toward the mountains, an attitude merely indifferent in the beginning, but later so enthusiastic that America would set an example for the world by enshrining its finest mountain areas in the national parks.

The earliest American settlers – particularly the New England Puritans, as the Bradford account in this collection indicates – were not notably interested in the peaks on their horizon. Struggling simply to survive, they had neither time nor energy to spare for climbing mountains, and there had as yet been no Romantic Movement to suggest that doing so could be anything but dangerous and dismal. To the extent that they thought of mountains at all, these earliest settlers might logically have supposed them to be inaccessible, cold, the haunt of Indians of unknown demeanor. The wonder is that climbs were made as soon as they were – in 1642, in the case of Mount Washington, and possibly in 1669 or 1671 in the case of the southern Appalachians. We cannot be sure of what motivated the earliest climbers, but simple curiosity certainly played a part. Darby Field may have been searching for the diamonds rumored to exist on the summit of Mount Washington, but that does not explain why so many others repeated the climb so soon after he returned with a negative report. John Lederer and Robert Fallam, perhaps the first colonists to explore the southern Appalachians, were paid to look for trade routes to the interior; they were motivated primarily by profit, but their missions certainly could have been accomplished without climbing as high as they seem to have done. Did they ascend to the "tops" of the mountains merely to survey the route across, or were they driven by something less practical?

Later climbing accounts more clearly show a genuine enthusiasm for the mountains themselves. The development of that enthusiasm – what might be called the early American version of Coleman's "mountain passion" – seems to have followed two distinct paths. One, which can be traced in this anthology through the accounts of Lederer and Fallam and the later Western explorers Pike, Bonneville, and Frémont, is closely allied with Manifest Destiny, the belief that America's westward expansion was not only inevitable, but sanctioned by Providence. Climbers who shared this view – many in this book did not – could perhaps believe it most fervently while on top of a high mountain, gazing down on vast reaches of new territory awaiting annexation into a growing nation and at the same time experiencing the religious impulse so often felt in high places. For such climbers the act of conquering a mountain, useless in itself, had value as a sort of mental rehearsal for conquering the territory below. Certainly this was the case for Alexander Spotswood, a colonial Virginia governor for whom the 1716 ascent of a modest peak in the Blue Ridge provided a moving vision of an expansive and prosperous future:

> For hours the old veteran chief sat on the identical spot which he first occupied, drinking in rapture from the vision which he beheld . . . There lay the valley of Virginia, that garden spot of the earth, in its first freshness and purity, as it came from the hands of its Maker . . . Who could look upon it, as it spread out far to the east and west, until it was lost in the dim and hazy horizon, and not feel deeply impressed with the Majesty of its Author?
>
> Governor Spotswood carried his thoughts into the future, and imagined the fine country which he beheld, peopled and glowing under the hands of husbandmen, and all his bright anticipations were more than realized.

Manifest Destiny also informs what many feel is the greatest classic of American mountaineering literature, Clarence King's *Mountaineering in the Sierra Nevada*. Mountains, with their high tops and pyramidal shape, were for King a natural symbol of hierarchy and achievement, both for the country in which they rise and for the men and women who climb them. Mountains were a reminder for him that both men and nations ought to rise to their greatest potential, and it is not surprising that King was the principal player in the competition for the first ascent of Mount Whitney, the highest point of the continental United States. For him, as for Spotswood, mountaineering was a contest, a distillation of personal ambition and the acquisitive, territorial spirit of Manifest Destiny.

Not all the climbers in this book saw the mountains as stepping stones to national or personal ascendancy. What might be called a dissenting view – one in which mountains were admired primarily for their own beauty and for the powerful effect they could have on the climber – developed early, being clearly seen first in writers such as Mark Catesby, who probably never actually climbed a peak but whose descriptions of the southern Appalachians show a genuine interest in their structure and natural history. William Bartram, whose journals influenced such poets as Coleridge and Wordsworth, sat squarely in this Romantic tradition; he went to the mountains not as the vanguard of a conquering nation but solely to see what they had to show him. This view reached its fullest expression in the mountain writings of Henry David Thoreau and John Muir. Thoreau – whose climbing was modest compared to his literary achievement – wrote at times from the standpoint of the scientist and at times from that of the philosopher. He observed clearly both the mountains themselves and the profound effects they can have on those who climb them, so that even his climbing essays are as much about men as mountains. Muir, the lesser writer, was the better mountaineer; certainly none of the writers in this book climbed as many mountains as he, or knew them better, or helped us to know them so well. More than any other American of his time, Muir was fired by something comparable to Coleman's *passion des montagnes*, and when he retired from climbing that passion continued to work in him, driving him to become a founder of the Sierra Club and to fight for the preservation of forest and mountain areas. To the extent that this second strain of American mountaineering influenced John Muir, it can be considered a root not only of a style of climbing, but also of the modern environmental movement.

The period covered by this anthology, 1642 to 1873, is in some ways arbitrary. Mountaineering in the New World actually started much earlier, with its native inhabitants. Well before the arrival of Pizarro, the Incas had already climbed Andean peaks as high as 22,000 feet, and in western North America, pre-Columbian artifacts have occasionally been found on 14,000-foot summits. Presumably, none of these Native American ascents was recorded at the time in writing, though some of them may be celebrated in folklore. The first European to climb a high peak in North America was Diego de Ordaz, who, in search of sulphur for the arsenal of the conquistador Cortez, ascended to the summit crater of the Mexican volcano Popocatepetl in 1519. The first Europeans to encounter mountains in what would become the Thirteen Colonies were the six hundred members of the 1540 expedition led by Hernando de Soto, who penetrated the southern Appalachians with the hope of stumbling across the same sort of luck that had befallen Pizarro and Cortez. De Soto's route is not known for certain, but he may have traveled through Hickory Nut Gap to the French Broad River in Tennessee and then southward into the complicated Toxaway region, among whose peaks he was for a time quite bewildered. A quarter century later another Spaniard, one Juan Pardo, set out from the North Carolina coast toward the Blue Ridge. With him he had just thirty men, and his orders were "to discover and conquer the interior country from there to Mexico." Unfortunately for him, the Cherokee Indians proved more resistant to conquest than either the Incas or the Aztecs; Pardo failed to cross the mountains, and, after returning the following year for a second attempt, disappeared completely. These early forays are not included in this collection because the Spanish chroniclers of the day were largely mute on the subject of mountains, and because there is little reason to suppose that any of these Spaniards ever actually reached a mountaintop.

It seemed most logical to begin this anthology with the first recorded mountain ascent, by a European, in territory that is now the United States – the 1642 ascent of Mount Washington by Darby Field. Choosing an appropriate cutoff date was not so easy. I chose the year 1873 for two reasons. First, it allowed me to include two accounts that many regard as America's finest mountaineering stories, Clarence King's "Ascent of Mount Tyndall" and John Muir's "A Near View of the High Sierra." Second, it seems to me that American mountaineering began to undergo a fundamental change about that time. It was in 1873 that Mount Whitney was finally climbed. Whitney is the highest point in the continental United States, and Clarence King wanted badly to make the first ascent. He tried to climb it twice in 1864 and again in 1871, failing each time. On the 1871 attempt his view was obscured by clouds; King thought he had reached the summit, but in fact had only climbed a nearby peak several hundred feet lower. When informed of his error two years later, he rushed back to the mountains from the East Coast and finally reached the true summit on September 19, 1873 – a month after the first ascent had been made by three vacationing fishermen, who reportedly relished the fact that they had bested the renowned King.

The sort of competition that characterized the Whitney ascent, mild as it was, is entirely lacking in the accounts in this anthology. In the three decades after 1873, by contrast, increasingly rancorous controversies would surround the ascents of Mount Rainier, the Grand Teton, and Mount McKinley. Previously a thoroughly peripheral activity, mountaineering grew increasingly popular and all too often became the object of the sort of publicity and competition that still plague the sport today.

But all that happened later. The accounts that follow are the testament of an earlier era of mountain climbing – less technically advanced, certainly, but also, like the nation itself, more innocent. For that alone they are worth preserving.

Prelude: From William Bradford's *History of Plymouth Plantation*, 1620

WILLIAM BRADFORD, WE can be reasonably sure, never climbed a mountain in his life. But his *History of Plymouth Plantation*, a chronicle of the Pilgrims' voyage to and arrival in the New World, contains what may be the first reference to a mountain in American literature, and is excerpted below as a sort of prelude to the accounts that follow it.

New England in 1620 was for Europeans a raw and dangerous place, and, like most others at the time, Bradford found its wild, mountainous landscape abhorrent. In the *History* he ignored that landscape completely, except for the brief passage excerpted below, in which he seems to bring the subject up solely for religious purposes. He clearly has little interest in the landscape itself, but mentions it in order to invest the Puritan arrival in New England with a biblical significance, comparing the Puritans' flight from Europe with the Jewish Exodus, their landing on the treacherous New England coast with that of the Apostle Paul on the island of Malta, and their struggles in the New World with the forty years' wandering in the wilderness. The landscape is more meaningful to him as metaphor than reality, and it is thus not surprising that the one time he does mention a mountain, it is the biblical Mount Pisgah rather than any actual eminence in New England. Descriptions of the unexplored mountains of the New World would have to wait for a generation more secure on the land and less consumed with religious zeal.

The spelling and punctuation in this selection, as in those that follow, is as in the original.

But hear I cannot but stay and make a pause, and stand half amased at this poor peoples presente condition; and so I thinke will the reader too, when he well considers the same. Being thus passed the vast ocean, and a sea of troubles before in their preparation . . . they had now no freinds to wellcome them, nor inns to entertaine or refresh their weatherbeaten bodys, no houses or much less townes to repaire too, to seeke for succoure. It is recorded in scripture, as a mercie to the apostle & his shipwraked company, that the barbarians shewed them no smale kindnes in refreshing them, but these savage barbarians, when they mette with them . . . were readier to fill their sids full of arrows then otherwise. And for the season it was winter, and they that know the winters of that cuntrie know them to be sharp & violent, & subjecte to cruell & feirce stormes, deangerous to travill to known places, much more to serch an unknown coast. Besids, what could they see but a hidious and deso-late wildernes, full of wild beasts and willd men? and what multituds ther might be of them they knew not. Nether could they, as it were, goe up to the tope of Pisgah, to vew from this willdernes a more goodly cuntrie to feed their hops; for which way soever they turnd their eys (save upward to the heavens) they could have little solace or content in respecte of any outward objects. For sumer being done, all things stand upon them with a wetherbeaten face; and the whole countrie, full of woods & thickets, represented a wild & savage heiw. If they looked behind them, ther was the mighty ocean which they had passed, and was now as a maine barr & goulfe to seperate them from all the civill parts of the world. . . . What could now sustaine them but the spirite of God & his grace?

Darby Field Climbs
Mount Washington, 1642

L ITTLE IS KNOWN about Darby Field, the man generally credited with making the first recorded mountain climb in what is today the United States. We don't even know if the account below was related directly by Field to Massachusetts Governor John Winthrop, from whose journal it is excerpted, or whether it was already a secondhand story when it reached the governor. Winthrop does tell us Field was an Irishman, but the modern Fields who claim to be his descendants say he was an Englishman, born around 1610 in Lincolnshire. He reportedly emigrated to Boston, Massachusetts, in 1636, and later owned an estate at Oyster River, in New Hampshire. In 1638 he relocated to Exeter, where the following year he joined other settlers in signing a governmental agreement known as the "Exeter Combination." Ten years later he moved again, to Dover, New Hampshire, where he is recorded on the tax rolls and where he died in 1649.

The only surviving remnants of Field's Mount Washington climb are two entries in the journal Winthrop kept from 1630 to 1649. (It was not published until 1790; in the interim the original was cared for by, among others, Cotton Mather.) The entry concerning Field, sandwiched between accounts of the day-to-day life of the young colony, is detailed enough that historians have ventured to reconstruct Field's route on the peak: through the valley of the Ellis River, then to the 6,288-foot summit via what is today called Boott Spur, the mountain's great southeastern ridge. Winthrop does not indicate precisely when Field made the climb. One historian claims it was in June, but that seems unlikely. Winthrop's editor dated the first of the journal entries below June 8, 1642, and that entry mentions two ascents, one made "about a month after" the first. Even if it only took a few days for word of the second climb to reach the governor, the first climb could not have taken place much later than the first or second week of May. Given the notoriously bad winter weather on Mount Washington, it is hard to imagine the climb being made very much earlier than that. Winthrop mentions that it was "very cold" and that the climbers ascended on bare rock above "valleys filled with snow," conditions fairly typical following stretches of settled spring weather. Taken together, the evidence argues that Field made the climb in April or May of 1642.

In 1642 the American interior was still very much *terra incognita* to Europeans, so it is not surprising that this account focuses on the more pragmatic aspects of the journey – on distances from the nearest settlement, on the absence of such useful vegetation as trees and grass, on the presence of falls that might impede navigation of the rivers. But Winthrop's journal, sparely written as it is, still gives us a good feel for the ascent. In it we can follow the climbers as they ascend bare rock past stunted trees, as they gain distant views and experience the novel sensation of looking down on the tops of clouds, and as they misjudge distances in the clear air of high altitude (Saco, actually nearly seventy miles away, appears to the climbers "as if it had been 20 miles").

Field climbed the mountain at least twice and, as Winthrop mentions, "divers others" made the ascent that same year. Of those "others" mentioned by name, little is known of Gorge, though he appears to have been Thomas Gorges, a deputy of Sir Ferdinando Gorges, one of the moving forces behind English colonization of the New World. Richard Vines (1585–1651) was an agent of Sir Ferdinando and later a colonial administrator who lived in Saco. Field, Gorges, and Vines, plus the "five or six others" mentioned below, add up to at least eight climbers who made the ascent of Mount Washington in 1642. Those who visit the peak today and deplore the crowds on its top should bear in mind that the climb has been a popular one for more than three centuries.

[June 8, 1642] One Darby Field, an Irishman, living about Pascataquack, being accompanied with two Indians, went to the top of the white hill. He made his journey in 18 days. His relation at his return was, that it was about one hundred miles from Saco, that after 40 miles travel he did, for the most part, ascend, and within 12 miles of the top was neither tree nor grass, but low savins, which they went upon the top of sometimes, but a continual ascent upon rocks, on a ridge between two valleys filled with snow, out of which came two branches of Saco river, which met at the foot of the hill where was an Indian town of some 200 people. Some of them accompanied him within 8 miles of the top, but durst go no further, telling him that no Indian ever dared to go higher, and that he would die if he went. So they staid there till his return, and his two Indians took courage by his example and went with him. They went divers time through the thick clouds for a good space, and within 4 miles of the top they had no clouds, but very cold. By the way, among the rocks, there were two ponds, one a blackish water and the other reddish. The top of all was plain about 60 feet square. On the north side there was such a

precipice, as they could scarce discern to the bottom. They had neither cloud nor wind on the top, and moderate heat. All the country about him seemed a level, except here and there a hill rising above the rest, but far beneath them. He saw to the north a great water which he judged to be about 100 miles broad, but could see no land beyond it. The sea by Saco seemed as if it had been within 20 miles. He saw also a sea to the eastward, which he judged to be the gulf of Canada: he saw some great waters in parts to the westward, which he judged to be the great lake which Canada River comes out of. He found there much muscovy glass [probably mica], they could rive out pieces of 40 feet long and 7 or 8 broad. When he came back to the Indians, he found them drying themselves by the fire, for they had a great tempest of wind and rain. About a month after he went again with five or six in his company, then they had some wind on the top, and some clouds above them which hid the sun. They brought some stones which they supposed had been diamonds, but they were most crystal.

———————— ▲ ————————

[October 6(?), 1642] Mention is made before of the white hills, discovered by one Darby Field. The report he brought of shining stones, etc., caused divers others to travel thither, but they found nothing worth their pains. Amongst others, Mr. Gorge and Mr. Vines, two of the magistrates of Sir Ferdinand Gorge his province, went thither about the end of this month [the end of September?]. They went up Saco River in birch canoes, and that way, they found it 90 miles to Pegwagget, an Indian town, but by land it is but 60. Upon Saco River, they found many thousand acres of rich meadow, but there are ten falls, which hinder boats, etc. From the Indian town, they went up hill (for the most part) about 30 miles in woody lands, then they went about 7 or 8 miles upon shattered rocks, without tree or grass, very steep all the way. At the top is a plain about 3 or 4 miles over, all shattered stones, and atop that is another rock or spire, about a mile in height, and about an acre of ground at the top. At the top of the plain arise four great rivers, each of them so much water, at the first issue, as would drive a mill; Connecticut river from two heads, at the N.W. and S.W. which join in one about 60 miles off, Saco river on the S.E., Amascoggen which runs into Casco Bay at the N.E., and Kennebeck, at the N. by E. The mountain runs E. and W. 30 or 40 miles, but the peak is above all the rest. They went and returned in 15 days.

John Josselyn Climbs Mount Washington, between 1663 and 1671

J OHN JOSSELYN, A native of Essex, England, first sailed for New England for a year-long visit in 1638. He came back in 1663 and lived for several years with his brother Henry, who had settled in the hamlet of Scarborough. In December 1671 he returned to England for good and proceeded to write two books about his experiences in the New World – *An Account of Two Voyages to New-England* and *New Englands Rarities Discovered.* Sometime during his second sojourn he made the ascent of Mount Washington described in the selection below. Just when is not certain; at least one researcher feels it was in 1663, but as Josselyn did not arrive in Scarborough until August 15 of that year, this seems a little unlikely.

Several things are interesting in this short account. In 1671, Josselyn already had what today might be called a degree of ecological awareness, a sensitivity to the interrelatedness of different parts of the landscape. He relates, for example, Mount Washington's gullies to the erosive action of "dissolved snow," though it is not clear whether he is referring thereby to avalanches, running water or something else. Similarly, he attributes the appearance of a great column of vapor to the action of sunlight on a lake – a notion that recalls the ancient idea of the *axis mundi,* the mysterious link between earth and the heavens. Also notable is the fact that Josselyn twice mentions how the terrain forced him to adopt a sort of "climbing technique," first using the shrubbery for support and later ascending "as if going up a pair of stairs." Thus does Josselyn let us know he was not merely walking, but climbing a mountain.

The selection below is excerpted from *New Englands Rarities Discovered,* first published in London in 1672.

Fourscore miles (upon a direct line) to the Northwest of *Scarborow,* a Ridge of Mountains runs Northwest and Northeast an hundred Leagues, known by the name of the *White Mountains,* upon which lieth Snow all the year, and is a Land-mark twenty miles off at Sea. It is rising ground from the Sea shore to these Hills, and they are inaccessible but by the Gullies which the dissolved Snow hath made; in these Gullies grow *Saven* Bushes, which being taken hold

of are a good help to the climbing Discoverer; upon the top of the highest of these Mountains is a large Level or Plain of a day's journey over, whereon nothing grows but Moss; at the farther end of this Plain is another Hill called the *Sugar-loaf,* to outward appearance a rude heap of massie stones piled one upon another, and you may as you ascend step from one stone to another, as if you were going up a pair of stairs, but winding still about the Hill till you come to the top, which will require half a days time, and yet it is not above a Mile, where there is also a Level of about an Acre of ground, with a pond of clear water in the midst of it; which you may hear run down, but how it ascends is a mystery. From this rocky Hill you may see the whole Country round about; it is far above the lower Clouds, and from hence we beheld a Vapour (like a great Pillar) drawn up by the Sun Beams out of a great Lake or Pond into the Air, where it was formed into a Cloud. The Country beyond these Hills Northward is daunting terrible, being full of rocky Hills, as thick as Mole-hills in a Meadow, and cloathed with infinite thick Woods.

John Lederer Reaches "the Top of the Apalataean Mountains," 1669 and 1670

A S WITH DARBY Field, little is known of the origins and early life of John Lederer. He was a German by birth, a physician, and apparently an accomplished traveler. In 1669, while in the young colony of Virginia, he was commissioned to find a route over the Appalachian Mountains to the headwaters of the Ohio River, where the French had imperial ambitions that rivalled England's. Lederer never made it completely across the range, though on two of his three attempts he probably succeeded in reaching the crest of the Blue Ridge. Shortly afterward he left Virginia for Maryland, where his friend William Talbot prepared an account of Lederer's travels for publication. The resulting volume, *The Discoveries of John Lederer*, was published in London in 1672 and is the source of the excerpts below.

Whether Lederer's feats constitute "mountain climbing" is left to the reader to decide. It is possible he never reached any mountaintops at all, but only ascended to high gaps in the range. In each of the two accounts excerpted below, however, his wording seems to indicate that he was atop a mountain – that is, if we can trust his word at all, which some historians are reluctant to do, since Lederer's writing is frequently marked by exaggerations and outright falsehoods. At one point in his narrative Lederer reports encountering silver tomahawks, huge lakes, and expansive deserts where clearly none exist. Elsewhere, he strains belief when he complains of "intense cold" on the twenty-sixth of August. One historian has even gone so far as to compare Lederer's accounts to the fantastic tales of Baron Münchhausen.

On the other hand, some of Lederer's purported "exaggerations" may be nothing of the sort. It is hardly likely that he saw, from the distant Blue Ridge, "the Atlantick-Ocean washing the Virginian-shore," but the claim may have been an honest mistake, made upon seeing the eastern horizon blend imperceptibly into blue haze. His assertion that at one point the terrain was steep enough to make his head swim has been cited as another tall tale, but it may in fact have been the natural response of a seventeenth-century Tidelander unused to mountain country. At any rate, there is little reason to doubt his claim of reaching the crest of the Blue Ridge. Had he consciously wished to embellish his accomplishment, it would have made far more sense to claim he'd gone all the way *across* the mountains, as in fact he had been commissioned to do.

Upon the ninth of March, 1669, (with three Indians whose names were Magtakunh, Hopottoguoh and Naunnugh) I went out at the falls of Pemaeoncock, alias York-River in Virginia, from an Indian village called Shickehamany, and lay that night in the woods, encountring nothing remarkable, but a rattle-snake of extraordinary length and thickness, for I judged it two yards and a half or better from head to tail, and as big about as a mans arm . . .

The fourteenth of March, from the top of an eminent hill, I first descried the Apalataean mountains, bearing due west to the place I stood upon: their distance from me was so great, that I could hardly discern whether they were mountains or clouds, until my Indian fellow-travellers prostrating themselves in adoration, howled out after a barbarous manner, *Okée poeze* i.e. God is nigh.

The fifteenth of March, not far from this hill, passing over the South-branch of Rappahanock-river, I was almost swallowed in a quicksand. Great

herds of red and fallow deer I daily saw feeding; and on the hill-sides, bears crashing mast like swine. Small leopards I have seen in the woods, but never any lions, though their skins are much worn by the Indians. The wolves in these parts are so ravenous, that I often in the night feared my horse would be devoured by them, they would gather up and howl so close round about him, though tethr'd to the same tree at whose foot I my self and the Indians lay: but the fires which we made, I suppose, scared them from worrying us all. Beaver and otter I met with at every river that I passed; and the woods are full of grey foxes.

Thus I travelled all the sixteenth; and on the seventeenth of March I reached the Apalataei. The air here is very thick and chill; and the waters issuing from the mountain-sides, of a blue color, and allumish taste.

The eighteenth of March, after I had in vain assayed to ride up, I alighted, and left my horse with one of the Indians, whilst with the other two I climbed up the rocks, which were so incumbred with bushes and brambles, that the ascent proved very difficult: besides the first precipice was so steep, that if I lookt down I was immediately taken with a swimming in my head; though afterwards the way was more easie. The height of this mountain was very extraordinary: for notwithstanding I set out with the first appearance of light, it was late in the evening before I gained the top, from whence the next morning I had a beautiful prospect of the Atlantick-Ocean washing the Virginian-shore; but to the north and west, my sight was suddenly bounded by mountains higher than that I stood upon. Here did I wander in snow, for the most part, till the four and twentieth day of March, hoping to find some passage through the mountains; but the coldness of the air and earth together, seizing my hands and feet with numbness, put me to a *ne plus ultra*; and therefore having found my Indian at the foot of the mountain with my horse, I returned back by the same way that I went.

———————— ▲ ————————

The six and twentieth of August [1670] we came to the mountains, where finding no horseway up, we alighted, and left our horses with two or three Indians below, whilst we went up afoot. The ascent was so steep, the cold so intense, and we so tired, that having with much ado gained the top of one of the highest, we drank the kings health in brandy, gave the mountain his name, and agreed to turn back again, having no encouragement from that prospect to proceed to a further discovery; since from hence we saw another mountain, bearing north and west to us, of a prodigious height . . . we unanimously agreed to return back, seeing no possibility of passing through the mountains: and finding our Indians with our horses in the place where we left them, we rode homewards without making any further discovery.

Robert Fallam Crosses the Blue Ridge, 1671

TWO YEARS AFTER John Lederer's unsuccessful attempts to reach the waters of the Ohio, the governor of Virginia, William Berkeley, sent out another expedition on the same mission. This party, which consisted of colonists Thomas Batts, Thomas Wood and Robert Fallam, accompanied by an Appomattox Indian named Perecute, succeeded in making the first recorded crossing of the Appalachians, thereby helping solidify England's claim to the interior of the continent. Theirs was only the first *recorded* crossing, however; the initials "M.A N I," mentioned by Fallam early in the expedition, were seen by the explorers on both sides of the mountains, indicating that someone had preceded them. Just who might have done so, however, is unknown.

Fallam kept a terse journal during the expedition. The following excerpt is from a copy made by one John Clayton about fifteen years after the fact and read before the Royal Society in London in 1688.

Sept. 8. We set out by sunrise and Travelled all day a west and by north course. About one of the clock we came to a Tree mark'd in the past with a coal M.A N I. About four of the clock we came to the foot of the first mountain went to the top and then came to small descent, and so did rise again and then till we came almost to the bottom was a very steep descent. We travelled all day over very stony, rocky ground and after thirty miles travill this day we came to our quarters at the foot of the mountains due west. We past the Sapony River twice this day.

Sept. 9. We were stirring with the Sun and travelled west and after a little riding came again to the Supany River where it was very narrow, and ascended the second mountain which wound up west and by south with several springs and fallings, after which we came to a steep descent at the foot whereof was a lovely descending Valley about six miles over with curious small risings. Our course over it was southwest. After we were over that, we came to a very steep descent, at the foot whereof stood the Tetera Town [near present-day Salem, Va.] in a very rich swamp between a branch and the main River of Roanoke circled about with mountains. We got thither about three of the clock after we had travelled twenty-five miles. Here we were exceedingly civilly entertain'd.

Saturday night, Sunday and monday [September 9, 10 and 11] we staid at the Toteras. Perceute [sic] being taken very sick of a fever and ague every afternoon, notwithstanding on tuesday morning about nine of the clock we resolved to leave our horses with the Toteras and set forward.

Sept. 12. We left the town West and by North we travell'd that day sometimes southerly, sometimes westerly as the path went over several high mountains and steep Vallies crossing several branches and the River Roanoke several times all exceedingly stony ground until about four of the clock Perceute being taken with his fit and verry weary we took up our quarters by the side of the Roanoke River almost at the head of it at the foot of the great mountain. Our course was west by north, having travill'd twenty-five miles. At the Teteras we hired one of their Indians for our Guide and left one of the Apomatock Indians there sick.

Sept. 13. In the morning we set forward early. After we had travelled about three miles we came to the foot of the great mountain and found a very steep ascent so that we could scarse keep ourselves from sliding down again. It continued for three miles with small intermissions of better way. right up by the path on the left we saw the proportions of the mon. When we were got up to the Top of the mountain and set down very weary we saw very high mountains lying to the north and south as far as we could discern. Our course up the mountain was west by north. A very small descent on the other side and as soon as over we found the vallies tending westerly. It was a pleasing tho' dreadful sight to see the mountains and Hills as if piled upon one another. . . .

Mark Catesby in the
Southern Appalachians, 1714

MARK CATESBY, A London-educated naturalist born about 1679, spent a decade in the New World beginning in 1710. The result of that trip and a subsequent, shorter one was his classic *Natural History of Carolina, Florida and the Bahama Islands,* published in England in 1731. The *Natural History* is distinguished both by Catesby's careful observations and by his beautiful color plates, hand-tinted drawings that were precursors of the work of a better-known artist named John James Audubon.

Catesby's account of the southern Appalachians, excerpted below from the *Natural History,* does not mention whether he reached any summits. It reflects the fact that Catesby was both artist and scientist, and is notable for its detailed and precise descriptions as well as for its early ecological consciousness, for the way Catesby notes the linkage between seemingly unrelated phenomena. Presaging the ideas of modern ecology, he saw clearly the relationship between geese and freshwater snails, between chestnuts and bears. The selection ends with an observation on how profoundly mountains can affect the creatures, both human and animal, living beneath them.

The *Apalachian* mountains have their southern beginning near the bay of *Mexico,* in the latitude of 30, extending northerly on the back of the *British* colonies, and running parallel with the sea coast, to the latitude of 40. By this parallel situation of the mountains and sea coast, the distances between the mountains and the maritime parts of most of our colonies of the Continent, must consequently be pretty near equal in the course of their whole extent: but as the geography of these extensive countries is hitherto imperfect, the western distances between the sea and mountains cannot be ascertained, though they are generally said to be above two hundred miles. The lower parts of the country, to about half way towards the mountains, by its low and level situation, differ considerably from those parts above them, the latter abounding with blessings, conducing much more to health and pleasure: but as the maritime parts are much more adapted for commerce, and luxury, these delightful countries are as yet left unpeopled, and possessed by wolves, bears, panthers, and other beasts.

A great part of these mountains are covered with rocks, some of which are of a stupendous height and bulk; the soil between them is generally black and sandy, but in some places differently coloured, and composed of pieces of broken rock, and spar, of a glittering appearance, which seem to be indications of minerals and ores, if proper search was made after them. Fossil coal fit for fuel hath been discovered on Colonel *Byrd's* estate in *Virginia.* Chesnuts and small oaks are the trees that principally grow on these mountains, with some *Chinkapin,* and other smaller shrubs; the grass is thin, mixt with vetch and wild peas; on some other tracts of these mountains is very little vegetable appearance.

▲

In the year 1714 I travelled from the lower part of St. *James's* river in *Virginia* to that part of the *Apalachian* mountains where the sources of that river rise, from which to the head of the *Savannah* river, is about four degrees distance in latitude. As some remarks I then made may serve to illustrate what I have now said, I hope it may not be amiss to recite so much of them as may serve for that purpose.

At sixty miles from the mountains, the river, which fifty miles below was a mile wide, is here contracted to an eighth part, and very shallow, being fordable in many places, and so full of rocks, that by stepping from one to another it was everywhere passable. Here we kill'd plenty of a particularly kind of wild geese; they were very fat by feeding on fresh water snails, which were in great plenty, sticking to the tops and sides of the rocks. The low lands joining to the rivers were vastly rich, shaded with trees that naturally dislike a barren soil, such as black walnut, plane, and oaks of vast stature. This low land stretched along the river many miles, extending back half a mile more or less, and was bounded by a ridge of steep and very lofty rocks, on the top of which we climbed, and could discern some of the nearer mountains, and beheld most delightful prospects, but the country being an entire forest, the meanders of the rivers, with other beauties, were much obscured by the trees. On the back of this ridge of rocks the land was high, rising in broken hills, alternately good and bad. Some miles further the banks of the river on both sides were formed of high perpendicular rocks, with many lesser ones scattered all over the river, between which innumerable torrents of water were continually rushing.

At the distance of twelve miles from the mountains we left the river, and directed our course to the nearest of them. But first we viewed the river, and crossed it several times, admiring its beauties, as well as those of the circumjacent parts. Ascending the higher grounds we had a large prospect of the mountains, as well as of the river below us, which here divided into narrow rocky Channels, and formed many little islands.

So soon as we had left the river, the land grew very rugged and hilly, increasing gradually in height all the way. Arriving at the foot of the first steep hill we pursued a Bear, but he climbing the rocks with much more agility than we, he took his leave. Proceeding further up, we found by many beaten tracts, and dung of bears, that the mountains were much frequented by them, for the sake of chesnuts, with which at this time these mountains abounded.

The rocks of these mountains seem to engross one half of the surface; they are most of a light grey color; some are of a coarse grain'd alabaster, others of a metallic lustre; some pieces were in form of slate and brittle, others in lumps and hard; some appeared with spangles, others thick, sprinkled with innumerable small shining specks like silver, which frequently appeared in stratums at the roots of trees when blown down.

————————— ▲ —————————

The larger rivers in *Carolina* and *Virginia* have their sources in the *Apalachian* mountains, generally springing from rocks and forming cascades and waterfalls in various manners, which being collected in their course, and uniting into single streams, cause abundance of narrow rapid torrents, which falling into the lower grounds, fill unnumerable brooks and rivulets, all which contribute to form and supply the large rivers.

————————— ▲ —————————

The rivers springing from the mountains are liable to great inundations, occasioned not only from the numerous channels feeding them from the mountains, but the height and steepness of their banks, and obstructions of the rocks.

When great rains fall on the mountains, these rapid torrents are very sudden and violent, an instance of which may give a general idea of them, and their ill consequences.

In September 1722, at Fort *Moor,* a little fortress on the *Savannah* river, about midway between the sea and mountains, the waters rose twenty-nine feet in less than forty hours. This proceeded only from what rain fell on the mountains, they at the Fort having had none in that space of time.

It came rushing down the river so suddenly, and with that impetuosity, that it not only destroyed all their grain, but swept away and drowned the cattle belonging to the garrison. Islands were formed, and others joined to the land. And in some places the course of the river was turned. A large and fertile tract of low land, lying on the south side of the river, opposite to the Fort, which was a former settlement of the *Savannah Indians,* was covered with sand three feet in depth, and made unfit for cultivation. This steril land was not carried from the higher grounds, but was washed from the steep banks of the river. Panthers, Bears and Deer were drowned, and found lodged on the limbs of trees.

Alexander Spotswood
Climbs "Mount George," 1716

A LEXANDER SPOTSWOOD BECAME acting governor of Virginia in 1710, by which time pressure on the colony to expand had become more acute than ever. The French were still active around New Orleans and in Canada, and Virginia was beginning to feel cramped as more and more settlers arrived. In the first year of Spotswood's administration he was authorized to send an exploratory expedition westward; this party, like John Lederer, climbed to the crest of the Blue Ridge but did not descend into the Shenandoah Valley below. Six years later a second expedition set out for the transmontane valley, this one led by Spotswood himself. His purpose, as he put it, was to encourage both settlement and trade with the Indians and "to satisfye my Self whether it was practicable to come at the Lakes." (Spotswood, having a wildly inaccurate idea of the location of the Great Lakes, thought the frontier with French Canada was much closer than it was.) The expedition set out in August of 1716, fully equipped with servants, extra horses, and a formidable quantity of libations, and traveling on horseback at a rather leisurely pace of about nine miles per day. On the eighth day out the party reached the base of the mountains. With their axmen clearing the way and only occasionally being forced to dismount, these "gay young cavaliers" climbed to a modest summit and "drank King George's health, and all the Royal Family's, at the very top of the Appalachian Mountains." The summit, dubbed "Mount George" by Spotswood, was not the "highest peak of the Blue Ridge," as the selection below claims, but was probably today's High Top, which overlooks Swift Run Gap near present-day Elkton, Virginia. After the ascent the cavaliers descended into the "Valley of Virginia," rather grandiloquently naming the first stream they encountered there the Euphrates.

Spotswood's expedition did not lead to immediate settlement of the valley and probably had little practical impact on the colony. Yet it became a part of the lore of the Old South as a result of its glorification in *The Knights of the Golden Horse-Shoe*, an early historical romance authored by William Alexander Caruthers and first published in 1841. Caruthers is considered the first important Virginia novelist, and *Knights* is considered the best of his books. It was reprinted several times, elevating Spotswood's rather modest accomplishment – Lederer, after all, had done as much nearly fifty years before – to legendary status. The fictionalized account centers on the expedition itself and the subsequent initiation of the rite of the "Golden Horse Shoe," with Caruthers probably taking his cue from this contemporary description:

> For this Expedition they were obliged to provide a great Quantity of Horse-Shoes; (Things seldom used in the lower Parts of the Country, where there are few Stones:) Upon which Account the Governor upon their Return presented each of his Companions with a Golden Horse-Shoe, (some of which I have seen studded with valuable Stones resembling the Heads of Nails) with this Inscription on the one Side: *Sic juvat transcendere montes* ["Thus does he rejoice to cross the mountains"]: And on the other is written the Tramontane Order.
>
> This he instituted to encourage Gentlemen to venture backwards, and make Discoveries and new Settlements; any Gentleman being entitled to wear this Golden Shoe that can prove his having drunk *His Majesty's Health* upon MOUNT GEORGE.

Caruthers's novel contains a number of exaggerations and errors. The expedition actually took place in 1716, not Caruthers's 1714, and was made up, not of the "army" referred to in the book, but of a total of sixty-three men, most of whom were servants. They suffered no real privations, nor were they attacked by Indians – the "battle" alluded to in the following excerpt is entirely fictional. Historians agree, however, that Caruthers's treatment of Spotswood's character was accurate. The governor, an early exponent of what would later be called Manifest Destiny, was indeed deeply inspired by the idea of crossing the mountains and expanding the colony across the continent, and he skillfully used the drama of the ascent to fire the imagination of his compatriots.

However loosely Caruthers may have played with the facts, his yarn evinces something of the spirit of mountain climbing. It is a better book because of the climbing in it, with the critics agreeing that *Knights* is the best of Caruthers's three novels at least partly because its focus on the mountain journey lends it a unity lacking in the others. And when the author, through his character Kate, says of Spotswood that "his thoughts soar forever over those blue mountains, and that very passion will carry him one day to their summits, and does it not ennoble his character?" we glimpse a man who, however modest his actual climbing, is a true mountaineer in spirit.

After a somewhat rainy and stormy night, the morning broke brightly and beautifully clear. The air was fresh and invigorating, and a long and sound

sleep after the fatigues of the day's march, left the luxurious young cavaliers with elastic and buoyant spirits. The brilliant songsters of the feathered tribes were startled from their first essay by the reveille from the martial instruments. The leaves of the trees were glittering with rain drops, and the autumnal forest flowers bursting into life and beauty with the heat of the morning sun. All nature looked calm and bright and beautiful, and mere existence seemed a pleasure, but it was a pleasure inviting to repose and contemplation.

--------------- ▲ ---------------

The route up to this time had been nearly in a straight line to the mountains, for the river along the banks of which they mainly marched, lay fortunately in that direction; but it became necessary now to diverge to the east, in order to take Germana in their way. It was fully a day's march, or more, out of their route, but such were the Governor's orders, and all obeyed with alacrity.

This day they began to exchange the monotonous pine barrens for forests more genial to the eye. The country, although nearly in a state of nature, was rich in all that pleases the eye and enlivens the heart. For the first time, regular parties were detailed to precede the main body of the troops, and skirt their flanks on each side, for the purpose of hunting. One of them accompanied the scout immediately in front, and it was the Governor's orders that each, in succession, should be under the direction of the veteran woodsman. As Joe predicted, however, they had but poor luck, a single herd of deer was encountered, and they, after a hot pursuit, only lost two of their number. Jarvis told the Governor's aids, at night, that "them everlasting trumpets would have to be spiked, else they would all starve when the provisions ran out."

That night they encamped among the head waters of the Mattapony River, having left the beautiful banks of the Pamunky far in their rear, and accomplished, during the day, even a better journey than on the previous one. All were now in fine spirits, notwithstanding the fortune of the hunting parties, upon which in a short time, not only the fate of the enterprise, but their very lives were to depend. As yet, however, provisions were abundant, without even trenching upon the stores of jerked beef, and hard bread and parched corn laid up in their wagons, and on the backs of their mules. With the young, and the gay, and the thoughtless, sufficient for the day were the evils thereof.

The camp fires were enlivened with many a song and story, and to tell the truth, the sparkling wine cup was not wanting to enliven the festivities of the gay young cavaliers. The novelty of the scene around them had not yet worn off, and bright hope painted to their mental vision more enrapturing beauties and brighter landscapes beyond. The Governor failed not to encourage their glowing anticipations, from his own store of imaginary pictures.

▲

The route to Germana was little varied by adventures or mishaps of any kind; but the country through which they passed was hourly becoming more bold and picturesque, and the scenery more grand and imposing. The land commenced to be what, in the language of the country, is called rolling. It was broken into long wavy or undulating lines, scarcely amounting to a hill, and yet relieving the eye, in a great measure, from the monotony of the dead level tide water country. The romantic and excited youths who surrounded the Governor, were already expressing themselves in raptures at the new views every moment bursting upon their vision. Many of them had never in their lives beheld any thing so lovely. At these raptures the old chief would smile, and sometimes encourage their enthusiasm, but always foretelling them of the Apalachian wonders which they would behold. Indeed, being a native of a bold and mountainous country himself, he longed as much as any of them to feast his eye on the top of a crag, from which he could behold a horizon with mountains piled upon mountains, one behind another, reaching, as it were, to meet the clouds.

▲

Gov. Spotswood was by no means singular in his ardent attachment to his native hills. It has often been remarked how ardent is the attachment to home of every mountaineer, and as this homely feeling is the basis of all true patriotism, it is a feeling to be admired and cherished. Philosophers may wonder why it is that the natives of these cloud capped regions should be more devotedly attached to them, than the tide-landers are to their ocean-washed homes, and they may endeavor to fathom the why and the wherefore, with no more success than hitherto. We simply state the fact from personal experience. It has been our fate to exchange a home, combining the grandest and the loveliest extremes of nature — the green valley and the rugged mountain cliff — the serenest pictures of domestic comfort, in juxtaposition with the wildest ravines and most towering precipices — for one within the reach of old Neptune's everlasting roar — and our heart still yearns towards our native mountains.

▲

Leaving Germana, the course of the expedition was directed for several days in a diagonal line towards the direct route to the mountains. That time brought our adventurers into a region of country such as many of them had never seen before. The land was thickly strewn with rocks, and stones, and pebbles. These were a subject of curiosity and admiration at first, but soon turned to one of annoyance, as will be seen as we progress with our narrative.

Several spurs of mountains stretching in broken lines from the main chain of the Blue Ridge, already presented their formidable barriers before them, and being able to grasp an extended view from their base, they thought that they had already arrived at the long desired point of their journey. Eager were the emulous young cavaliers in their struggles to see who should first lead their followers to the top of these heights, but, alas! they were only destined to meet disappointment, for the same interminable view of broken and rolling country met the view beyond, bounded still by that dim blue outline in the back ground, and seeming rather to recede as they advanced. Hearty was the laughter of the Scout — in which even the Governor joined — as they stood upon the highest summit of the first of them and surveyed with dismay, the mountains piled upon mountains beyond.

Governor Spotswood now, for the first time, began to have clear conceptions of the vast region which lay before him — the difficulties of the undertaking, and the hardships which would have to be endured before he accomplished his design.

—————————— ▲ ——————————

At length the army was again in motion — the horses having recovered the use of their legs, and the riders their spirits. They were now passing thro' a country wholly new, even to the scout, and one of surpassing magnificence and beauty. The forest crowned hills, and the bright sparkling streams tumbling over their rocky beds, succeeded each other with astonishing rapidity, exhibiting some of the finest landscapes in nature.

The general course of the expedition was along the banks of these water courses — supposed to have their rise near or beyond the mountains, but their devious windings were not pursued — so that they often crossed the same stream some twenty times a day, in pursuance of the more direct compass line of the old chief.

Towards night of the first day's march after leaving the "horse-shoe," some twenty miles, the great range of mountains began to appear distinctly in view, so that it was confidently predicted that another day's journey would bring them up to the base.

How gloriously the blue mountains loomed up in the distance to the astonished and delighted gaze of the young Cavaliers, who supposed themselves just ready to grasp the magnificent prize for which they had so long toiled! But as the next day's march drew towards its close, they were very much surprised to find the mountains still apparently as far off, as though they pursued an *ignis fatus* — so delusive were the distances to eyes accustomed so

long to view objects on a dead level. These daily disappointments and vexa-
tions at length, however, began to revive the Governor's youthful experience
and recollection of such things. Still that experience was not exactly in point,
because here, the towering heights were clothed in dense forests, over which
the changing seasons were now throwing the gorgeous drapery of their autumnal hues, so that he was nearly as much at fault as his juniors.

In enthusiastic admiration of the matchless succession of panoramas
which hourly greeted his sight, he was not a whit behind any of them. Often
would he halt his suite, as they preceded the main body over some high hill,
and all, with one voice, would burst out in admiration at the new scenes
presented, sometimes stretching far away into green, secluded valleys, and
then towering up from their very borders into the most majestic and precipitous heights. As they advanced nearer and nearer to the mountains, these
characteristics gradually thickened upon them, until now the army was often
closed up entirely between surrounding hills, and at the other times the front
ranks of the imposing array would be ascending one hill, while the rear guard
was descending another.

───────── ▲ ─────────

Now it so happened, that the tents of the encampment were pitched just
under one of those spurs of the mountains, which they were daily encountering
and which had more than once deceived them with the idea that they had at
last arrived at the foot of the Apalachee. Whether this was the real Blue Ridge,
(for the Blue Ridge and the Alleghanies were then all confounded together,)
they had not yet ascertained, but an incident now occurred which induced
them to believe, that they had at last arrived at the base of the true mountains.
While so many were crowded round the cock pits [cock fights were a nightly
entertainment on the expedition] absorbed in the national amusement, an
astounding crash was heard, like an avalanche coming down the mountains.
Some huge object seemed to be coming directly toward them, bending and
crashing the trees, and tracking its course in sparks of fire. Some thought a
volcanic irruption had occurred, while others supposed it to be an avalanche;
but in far less time, than we have taken to record it, a huge fragment of rock,
weighing several tons, and carrying before it a shower of lesser bodies of the
same sort, came leaping and bounding toward the very spot where the cock pit
was located. Fortunately a large tree stood directly between the crowd and the
track of the fragment, or hundreds would have been instantly killed. As it was,
several were badly hurt by the bursting of the rock and the scattering of its
fragments. Jarvis shouted at once, that it was the Indians, and in a few
moments his sagacity was verified, for the whole side of the mountain seemed
suddenly belted with a ribbon of fire. Appalling as the salutation had been, the

young cavaliers stood lost in admiration at the grand and novel sight, which now saluted their wondering eyes, until roused from their dangerous trance, by the loud and commanding voice of Lee, who was already on horse-back and calling his comrades to arm, by the command of the Governor. When he had drawn them sufficiently away from their dangerous propinquity to the base of the mountains, and while they were speedily mounting, a thought occurred to him, which was productive of the happiest results. He had ordered the camp-fires extinguished, but suddenly countermanded the order and directed them to be furnished with fresh fuel, while he galloped off, to communicate his scheme to the Governor.

He found the veteran already in the saddle, and eager for the contest, which he supposed about to ensue. His first order was to remove the tents and horses away from the base of the mountain, and out of reach of the new sort of artillery with which they were threatened. This was executed with alacrity and promptitude—the opposite side of the plain or valley furnishing an equally commodious site for the encampment and sure protection against the enemy. The next was to extinguish the fires, as before ordered at first, by Frank Lee, but here the latter interposed, and suggested to the Governor to have them burning, and to avoid all signs of the kind at the new camp ground. Scarcely were the tents and horses removed, before the wisdom of this course was made manifest—for the thundering missiles were again heard crashing down the mountain.

Frank also suggested, that a body of volunteers should be sent round the spur or projection from the main body of the mountain, and thus out-flank the enemy, while they were engaged in loosing and hurling down the huge frag-ments of rock. He expressed his belief that such a force, might ascend on foot, before daylight, and either get above them, or hold them in check, while the main body ascended more leisurely with the baggage.

The Governor listened with attention to this scheme and proposed that they should ascend the eminence behind them on the other side of the valley and reconnoitre, and suggested that then they could form a more accurate idea of the position of the enemy and the feasibility of the plan. Accordingly he took his aids-de-camp and those in whose sagacity he had confidence, and ascended the eminence. By the time they had attained the desired elevation, however, the whole scene on the opposite mountain had changed its appearance. The wind, which had been sometime blowing a moderate breeze from the north-west, suddenly chopped round to the north-east and blew almost a gale, sweep-ing the belt or cordon of fire with which the savages had surrounded them-selves on three sides, into magnificent eddies, and curling and sweeping over the mountains with a rapidity inconceivable to those who have never witnessed such a scene. For some moments, the Governor and his party were lost in admiration at the grandeur of the spectacle, and the army, the threatened battle, and everything else, but the sight before them, were forgotten for the moment. The towering objects around, threw fantastic and colossal shadows over the sides of the mountain, and sometimes the entranced officers imagined that they could see spires, and domes, and huge edifices encircled with the flames, when suddenly these fairy creations of the furious element would vanish and leave nothing behind but a cluster of pine trees, with the curling flames encircling their now livid trunks, and occasionally pouring in one continuous sheet from their centres, presenting again an almost exact resemblance to the stock of some huge furnace, burned white hot with the ungovernable fury of its own fire. Sometimes too, they imagined they saw a fearful array of grim warriors marshalled behind the long line of fire, but as the fury of the latter would become exhausted for lack of new combustibles in the course of the wind, or by the interposition of a ledge of rock, the warriors would dwindle into the trunks of black jacks, and mountain laurels and other products of the soil. The leaves were hung with magnificent festoons of crimson and purple, constantly changing its hues like the dying dolphin, as the fire burned out over one track, and pursued its resistless career to another.

Every one saw now, that they had indeed arrived at the veritable Blue Ridge, for the fire that had commenced in the spur beneath which the army had encamped, had by this time, swept around its base, and entered upon the wider field of the main mountain, revealing what the governor had been so fearful of not being able to find, the gap of the mountains.

------------ ▲ ------------

Only picked men, of course, were taken by each of the young gentlemen who volunteered [for the fictional campaign against the Indians], because if each had taken his fifty men, the party would have been entirely too unwieldy, besides weakening too much the main body upon whom, in any event, much the heaviest part of the fighting would in all probability fall. They numbered something less than a hundred and fifty, all told. The foremost of these were already ascending, by a winding path, the spur beneath which the main army were encamped, and in an opposite direction, as it seemed, to that route in which the Governor contemplated marching at daylight. Simply, one party purposed marching up the ravine on one side of the mountain, and the other party were to encircle it until they should meet the first, near the head of the *gap*. To one accustomed to the mountains, in our day, this would seem no very difficult undertaking, but it must be remembered that this sort of traveling was wholly new to every one, except the scout, and even he had never been tried upon such a gigantic scale. Any one who has ascended a mountain for the first time, through a trackless forest, may form some idea of the excessive toil and fatigue which our luxurious youths endured that night. Often and often did Lee and his inseparable companion, the scout, seat themselves upon some flat rock, or piece of table land, and wait for their wearied and straggling companions. For more than half a mile beneath, they could distinguish the sounds of the rolling stones, as they were precipitated beneath the tread of their followers, and every now and then the shrill whistle of some straggler, who had wandered from the main body. This last device was one of Jarvis' suggesting, in order to exclude the possibility of alarming the savage camp on the other face of the mountain, or, perchance of arresting the attention of some straggling party of hunters, who might be out on that side, for the purpose of supplying the camp. The latter danger was the scout's whole dread, and therefore he pushed so far ahead of the main body. His gun he kept constantly ready for use, not for game, for every one had been charged not to fire upon any sort of animal short of a two-legged one, as Joe expressed it, and even the noise of this he deprecated, if the flight of such an one could be arrested by any other means.

-------------------- ▲ --------------------

[Following the "battle" with the Indians] the Governor assembled the young gentry and the officers of rangers around him, to witness the interesting ceremony of planting the British standard upon the highest peak of the Blue Ridge, in the name of his sovereign. They still, however, called it under the general term of Apalachee, under the mistaken impression with which they set out, that there was but one chain of mountains.

After a toilsome struggle from the table land before described, and upon which the battle had been fought, they at length found themselves on the real summit of the long sought eminence, and the Governor planted the British standard upon the highest rock, with due form, and in the name of his royal master.

It was a bleak and barren spot, made up wholly of huge fragments of rock, piled up one upon the other, as if in some far remote age, they had been cast there by a violent convulsion of nature. It was fortunate, however, that it was thus barren of vegetation in one respect — for it gave them an uninterrupted view of what has since been called the VALLEY OF VIRGINIA! What a panorama there burst upon the enraptured vision of the assembled young chivalry of Virginia! Never did the eye of mortal man rest upon a more magnificent scene! The vale beneath looked like a great sea of vegetation in the momn-light, rising and falling in undulating and picturesque lines, as far as the eye could reach towards the north-east and south-west; but their vision was interrupted on the opposite side by the Alleghanies. For hours the old veteran chief stood on the identical spot which he first occupied, drinking in rapture from the vision which he beheld. Few words were spoken by any one, after the first exclamations of surprise and enthusiasm were over. The scene was too overpowering—the grand solitudes, the sublime stillness, gave rise to profound emotions which found no utterance. Nearly everyone wandered off and seated himself upon some towering crag, and then held communion with the silent spirit of the place. There lay the valley of Virginia, that garden spot of the earth, in its first freshness and purity, as it came from the hands of its Maker. Not a white man had ever trod that virgin soil, from the beginning of the world. What a solemn and sublime temple of nature was there—and who could look upon it, as it spread far out to the east and west, until it was lost in the dim and hazy horizon, and not feel deeply impressed with the majesty of its Author.

Governor Spotswood carried his thoughts into the future, and imagined the fine country which he beheld, peopled and glowing under the hands of the husbandman, and all his bright anticipations were more than realized. At length he turned to Moore, who sat near him not less entranced, and said, "They call me a visionary, but what imagination ever conjured up a vision like that?"

William Byrd in the Blue Ridge Mountains, 1728

ADECADE AFTER ALEXANDER Spotswood made his climb of "Mount George," another wealthy Virginian, William Byrd II, was commissioned by the British Crown to survey the boundary between his home colony and neighboring North Carolina. Byrd led a team of surveyors from the Atlantic coast due west along the boundary line to the base of the Blue Ridge Mountains, where, in late fall of 1728, without apparently having climbed any peaks, the expedition turned back. The nature of the mission took the party far from roads and settlements, forcing the men who "advanced the line" to cross hills and rivers as they encountered them and to camp out each night beneath the sky. Surprisingly, the aristocratic Byrd – who had been educated in England, was a member of the Royal Society and possessed the largest private library in the colonies – took the rigors of the journey in stride, asserting after the experience that "mankind are the great Losers by the Luxury of Feather-Beds and warm apartments." Byrd's attitude stemmed in part from his romantic turn of mind, and partly from the fact that the expedition, like Spotswood's before it, was anything but a spartan one – as is evident from a note to the North Carolina contingent of the survey party in which Byrd mentioned that he and his fellow Virginians would be bringing with them "about 20 men furnish't with provision for 40 days. We shal have a Tent with us & a Marquis [an awning for shelter at mealtime] for the convenience of ourselves & Servants. We shal be provided with as much Wine & Rum as just enable us, and our men, to drink every Night to the Success of the following Day."

Byrd chronicled his impressions of the Appalachian wilderness in his delightful *History of the Dividing Line Betwixt Virginia and North Carolina.* For years this book, though its tone is highly satirical and it reads in places like a mock epic, had been regarded as an accurate account of the expedition. Then an earlier version of the *History* turned up, showing that the later work, written several years after the expedition, had been heavily embellished. The first version, known as *The Secret History,* is only half as long as the later account, and most of Byrd's enthusiasm for the mountain scene is absent from it. Some researchers have therefore argued that his appreciation for nature was largely feigned, inserted after the fact merely to please his audience back in Britain, where it had become fashionable to admire "Romantick" scenery.

Feigned or not, the *History* remains delightful reading. Unlike his predecessors in the American mountains, Byrd was intensely interested in the landscape, and he was a curious and observant traveler. His vivid and often humorous description of the Appalachian terrain contrasts sharply with the sparely written accounts that preceded it.

11. [October 11, 1728] At the Distance of 4 miles and 60 poles from the Place where we encampt, we came upon the River Dan a Second time; tho' It was not so wide in this Place as where we crosst it first, being not above a 150 yards over.

The West Shore continued to be cover'd with the Canes above mentioned, but not to so great a Breadth as before, and 'tis Remarkable that these canes are much more frequent on the West Side of the River than on the East, where they grow generally very scattering.

It was Still a beautiful Stream, rolling down its limpid and murmuring waters among the Rocks, which lay scatter'd here and there, to make up the variety of the Prospect.

It was about two Miles from this River to the End of our Day's Work, which led us mostly over Broken Grounds and troublesome Underwoods. Hereabout, from one of the Highest hills, we made the first Discovery of the Mountains, on the Northwest of our course. They seem'd to lye off at a vast Distance, and lookt like Ranges of Blue clouds rising one above another.

14. There having been great Signs of Rain yesterday Evening, we had taken our Precautions in Securing the Bread, and trenching in our Tent.

The men had also Stretcht their Blankets upon Poles, Penthouse fashion, against the Weather, so that nobody was taken unprepar'd.

It began to fall heavily about three o'clock in the Morning, and held not up till near Noon. Everything was so thoroughly Soakt, that we laid aside all thoughts of decamping that Day.

This gave leizure to the most expert of our Gunners to go and try their Fortunes, and they succeeded so well, that they return'd about Noon with three fat Deer, and 4 wild Turkeys. Thus Providence took care of us, and however short the Men might be in their Bread, 'tis certain they had Meat at full Allowance.

The Cookery went on Merrily all Night long, to keep the Damps from entering our Pores; and in truth the Impressions of the Air are much more powerful upon empty Stomachs.

In such a Glut of Provisions, a true Woodsman, when he has nothing else to do, like our honest countrymen the Indians, keeps eating on, to avoid the imputation of Idleness; Though, in a Scarcity, the Indian will fast with a much better Grace than they. They can Subsist Several days upon a little Rocka-hominy, which is parcht Indian Corn reduc'd to powder. This they moisten in the hollow of their Hands with a little water, and 'tis hardly credible how small a Quantity of it will Support them. Tis true they grow a little lank upon it, but to make themselves feel full, they gird up their Loins very tight with a Belt, taking up a Hole every day. With this Slender Subsistence they are able to travel very long Journeys; but then, to make themselves Amends, when they do meet with better chear, they eat without ceasing, till they have raven'd themselves into another Famine.

17. . . . Near our Camp we found a prickly Shrub, riseing about a foot from the Ground, something like that which bears the Barberry, tho' much Smaller. The Leaves had a fresh, agreeable Smell, and I am perswaded the Ladies would be apt to fancy a Tea made of them, provided they were told how far it came, and at the Same time were obliged to buy it very dear.

About a Mile to the South-West of our Camp rose a regular Mount that commanded a full Prospect of the Mountains, and an Extensive View of the Flat Country. But being, with respect to the high Mountains, no more than a Pimple, we call'd it by that Name.

Presently after Sunset we discovered a great Light towards the West, too bright for a fire, and more resembling the Aurora Borealis. This, all our Woodsmen told us, was a Common Appearance in the High Lands, and generally foreboded bad Weather. Their Explanation happen'd to be exactly true, for in the Night we had a Violent Gale of Wind, accompany'd with Smart Hail, that rattled frightfully amongst the Trees, tho' it was not large enough to do us any Harm.

18. The Irvin runs into the Dan about four Miles to the Southward of the Line, and seem'd to roll down its Waters from the N.N.W. in a very full and Limpid stream, and the Murmur it made, in tumbling over the Rocks, caus'd the Situation to appear very Romantick, and had almost made some of the Company Poetical, tho' they drank nothing but Water.

――――――― ▲ ―――――――

The Whole Distance the Surveyors advanc'd the Line this day amounted to 6 Miles and 30 Poles, which was no small journey, considering the Grounds we had traverst were exceedingly rough and uneven, and in many Places intolerably entangled with Bushes. All the Hills we ascended were encumber'd with Stones, many of which seem'd to contain a Metallick Substance, and the Vallies we crosst were interrupted with Miry Branches. From the Top of every Hill we cou'd discern distinctly, at a great Distance to the Northward, three or four Ledges of Mountains, rising one above another; and on the highest of all rose a Single Mountain, very much resembling a Woman's Breast.

19. About four Miles beyond the River Irvin, we forded Matrimony Creek, call'd so by an unfortunate marry'd man, because it was exceedingly noisy and impetuous. However, tho' the Stream was Clamorous, yet, like those Women who make themselves plainest heard, it was likewise perfectly clear and unsully'd.

Still half a Mile further we saw a Small Mountain, about five Miles to the North-west of us, which we call'd the Wart, because it appeared no bigger than a Wart, in Comparison of the great Mountains which hid their haughty Heads in the Clouds.

We were not able to extend the Line more than 5 Miles and 135 Poles, notwithstanding we began our March Early in the Morning and did not encamp till it was almost dark.

We made it the later by endeavouring to Quarter in some convenient Situation, either for Grass or Canes. But Night Surprising us, we were oblig'd to Lodge at last upon High and uneven Ground, which was so overgrown with Shrubs and Saplings, that we cou'd hardly see ten yards around us.

The most melancholy part of the Story was, that our Horses had Short Commons. The poor Creatures were now grown so weak that they Stagger'd when we mounted them. Nor wou'd our own Fare have been at all more plentiful, had we not been so provident as to carry a Load of Meat along with us. Indeed, the Woods were too thick to shew us any sort of Game but one Wild Turkey, which help'd to enrich our Soup.

To make us amends, we found abundance of very Sweet Grapes, which, with the help of Bread, might have furnish'd out a good Italian Repast, in the Absence of more Savoury Food.

The men's Mouths water'd at the Sight of a Prodigious Flight of Wild Pigeons which flew high over our Heads to the Southward. . . .

20. It was now Sunday, which we had like to have spent in Fasting as well as Prayer; for our Men, taking no Care for the Morrow, like good Christians, but bad Travellers, had improvidently Devour'd all their Meat for Supper.

They were order'd in the Morning to drive up their Horses, lest they shou'd stray too far from the Camp and be lost, in case they were let alone all day. At their Return they had the very great Comfort to behold a monstrous fat Bear, which the Indian had kill'd very Seasonably for their Breakfast.

We thought it still necessary to make another Reduction of our Bread, from four to three Pounds a Week to every man, computing that we had still enough in that Proportion to last us Three weeks longer.

The Atmosphere was so smoaky all around us, that the Mountains were again growing invisible. This happen'd not from the Hazyness of the Sky, but from the fireing of the Woods by the Indians, for we were now near the Route the Northern Savages take when they go out to War against the Cataubas and other Southern Nations.

21. The smoak continued still to Veil the Mountains from our Sight, which made us long for Rain, or a brisk Gale of Wind, to disperse it. Nor was the loss of this wild Prospect all our concern, but we were apprehensive lest the Woods shou'd be burnt in the Course of our Line before us, or happen to take fire behind us, either of which wou'd effectually have Starv'd the Horses, and made us all Foot Soldiers. But we were so happy, thank God! as to escape this Misfortune in every Part of our Progress.

23. At the Distance of 62 Poles from where we lay, we crost the South Branch of what we took for the Irvin, nor was it without Difficulty we got over, tho' it happen'd to be without Damage.

Great part of the way after that was Mountainous, so that we were no sooner got down one Hill, but we were oblig'd to climb up another. Only for the last Mile of our Stage, we encounter'd a Locust Thicket that was level but interlac'd terribly with Bryars and Grape Vines.

We forded a large creek, no less than five times, the Banks of which were so steep that we were forc'd to cut them down with a Hough.

We gave it the Name of Crooked creek, because of its frequent Meanders. The Sides of it were planted with Shrub-Canes, extremely inviting to the Horses, which were now quite jaded with clambering up so many Precipices, and tugging thro' so many dismal Thickets, notwithstanding which we pusht the Line this day Four Miles and 69 Poles. The men were so unthrifty this Morning as to bring but a Small Portion of their Abundance along with them. This was the more unlucky, because we cou'd discover no Sort of Game the whole livelong Day. Woodsmen are certainly good Christians in one respect, at least, that they always leave the Morrow to care for itself; tho' for that very reason they ought to pray more fervently for their Dayly Bread than most of them remember to do.

The Mountains were still conceal'd from our Eyes by a cloud of Smoak. As we went along we were alarmed at the Sight of a great Fire which shewed itself to the Northward. This made our small Corps march in closer Order than we us'd to do, lest perchance we might be waylaid by Indians. It made us look out Sharp to see if we could discover any Track or other Token of these insidious Forresters, but found none. In the mean time we came often upon the Track of Bears, which can't without some Skill be distinguisht from that of Human Creatures, made with Naked Feet. And Indeed a Young Woodsman wou'd be puzzled to find out the Difference, which consists principally in a Bear's Paws being something Smaller than a Man's foot and in its leaving sometimes the Mark of its Claws in the Impression made upon the Ground.

25. The Air clearing up this Morning, we were again agreeably surprized with a full Prospect of the Mountains. They discover'd themselves both to the North and South of us, on either side, not distant above ten Miles, according to our best Computation.

We cou'd now see those to the North rise in four distinct Ledges, one above another, but those to the South form'd only a Single Ledge, and that broken and interrupted in many Places; or rather they were only single Mountains detacht from each other.

One of the Southern Mountains was so vastly high, it seem'd to hide its head in the Clouds, and the West End of it terminated in a horrible Precipice, that we call'd the Despairing Lover's Leap. The Next to it, towards the East, was lower, except at one End, where it heav'd itself up in the form of a vast Stack of Chimnys.

The Course of the Northern Mountains seem'd to tend West-South-West, and those to the Southward very near West. We cou'd descry other Mountains ahead of us, exactly in the Course of the Line, tho' at a much greater distance. In this Point of View, the Ledges on the right and left both seem'd to close and form a Natural Amphi-Theater.

Thus, 'twas our Fortune to be wedg'd in betwixt these two Ranges of Mountains, insomuch that if our Line had run ten Miles on either Side, it had butted before this day either upon one or the other, both of them now Stretching away plainly to the Eastward of us.

It had rain'd a little in the Night, which disperst the smoak and opened this Romantick Scene to us all at once, tho' it was again hid from our Eyes as we mov'd forwards by the rough Woods we had the Misfortune to be engag'd with.

26. We found our way grow still more Mountainous, after extending the Line 300 Poles farther. We came then to a Rivulet that ran with a Swift Current towards the South. This we fancy'd to be another Branch of the Irvin, tho' some of these men, who had been Indian Traders, judg'd it rather to be the head of the Deep River, that discharges its Stream into that of Pee Dee; but this seem'd a wild Conjecture.

The Hills beyond that River were exceedingly lofty, and not to be attempted by our Jaded Palfreys, which could now hardly drag their Legs after them upon level Ground. Besides, the Bread began to grow Scanty, and the Winter Season to advance space upon us.

We had likewise reason to apprehend the Consequences of being intercepted by deep Snows, and the Swelling of the many Waters between us and Home. The first of these Misfortunes would Starve all our horses, and the Other ourselves, by cutting off our Retreat, and obliging us to Winter in these Desolate Woods. These considerations determin'd us to Stop short here, and push our Adventures no farther.

John Brickell Visits
the "Charokee Mountains," 1730

JOHN BRICKELL SET out from the North Carolina coast "to view the mountains" in late winter of 1730, at which time he was probably about twenty years old. Before and after the mountain excursion described below he had traveled extensively through the region, and in 1737, after returning to England, his *Natural History of North Carolina* was published in Dublin. Most of Brickell's book was actually plagiarized from an earlier volume, John Lawson's *History of Carolina*, which had first appeared more than twenty-five years earlier. The description of the "Charokee Mountains," however, is his own.

Brickell "approached to the top of one of the mountains" and succeeded in crossing this ridge, then in climbing to the top of a much higher one further west. His precise route is unknown. The only real hazard he and his men encountered was in convincing the Indians they met that their motivation was not warfare but simply "a curiosity in viewing the mountains." The danger was not imaginary; Lawson, as Brickell was well aware, had been captured, probably tortured, and then killed by Indians in 1712. Brickell was more fortunate, however, with a gift for diplomacy that saw him safely to the mountains and back home again.

Thus I have given the most exact Account of the *Indians* of *Carolina* Conjuring over the *Sick, stolen Goods,* and the Nature and Manner of burying their dead. I shall therefore make a small Degression, to inform my Readers with the manner of our Travelling up to the *Charokee Mountains,* having already set forth the many and different Observations we made in this spacious Country, and then proceed to the *Indian Distempers,* some of which I have been Eyewitness to.

The latter end of *February, Anno. Dom.* 1730, we set out on our intended Journey, being in Number Ten *White Men,* and Two *Indians,* who served for our Huntsmen and Interpreters. Having provided a sufficient quantity of *Firearms, Ammunition, Horses,* two *Mariners Compasses, Rum, Salt, Pepper, Indian Corn,* and other Necessaries, we began our Journey; and after we had passed the *Christian Plantations,* our Accommodations were as follows: All the Day we were diverted with variety of beautiful and strange Objects; in the Evening we encamped an Hour before Sunset, tyed our Horses to Trees near us, which we made the *Indians* climb up to procure a sufficient quantity of *Moss* for their Food, and to make Beds for us to lie upon, which was generally under the shade of some large Tree: Our next Business was to send the *Indians* to Hunt; our Care in the meantime was to make a large Fire of the broken pieces of Timber which we found in plenty lying dispersed up and down the Woods; this we piled up in order to continue burning all Night, which prevented all manner of Wild Beasts and pernicious *Insects* being troublesome, or approaching us or our Horses.

▲

It would not be proper to trouble the Reader with the Adventures of each Day, and the many Observations we made therein, these being sufficiently set forth already: Let it suffice to inform them, that after fifteen Days Journey, we

A Draught of the
CHEROKEE COUNTRY,
On the West Side of the Twenty four Mountains,
commonly called Over the Hills;
Taken by Henry Timberlake, *when he*
was in that Country, in March 1762.

arrived at the foot of the Mountains, having met with no Human Specie all the way. It seems upon our first arrival we were discovered by a Party of the *Iriquois Indians,* who, as I said before, are very powerful, and continually at War, wandering all over the Continent between the two Bays of *Mexico* and *St. Lawrence.* As soon as they had discovered us they disappeared, (as we were afterwards informed) and gave Notice thereof to their King, who sent immediately an Ambassador, or one of his Attendants, painted as red as *vermillion,* together with a strong Party of his Men, armed with Bows and Arrows.

When they appeared the second time, the Retinue halted at about half a Mile distant from us and the Ambassador attended with one Person, came to the place where we were (which was in a large *Savanna*) with a green Bough in his Hand, and gave us to understand that he was sent to us by Order of his King, who desired to know whether we came for Peace or War, or what other Business had brought us to those Parts; In such like Speeches he accosted us. We assured him by our *Indian* Interpreters, that we were come in a friendly manner, with no other Design than a Curiosity of viewing the Mountains. When we had thus satisfied him he sat down with us, and dispatched the other Person that attended him, to acquaint the King with the Reasons of our coming.

During his Absence, we entertained the Ambassador with *Punch,* and made him a Present of some few Toys, which he accepted of, and was highly pleased therewith. About four Hours after the Messenger returned, whom the Ambassador received at a little distance from us, where they discoursed for some time, and at his return told us, that the Message from the King was, to desire us to make him a Visit, assuring us at the same time of his Friendship. This Message occasioned several Debates to arise amongst us, concerning the consequence that might attend it; we seemed unwilling to go, which he perceiving, assured us in the strongest Terms of our safety, and the Sincerity and Friendship of the King. At length, rather than incur his Displeasure (notwithstanding we were determined to sell our Lives at the dearest rate, if we met with any opposition) we complied, and arrived about six o'Clock at the *Indian* Town (attended with the Guards that came with the Ambassador, who marched at some distance from us) and were conducted to the State House, where the King was seated with his *War Captains* and *Councellors,* who got up and placed us next to him; after we had paid our due acknowledgements to him, and made him some Presents, he then began to enquire the Reasons of our coming thither, and among other things, *How his Brother did,* meaning the Governor; and many other such like Speeches passed between us. After we had satisfied him in each particular that he demanded, he bid us welcome, shaking Hands with each of us; assuring us of his Friendship, and the great Regard he had for those of our Nation. The few Presents we gave (which were *Knives,*

Glass Beads, Punch, and the like) had made so favourable an Impression in the Breast of his Majesty, and all his Councellors, in our behalf, that the King's Orders were issued out immediately, strictly charging all his Subjects to treat us in the most friendly manner, and supply us with whatever we had occasion for during our Pleasure to stay amongst them. After all these Speeches were ended, towards Night we were dismissed, and conducted to one of the King's Houses (being an Apartment prepared for us) where we lay upon Benches, with the Skins of Beasts for our Covering; and this was the best Lodging we met with since our departure from the *Christians.* They took particular Care of our Horses, and treated us with all the good Nature possibly to be expected from them, supplying us with sufficient quantities of Provision, such as *Venison, Wildfowl, Fish,* and various kinds of dried *Fruits, Pulse,* and *Water,* no stronger Liquors are to be met with amongst these People.

——————— ▲ ———————

Two Days after our Arrival, we requested the King to have Liberty to depart, in order to view the Mountains, which he seemed very unwilling to comply with, pressing us to continue longer with him, urging many Arguments to persuade us, and that we had not as yet sufficiently refreshed ourselves after our late Fatigue. But we assured him that our Governor had given us strict Orders at our Departure, to be as expeditious as we possibly could in our return home. These Considerations at length moved him to a compliance sooner than he intended. But the chief Reason of our departing so soon was, that if we had remained there much longer, we should be deprived of all our *Rum,* which was a great support to us in this long and tedious Journey. The King then offered us a Party of his Men to guard us in the Mountains, least we should be molested by any *Indians* that might be Hunting in them, during our stay there. We most gratefully returned him our due Acknowledgements for his kind offer, and the many Favours he had already conferred upon us, and most humbly beg'd to be excused, which he readily granted us.

Having thus obtained our License of Departure, we made him a Present of a Bottle of *Rum,* in lieu whereof he gave us *Indian Corn, Venison* and some dried *Fruits,* for our support in the Mountains, where Provisions are scarce. All things being prepared as usual, we set out the next Morning about six o'Clock, continuing our Journey still *Westward:* The King and his Guards conducted us about half a Mile, wishing us Health, and intreating us at the same time, to make him a Visit at our Return, which we did not, taking a Tour another way.

About the Evening we approached to the top of one of these Mountains, where we refreshed, being all in perfect Health. Here we had the greatest difficulty to be supplied with Moss for Provision for our Horses, but after some time searching, we found what was sufficient for them; then making a great

Fire, and our Beds for that Night of the withered Leaves of the Trees, which we gathered for that Purpose. The next Morning very early having refreshed ourselves, we set forward, and in the Evening got on the other side of the first Ridge of Mountains into a most beautiful Valley, adorned with *Woods, Savannas,* and a very rich Soil, here we encamped this Night, being the longest Days Journey we made from our first setting out, by reason that we were destitute of Water in these barren places, for our Selves and Horses, only what we met with by chance in the hollow parts of the Rocks, which our Horses would hardly drink.

The next Morning we set forward with a great deal of chearfulness, having plenty of Water, and all manner of Provisions. In this Days Journey we discovered an *Indian* in the solitary parts of the Woods, but as soon as he espyed us, he fled, notwithstanding we made signs to him to come to us, but in vain, for he quickly vanished out of our sight, that we could not learn what Nation he belonged to, or whether there were any more with him in those Parts. After two Days Journey we arrived at another Ridge of rocky Mountains, with large Trees in several Places, but little or no Pasture like the former, but much higher, having a beautiful Prospect of large Woods and Forrests, as far as our sight would permit. From this Mountain we returned, making our Journey Eastward; meeting with nothing worthy of Observation, but what we have already made mention of; and in thirty two Days, to our great Satisfaction, arrived amongst the *Christians,* our Company being all in perfect Health, having had no Misfortune all the way, but the loss of one of our Compasses.

William Bartram Climbs Oconee Mountain and Mount Magnolia, 1776

WILLIAM BARTRAM AND his father, John, were leaders in the development of natural science in America. John, a botanist and a devout Quaker, established the first botanical garden in the colonies and was acquainted with Thomas Jefferson, Benjamin Franklin, and such leading European naturalists as Linnaeus and Peter Kalm. The younger Bartram shared his father's love of natural history, but at first tried to pursue a more respectable career, trying his hand variously as a farmer, merchant, planter, and trader. At these, however, he was a failure; at one point he had to flee his creditors, and his whereabouts were for a time unknown.

Such troubles may have contributed to the fact that William felt more at home in the woods than the parlor. On April 22, 1775, three days after the first shots of the American Revolution rang out in Lexington and Concord, he set out from Charleston for the wilds of the Appalachian Mountains, writing later that he thought of himself as old King Nebuchadnezzar, "expelled from the society of men, and constrained to roam in the mountains and wilderness." He wandered for five years, traveling light, remaining out of touch with civilization for months at a time and necessarily going it alone, as the mountains were still largely considered hazardous for whites. He soon managed to gain the trust of the "dangerous" Indians, who occasionally guided him through the wilderness and helped him find the botanical wonders he was seeking. He climbed a number of peaks in the southern Appalachians, and also kept a journal, which, in 1791, after he'd reentered civilization, was published in London as *Travels through North and South Carolina*.

Bartram's *Travels* was an immediate and influential best-seller, appearing in quick succession in Ireland, France, Germany and Holland. Critics would later call the book one of the first instances of modern nature writing, and the poets Wordsworth and Coleridge were inspired by Bartram's vivid and sympathetic descriptions of the New World wilderness. Wordsworth in particular used the *Travels* to include America in his poetic vision. Consider, for example, his poem "Ruth," in which a wild, wandering American – not unlike Bartram himself – visits England and tells

    . . . of the magnolia spread
High as a cloud, high overhead!
– Of flowers that with one scarlet gleam
Cover a hundred leagues, and seem
To set the hills on fire.

Wordsworth had never been to the American wilderness, but he saw it plainly through Bartram's eyes.

In the selection below, taken from the *Travels*, Bartram makes two ascents while crossing the rugged Nantahala Mountains in the vicinity of "Keowe," near present-day Franklin, North Carolina.

I waited two or three days at this post, expecting the return of an Indian who was out hunting. This man was recommended to me as a suitable person for a protector and guide to the Indian settlements over the hills, but upon information that he would not be in shortly, and there being no other person suitable for the purpose, rather than be detained, and perhaps thereby frustrated in my purposes, I determined to set off alone and run all risks.

I crossed the river at a good ford just below the old fort. The river here is just one hundred yards over. After an agreeable progress for about two miles over delightful strawberry plains and gently swelling green hills, I began to ascend more steep and rocky ridges. Having gained a very considerable elevation, looking round, I enjoyed a very comprehensive and delightful view. Keowe, which I had but just lost sight of, appeared again, and the serpentine river speeding through the lucid green plain apparently just under my feet. After observing this delightful landscape, I continued on again three or four miles, keeping the trading path, which led me over uneven rocky land, crossing rivulets and brooks, and rapidly descending over rocky precipices, when I came into a charming vale, embellished with a delightful glittering river which meandered through it and crossed my road. On my left hand, upon the grassy bases of the rising hills, appeared the remains of a town of the ancients, as the tumuli, terraces, posts or pillars, old peach and plum orchards, etc. sufficiently testify. These vales and swelling bases of the surrounding hills afford vast crops of excellent grass and herbage fit for pasturage and hay.

———————— ▲ ————————

Having crossed the vales, I began to ascend again the more lofty hills of ridges, then continued about eight miles over more gentle pyramidal hills, narrow vales and lawns, the soil exceedingly fertile, producing lofty forests and odoriferous groves of Calycanthus, near the banks of rivers, with Halesia,

Philadelphus inodorus, Rhododendron ferrugineum, Azalea, Stewartia montana. . . . At once the mounts divided and disclosed to view the ample Oconee vale, encircled by a wreath of uniform hills, their swelling bases clad in cheerful verdure over which, issuing from between the mountains, plays along a glittering river, meandering through the meadows. Crossing these at the upper end of the vale, I began to ascend the Oconee Mountain. On the foot of the hill were ruins of the ancient Oconee town. The first step after leaving the verdant beds of the hills was a very high, rocky chain of pointed hills, extremely well timbered. . . .

My next flight was up a very high peak, to the top of the Oconee Mountain, where I rested; and turning about, found that I was now in a very elevated situation, from whence I enjoyed a view inexpressibly magnificent and comprehensive. The mountainous wilderness which I had lately traversed, down to the region of Augusta, appearing regularly undulated as the great ocean after a tempest; the undulations gradually depressing, yet perfectly regular, as the squamae of fish or imbrications of tile on a roof. The nearest ground to me was of a perfect full green, next more glaucous, and lastly almost blue as the ether with which the most distant curve of the horizon seemed to be blended.

My imagination thus wholly engaged in the contemplation of this magnificent landscape, infinitely varied and without bound, I was almost insensible or regardless of the charming objects more within my reach: a new species of rhododendron, foremost in the assembly of mountain beauties; next the flaming azalea, Kalmia latifolia, Robinia, snowy mantled Philadelphus inodorus, perfumed Calycanthus, etc.

———————— ▲ ————————

After being recovered of the fatigue and labor in ascending the mountain, I began again to prosecute my task. Proceeding through a shady forest, I soon after gained the most elevated crest of the Oconee Mountain and then began to descend the other side. The winding, rough road carried me over rocky hills and levels shaded by incomparable forests, the soil exceedingly rich and of an excellent quality for the production of every vegetable suited to the climate. It seemed peculiarly adapted for the cultivation of vines, olives, the almond tree, fig, and perhaps the pomegranate, as well as peaches. . . . I passed again steep, rocky ascents and then rich levels, where grew many trees and plants common in Pennsylvania, New York, and even Canada . . . but what seems remarkable, the yellow Jessamine, which is killed by a very slight forest in Pennsylvania, here on the summit of the Cherokee Mountains associates with the Canadian vegetables and appears roving with them in perfect bloom and gaiety. . . . Then I entered a charming narrow vale through which flows a rapid large creek, on whose banks are happily associated the shrubs already recited, together with the following: Staphylea, Euonymus Americana, Hamamelis, Azalea (various species), Aristolochia frutescens, s. odoratissima, which rambles over the trees and shrubs on the prolific banks of these mountain brooks. Passed through magnificent high forests and then came upon the borders of an ample meadow on the left, embroidered by the shade of a high circular amphitheater of hills, the circular ridges rising magnificently one over the other. On the green turfy bases of these ascents appear the ruins of a town of the ancients. The upper end of this spacious green plain is divided by a promontory or spur of the ridges before me, which projects into it. My road led me up into an opening of the ascents through which the glittering brook which watered the meadows ran rapidly down, dashing and roaring over high rocky steps. Continued, yet ascending, until I gained the top of an elevated rocky ridge, when appeared before me a gap or opening between other yet more lofty ascents, through which I continued as the rough rocky road led me, close by the winding banks of a large rapid brook which, at length turning to the left, pouring down rocky precipices, glided off through dark groves and high forests, conveying streams of fertility and pleasure to the fields below.

The surface of the land now for three or four miles was level, yet uneven, occasioned by natural mounds or rocky knobs, but covered with a good staple of rich earth, which affords forests of timber trees and shrubs. After this, gently descending again, I traveled some miles over a varied situation of ground, exhibiting views of grand forests, dark detached groves, vales, and meadows, as heretofore, and producing the like vegetable and other works of nature. The meadows afforded exuberant pasturage for cattle, and the bases of the encircling hills, flowering plants, and fruitful strawberry beds. I observed frequently ruins of the habitations or villages of the ancients. Crossed a delightful river, the main branch of Tugilo, when I began to ascend again, first over swelling turfy ridges, varied with groves of stately forest trees; then ascending again more steep, grassy hillsides, rested on the top of Mount Magnolia, which appeared to me to be the highest ridge of the Cherokee Mountains, which separate the waters of Savannah River from those of the Tanase or greater main branch of the Cherokee River. This, running rapidly a northwest course through the mountains, is joined from the northeast by the Holstein. Thence taking a west course yet amongst the mountains, receiving into it from either hand many large rivers, it leaves the mountains, immediately after being joined by a large river from the east, becomes a mighty river by the name of Hogehege, thence meanders many hundred miles through a vast country consisting of forests, meadows, groves, expansive savannahs, fields, and swelling hills, most fertile and delightful, flows into the beautiful Ohio, and in conjunction with its transparent waters becomes tributary to the sovereign Mississippi.

This exalted peak I named Mount Magnolia, from a new and beautiful species of that celebrated family of flowering trees which here, at the Cascades of Falling Creek, grows in a high degree of perfection. I had, indeed, noticed this curious tree several times before, particularly on the high ridges betwixt Sinica and Keowe and on ascending the first mountain after leaving Keowe, when I observed it in flower, but here it flourishes and commands our attention.

———————— ▲ ————————

Having collected some valuable specimens . . . I continued my lonesome pilgrimage. My road for a considerable time led me winding and turning about the steep rocky hills, the descent of some of which were very rough and troublesome because of fragments of rocks, slippery clay and talc. After this I entered a spacious forest, the land having gradually acquired a more level surface. A pretty grassy vale appeared on my right, through which my wandering path led me, close by the banks of a delightful creek which, sometimes falling over steps of rocks, glided gently with serpentine meanders through the meadows.

After crossing this delightful brook and mead, the land rises again with sublime magnificence, and I am led over hills and vales, groves and high forests, vocal with the melody of the feathered songsters, the snow-white cascades glittering on the sides of the distant hills.

It is now afternoon. I approach a charming vale, amidst sublimely high forests, awful shades! Darkness gathers around; far-distant thunder rolls over the trembling hills. The black clouds with august majesty and power move slowly forwards, shading regions of towering hills and threatening all the destruction of a thunderstorm. All around is now still as death. Not a whisper is heard, but a total inactivity and silence seem to pervade the earth. The birds, afraid to utter a chirrup, in low tremulous voices take leave of each other, seeking covert and safety. Every insect is silenced, and nothing heard but the roaring of the approaching hurricane. The mighty cloud now expands its sable wings, extending from north to south, and is driven irresistibly on by the tumultuous winds, spreading its livid wings around the gloomy concave, armed with terrors of thunder and fiery shafts of lightning. Now the lofty forests bend low beneath its fury; their limbs and wavy boughs are tossed about and catch hold of each other; the mountains tremble and seem to reel about, and the ancient hills to be shaken to their foundations. The furious storm sweeps along, smoking through the vale and over the resounding hills. The face of the earth is obscured by the deluge descending from the firmament, and I am deafened by the din of the thunder. The tempestuous scene damps my spirits, and my horse sinks under me at the tremendous peals, as I hasten on for the plain. . . .

Jeremy Belknap on
Mount Washington, 1784

URING MUCH OF the century following John Josselyn's Mount Washington ascent, Indian hostilities (fueled by the Canadian French
and culminating in the French and Indian War) made the northeastern interior a dangerous place for the British colonist. For all of New
England, the mountaineering historians Laura and Guy Waterman list just a
few fragmentary references to climbs during this period: a real estate deal
consummated on Killington Peak; a few soldiers on Monadnock in 1725; Ira
Allen, brother of Ethan Allen, on Mount Mansfield in 1772; perhaps a man
named Nicholas Austin in the southern Presidential Range in 1774; and, on
Mount Washington, the occasional parties mentioned in the account below.

It was not until well after the Treaty of Paris in 1763 that Americans could
safely visit the northeastern mountains, and not until 1784 that the region was
tame enough to be traversed by a citified minister, historian, and amateur
scientist such as Jeremy Belknap, who led a large and well-equipped expedition from Boston to Mount Washington that summer. Accompanying him
were the Reverend Manasseh Cutler, a member of the Academy of Arts and
Sciences and perhaps the first serious botanist of the region, and about ten
others. The whole party, laden with guns and an assortment of odd-looking
scientific instruments, made quite a stir as it proceeded past the raw frontier
settlements of the northern mountains. After reaching a camp near present-
day Pinkham Notch, the climbers proceeded up the Cutler River to either
Boott Spur or Lion's Head and then up the mountain's east slope to the
summit. Belknap, who wrote afterward that he was "the heaviest person in
the party" and therefore "not the nimblest," dropped out after a couple of
hours and never came close to the top. Those who continued were met with
heavy clouds that completely obscured the view from the summit. The dense
fog prevented the party from making most of its planned scientific observations, though it did not prevent Belknap from later estimating the peak's
height to be near ten thousand feet.

The exact route of the descent is unclear. The climbers apparently tried
to take a more direct line than they had on the ascent, perhaps starting down
the rugged terrain leading into Tuckerman Ravine. They soon fell behind the
local man who was acting as guide; from far down the mountain, he advised

them to climb back up to gentler slopes and try a different route. They did so, but were overtaken by darkness just below treeline and forced to make what was probably the first unplanned bivouac on Mount Washington. The entire party returned safely to camp the next day.

Afterward there was some question about whether the climbers, groping blindly through the dense cloud, actually reached the true summit. The Watermans think it likely that they did, since there are no false tops that might have fooled them along their presumed ascent route. Regardless, the ascent is notable for several reasons. It was the first American climb to be documented firsthand and in detail by several participants, and it marked the first visit by serious scientists to a high American peak. Finally, various accounts of the expedition were widely published, generating considerable public interest in the White Mountains and leading eventually to the explosion of mountain climbing that was to take place in the first half of the nineteenth century.

The selection below, based partly on Belknap's own experiences on the lower part of the mountain and partly on the experiences of his companions, is excerpted from Belknap's *History of New Hampshire*, first published in 1792.

From the earliest settlement of the country, the White mountains have attracted the attention of all sorts of persons. They are undoubtedly the highest land in New-England, and in clear weather, are discovered before any other land, by vessels coming in to the eastern coast; but by reason of their white appearance, are frequently mistaken for clouds. They are visible on the land at the distance of eighty miles, on the south and southeast sides; they appear higher when viewed from the northeast, and it is said, they are seen from the neighborhood of Chamble and Quebec. The Indians gave them the name of Agiocochook: They had a very ancient tradition that their country was once drowned, with all its inhabitants, except one Powaw and his wife, who, foreseeing the flood, fled to these mountains, where they were preserved, and that from them the country was re-peopled. They had a superstitious veneration for the summit, as the habitation of invisible beings; they never ventured to ascend it, and always endeavoured to dissuade every one from the attempt. From them, and the captives, whom they sometimes led to Canada, through the passes of these mountains, many fictions have been propagated, which have given rise to marvellous and incredible stories; particularly, it has been reported, that at immense and inaccessible heights, there have been seen carbuncles, which are supposed to appear luminous in the night. Some writers, who have attempted to give an account of these mountains, have ascribed the whiteness of them, to shining rocks, or a kind of white moss; and the highest summit has been deemed inaccessible, on account of the extreme cold, which threatens to freeze the traveller, in the midst of summer.

Nature has, indeed, in that region, formed her works on a large scale, and presented to view, many objects which do not ordinarily occur. A person who is unacquainted with a mountainous country, cannot, upon his first coming into it, make an adequate judgment of heights and distances; he will imagine every thing to be nearer and less than it really is, until, by experience, he learns to correct his apprehensions, and accommodate his eye to the magnitude and situation of the objects around him. When amazement is excited by the grandeur and sublimity of the scenes presented to view, it is necessary to curb the imagination, and exercise judgment with mathematical precision; or the temptation to romance will be invincible.

The White mountains are the most elevated part of a ridge, which extends N.E. and S.W. to an immense distance. The area of their base, is an irregular figure, the whole circuit of which, is not less than sixty miles. The number of summits within this area, cannot at present be ascertained, the country round them being a thick wilderness. The greatest number which can be seen at once, is at Dartmouth, on the N.W. side, where seven summits appear at one view, of which four are bald. Of these, the three highest are the most distant, being on the eastern side of the cluster; one of these is the mountain which makes so majestic an appearance all along the shore of the eastern counties of Massachusetts: It has lately been distinguished by the name of *Mount WASH-INGTON.*

To arrive at the foot of this mountain, there is a continual ascent of twelve miles, from the plain of Pigwacket, which brings the traveller to the height of land, between Saco and Amariscoggin rivers. At this height there is a level of about a mile square, part of which is a meadow, formerly a beaver pond, with a dam at each end. Here, though elevated more than three thousand feet above the level of the sea, the traveller finds himself in a deep valley. On the east is a steep mountain, out of which issue several springs, one of which is the fountain of Ellis river, a branch of Saco, which runs south; another of Peabody river, a branch of Amariscoggin, which runs north. From this meadow, toward the west, there is an uninterrupted ascent, on a ridge, between two deep gullies, to the summit of Mount Washington.

The lower part of the mountain is shaded by a thick growth of spruce and fir. The surface is composed of rocks, covered with very long green moss, which extends from one rock to another, and is, in many places, so thick and strong, as to bear a man's weight. This immense bed of moss, serves as a sponge, to retain the moisture brought by the clouds and vapours, which are frequently rising and gathering round the mountains; the thick growth of

wood, prevents the rays of the sun from penetrating to exhale it; so that there is a constant supply of water deposited in the crevices of the rocks, and issuing in the form of springs, from every part of the mountain.

The rocks which compose the surface of the mountain, are, in some parts, slate, in others, flint; some specimens of rock chrystal have been found, but of no great value. No lime stone has yet been discovered, though the most likely rocks have been tried with aquafortis. There is one precipice, on the eastern side, not only completely perpendicular, but composed of square stones, as regular as a piece of masonry; it is about five feet high, and from fifteen to twenty in length. The uppermost rocks of the mountain, are the common quartz, of a dark grey colour; when broken, they shew very small shining specks, but there is no such appearance on the exterior part. The eastern side of the mountain, rises in an angle of 45 degrees, and requires six or seven hours of hard labour to ascend it. Many of the precipices are so steep, as to oblige the traveller to use his hands, as well as feet, and to hold by the trees, which diminish in size, till they degenerate to shrubs and bushes; above these, are low vines, some bearing red, and others blue berries, and the uppermost vegetation is a species of grass, called wintergrass, mixed with the moss of the rocks.

Having surmounted the upper and steepest precipice, there is a large area, called the plain. It is a dry heath, composed of rocks covered with moss, and bearing the appearance of a pasture, in the beginning of the winter season. In some openings, between the rocks, there are springs of water, in others dry gravel. Here the grous or heath bird resorts, and is generally out of danger; several of them were shot by some travellers in October, 1774. The extent of this plain is uncertain; from the eastern side, to the foot of the pinnacle, or sugar-loaf, it is nearly level, and it may be walked over in less than an hour. The sugar loaf, is a pyramidal heap of grey rocks, which, in some places, are formed like winding steps. This pinnacle has been ascended in one hour and a half. The traveller having gained the summit, is recompensed for his toil, if the sky be serene, with a most noble and extensive prospect. On the S.E. side, there is a view of the Atlantic ocean, the nearest part of which, is sixty-five miles, in a direct line. On the W. and N. the prospect is bounded by the high lands, which separate the waters of Connecticut and Amariscoggin rivers, from those of Lake Champlain and St. Lawrence. On the south, it extends to the southernmost mountains of New-Hampshire, comprehending a view of the Lake Winipiseogee. On every side of these mountains, are long winding gullies, beginning at the precipice below the plain; and deepening in the descent. In winter, the snow lodges in these gullies; and being driven, by the N.W. and N.E. wind, from the top, is deepest in those which are situated on the southerly side. It is observed to lie longer in the spring on the south, than on the N.W. side, which is the case with many other hills in New-Hampshire.

A ranging company, who ascended the highest mountain, on the N.W. part, April 29th, 1725, found the snow four feet on that side; the summit was almost bare of snow, though covered with white frost and ice, and a small pond of water, near the top, was hard frozen.

In 1774, some men, who were making a road through the eastern pass of the mountain, ascended the mountain to the summit, on the 6th of June, and on the south side, in one of the deep gullies, found a body of snow thirteen feet deep, and so hard, as to bear them. On the 19th of the same month, some of the same party ascended again, and in the same spot, the snow was five feet deep. In the first week of September, 1783, two men, who attempted to ascend the mountain, found the bald top so covered with snow and ice, then newly formed, that they could not reach the summit; but this does not happen every year so soon; for the mountain has been ascended as late as the first week in October, when no snow was upon it; and though the mountains begin to be covered, at times, with snow, as early as September, yet it goes off again, and seldom gets fixed till the end of October, or the beginning of November; but from that time it remains till July. In the year 1784, snow was seen on the south side of the largest mountain, till the 12th of July; in 1790, it lay till the month of August.

During this period, of nine or ten months, the mountains exhibit more or less of that bright appearance, from which they are denominated white. In the spring, when the snow is partly dissolved, they appear of a pale blue, streaked with white; and after it is wholly gone, at the distance of sixty miles, they are altogether of the same pale blue, nearly approaching a sky colour; while at the same time, viewed at the distance of eight miles or less, they appear of the proper colour of the rock. These changes are observed by the people who live within constant view of them; and from these facts and observation, it may with certainty be concluded, that the whiteness of them is wholly caused by the snow, and not by any other white substance, for in fact, there is none. There are indeed in the summer months, some streaks, which appear brighter than other parts; but these, when viewed attentively with a telescope, are plainly discerned to be the edges or the sides of the long deep gullies, enlightened by the sun, and the dark parts are the shaded sides of the same; in the course of a day, these spots may be seen to vary, according to the position of the sun.

A company of gentlemen visited these mountains in July, 1784, with a view to make particular observations on the several phenomena which might occur. It happened, unfortunately, that thick clouds covered the mountains almost the whole time, so that some of the instruments, which, with much labour, they had carried up, were rendered useless. These were a sextant, a telescope, an instrument for ascertaining the bearings of distant objects, a barometer, a thermometer and several others for different purposes. In the barometer, the mercury ranged at 22,6, and the thermometer stood at 44 degrees. It was their intention to have placed one of each at the foot of the mountain, at the same time that the others were carried to the top, for the purpose of making corresponding observations; but they were unhappily broken in the course of the journey, through the rugged roads and thick woods, and the barometer, which was carried to the summit, had suffered so much agitation, that an allowance was necessary to be made, in calculating the height of the mountain, which was computed in round numbers, at five thousand and five hundred feet above the meadow, in the valley below, and nearly ten thousand feet above the level of the sea. They intended to have made a geometrical mensuration of the altitude; but in the meadow, they could not obtain a base of sufficient length, nor see the summit of the sugar loaf; and in another place where these inconveniences were removed, they were prevented by the almost continual obscuration of the mountains, by clouds.

Their exercise, in ascending the mountain, was so violent, that when Doctor Cutler, who carried the thermometer, took it out of his bosom, the mercury stood at fever heat, but it soon fell to 44°, and by the time that he had adjusted his barometer and thermometer, the cold had nearly deprived him of the use of his fingers. On the uppermost rock, the Rev. Mr. Little began to engrave the letters N.H., but was so chilled with the cold, that he gave the instruments to Col. Whipple, who finished the letters. Under a stone, they left a plate of lead, on which their names were engraven. The sun shone clear while they were passing over the plain, but immediately after their arrival at the highest summit, they had the mortification to be inveloped in a dense cloud, which came up the opposite side of the mountain. This unfortunate circumstance, prevented their making any farther use of their instruments. Being thus involved, as they were descending from the plain, in one of the long, deep gullies, not being able to see to the bottom, on a sudden, their pilot slipped, and was gone out of sight, though happily, without any other damage, than tearing his clothes. This accident obliged them to stop. When they turned their eyes upward, they were astonished at the immense depth and steepness of the place, which they had descended by fixing their heels on the prominent parts of the rock, and found it impracticable to reascend the same way; but having discovered a winding gully, of a more gradual ascent, in this they got up to the plain, and then came down on the eastern side; this deep gully, was on the S.E. From these circumstances, it may be inferred, that it is more practicable and safe, to ascend or descend on the ridges, than in the gullies of the mountain.

These vast and irregular heights, being copiously replenished with water, exhibit a great variety of beautiful cascades; some of which fall in a perpendicular sheet or spout, others are winding and sloping, others spread, and form a bason in the rock, and then gush in a cataract over its edge. A poetic fancy may find full gratification amidst these wild and rugged scenes, if its ardor be not checked by the fatigue of the approach. Almost every thing in nature, which can be supposed capable of inspiring ideas of the sublime and beautiful, is here realized. Aged mountains, stupendous elevations, rolling clouds, impending rocks, verdant woods, chrystal streams, the gentle rill, and the roaring torrent, all conspire to amaze, to soothe and to enrapture.

André Michaux Climbs Roan Mountain in the Unaka Mountains, 1795

ANDRÉ MICHAUX WAS born in 1746 near the palace at Versailles, France. For generations, his family had managed a part of the royal domain, so it was natural that the young Michaux's interest in plants would be encouraged. At the age of twenty-three he married Cécile Claye, and the couple had a son, François André. Cécile died shortly afterward; the despondent Michaux proceeded to lose himself in the study of the sciences, particularly botany. He made botanizing expeditions in England, the Pyrenees, and as far away as Persia before the French government, in 1785, asked him to go to America to look for useful trees and shrubs. Later that year he and his son were established on a plantation he had purchased near Charleston, South Carolina. (François André, who frequently accompanied his father on expeditions, went on to become a renowned botanist in his own right.)

In the New World, Michaux was a respected scientist who moved in high circles, being acquainted with the likes of James Madison and Thomas Jefferson. But he also enjoyed the rough life of the wilderness, and his devotion to botanical discovery made him a formidable traveler. He once confided that he feared "nothing so much as leaving discoveries to be made by those who shall come after me"; accordingly, he ranged widely, often returning to the same ground at different times of the year to collect specimens in flower and later in fruit. Knowing that different plant species were to be found at different elevations, he literally looked high and low to make his discoveries. After exploring the mountains of the Carolinas he traveled to the swamps of Florida, and later ranged north as far as the treeline in the Hudson Bay region.

Michaux's rigorous itineraries and single-minded devotion to botany seem to have left him little time for writing, for his journal is spare and to the point. In the first of the brief excerpts below, written during the period he made the first ascent of 6,391-foot Roan Mountain (Michaux's "Round Mountain"), any mention of the mountains is a mere afterthought, squeezed in between lists of the plants he encountered and practical notations about distances and habitations. If Michaux ever enjoyed the act of climbing or the view from atop a peak, he never thought it worth mentioning in his journal. Even when his feet were frozen, as in the second of the excerpts below, he made only the briefest mention of it.

Michaux wrote in French. The following selections are from a translation made for Ruben Gold Thwaites's turn-of-the-century collection, *Early Western Travels.*

Sunday 3rd of May started for the Mountains; at a distance of 14 miles from Burke is Wagely's house.

The Lineville Mountains at whose foot this house is situated, abound in *Magnolia auriculata.* They were then in flower. From Wagely's to Captain Young's is 8 Miles.

The 4th of May left Young's. The distance to Ainswort's is 2 miles but by going to the right one reaches the foot of a very high Mountain 3 Miles from Young's. The summit is 5 Miles from Young's.

From the summit of the Mountain at Young's to Bright's, called Bright's Settlement, the distance is 3 Miles and from Bright's to Davin Port's 2 Miles, making 10 Miles in all from Young's to Davin Port's.

The 5th of May herborized in the vicinity of the dwellings of Davin Port and Wiseman.

The 6th started for the Mountains, namely: Round Mountain and Yellow Mountain; Toe River flows between these Mountains. All the *Convallaria* were in flower as well as the *Podophyllum diphyllum* and *umbellatum.*

Sunday 10th of May 1795 returned from the Mountains to the dwelling of Davin Port.

The 11th herborized on the Mountains facing the dwelling. The distance to the summit of the Bleue Ridges at the part called Rompback is about 3 Miles; on the first Mountains are to be seen in very great abundance the *Azalea foliis apice glandulosis, Azalea lutea.* There is no other Azalea on the Hills surrounding the dwellings of Davin Port and Wiseman but this yellow-flowered species. That on the River banks is generally that with carnation flowers and that with white flowers.

The 12th ascended the summit of the Blueridges, *Rhododendron minus* in flower, *Cypripedium Luteum.*

The 13th of May started to continue my journey. At Noon arrived at the foot of Yellow Mountain 10 Miles. In the evening came to sleep at the house of John Miller 12 Miles from the Mountain. Thus there are 22 Miles from Davin Port's to Miller's; at a distance of half a mile one commences to cross Doe River.

─────────── ▲ ───────────

Sunday the 24th of January 1796 arrived at a Creek at a distance of 29 Miles near which one Chapman keeps lodgings at 3-1/2 miles; MacFaddin on Big Brown keeps a ferry and lodgings. Total 32-1/2 Miles.

The 25th Rain and Snow.

The 26th started for Green river. The ground was covered with snow, the Roads rough and my horse fell lame. I was obliged to walk. I made 12 miles. I was unable to light a fire because the trees and wood were all frosted. I spent the night nearly frozen. About 2 o'clock the Moon rose and I resolved to return to MacFaddin's where I arrived at 10 o'clock in the morning.

The 27th being overcome by cold and weariness, having traveled afoot, having eaten nothing since the morning of the previous day and not having slept during the night, the toes of my right foot became inflamed. I bathed my feet in cold water several times during the following night and no sores resulted therefrom but for several days the toes were numb as if deprived of sensation.

Charles Turner
Climbs Katahdin, 1804

C HARLES TURNER, JR., a Massachusetts farmer and congressman, was born in 1760 in Duxbury. A lieutenant commander in the State Militia from 1798–1812, he worked several summers as a surveyor in the New England interior. It was while surveying "north of the District of Maine" in 1804 that he made the first recorded ascent of 5,267-foot Mount Katahdin, which he spelled variously as "Catardin" or "Natardin" in his correspondence. He included an account of the climb in a letter written that summer; the extract of the letter reprinted below was first published in 1819 in the *Collections of the Massachusetts Historical Society*.

Turner's account is notable for its early reference to the Indian legend of Pamola, an evil spirit who would kill anyone who ventured high on the peak. Pamola is reminiscent of the similar spirit mentioned by Darby Field in 1642; in both cases, belief in such spirits was not strong enough to prevent at least some Indians from accompanying whites to the mountaintop.

As might be expected of a surveyor, Turner gives us an accurate description of the physical configuration of Katahdin. Lacking the necessary instruments, he was unable to estimate the peak's height, though he observed that the elevation was "so great as sensibly to effect respiration." He also noted that the high tableland of the mountain would have afforded an excellent baseline with which to map "all the principal highlands and mountains" in the district. Having left the tools of his trade behind, however, he could do little more than describe the "enchanting" view.

On Monday, August 13th, 1804, at 8 o'clock, A.M. we left our canoes at the head of boat-waters, in a small clear stream of spring water, which came in different rivulets from the mountain, the principal of which (as we afterwards found) issued from a large gully near the top of the mountain. At 5 o'clock, P.M. we reached the summit of the mountain. Catardin is the southernmost and highest of a collection of eight or ten mountains, extending from it north east and north west. Round this mountain, on the west, south and east sides is a table land extending about four miles, rising gradually to the foot of the mountain. This table land is much elevated and overlooks all the country except the mountains; when viewed from the mountain however it appears like a plane. Leaving the table land, and following a ridge, we endeavoured to gain the summit, at the west end, which appeared most easy of access. From the head of the table land, which we considered as the base of the mountain, we ascended on an elevation, making an angle with the horizon of from 35 to 46 degrees, about two miles. This mountain is composed of rocks, which appear to have been broken or split. The rocks, except at and near the top, are of a coarse grain, of light grey colour, and most of them are crumbling, and of these crumbles the soil, if such it may be called, is composed. The rocks near the top are of finer contexture and of a bluish colour. The table land was formerly covered with wood of various kinds; with hard woods near the streams where the soil was good; but with spruce in other parts, the trees lessening in height as we approached and ascended the mountain, until they became dwarfs of only two feet in height, and finally came to nothing at about a half mile from the summit. The rocks and soil in the ascent were covered with a deep green moss. The table land and mountain on the south and east have been burnt over, and are entirely bare, except near the springs and streams. The ridge between the streams on the west seemed to have escaped the fire, and this circumstance enabled us to ascend with greater facility. The south and east sides were from their steepness inaccessible. Having reached the top, we found ourselves on a plane of rocks with coarse gravel in the interstices, and the whole covered with a dead bluish moss. This plane, the westerly part of which was very smooth, and descending a little to the northward, contained about eight hundred acres. The elevation was so great as to sensibly affect respiration. The day was very calm and sultry, and our toil so great, that when we had found several springs of very clear cold water, our company were inclined to drink of them too freely. Some felt the ill effects immediately, and others were taken with vomitting in the course of the night following; indeed our whole company, which consisted of eleven, found, on the following morning, our throats sore and inflamed. Whether this arose wholly from some ill quality in the water, or partly from eating a variety of fruits, such as raspberries, blue whortleberries, black currants, boxberries and bog cranberries, which we found in abundance from the place where we left our boats to near the top, we could not determine. Though to us, in our thirsty and fatigued condition, the pure spring brought to our minds the fabled nectar of the poets, yet we found that it had a very perceptible astringent quality, and appeared to be impregnated with minerals.

Having arrived at the highest point, which is towards the east end, we found ourselves above all the mountains within our horizon. We could not determine our actual elevation, not having instruments, nor being otherwise prepared to measure the height of the mountain. From this point our view was enchanting; the air however had during the day become a little smoky, which prevented our distinguishing distant objects with that clearness which we could have wished. The plane on the top of the mountain, being nearly a mile and an half in length, would have afforded a base or leg, by which, with correct instruments, we might have determined with a great degree of exactness, the situations and distances of all the principal highlands and mountains in the District of Maine, and the situation and extent of the principal lakes. Here we could see, due north from us, the lake or cross pond, which is the main reservoir of the Aroostook branch of St. John's River, and several smaller lakes. . . . Amongst the collection of mountains near the Catardin, is one lying N.N.W. called by the English Fort Mountain, from its shape; its base being an oblong square or parallelogram, extending N.E. and S.W. and ascending at the sides and ends in an angle of about 45 degrees to a sharp ridge; which ridge is about one mile in length, and is covered with verdure. North of Fort Mountain appears an irregular mountain, on the S. side of which, and near the top, appears an extensive ledge of smooth white rock which glittered like isingglass. We could clearly discern the high lands, from the Bay of Chaleur westerly, which divide the District of Maine from the Province of Quebec. E.N.E. from us lay Peaked Mountain, over which Bingham's easterly line runs. Mount Desert was also distinctly in view. We could discern the range of high fertile lands extending N. and S. between the Penobscot and Scodic waters; and those between the Penobscot and Aroostook waters, and St. John's River. But the sun was now declining in the west, and we took leave of the summit of the mountain, after having deposited the initials of our names (William Howe, Amos Patten, Joseph Treat, Samuel Call, William Rice, Richard Winslow, Charles Turner, Jun.) and the date, cut upon sheet lead, and a bottle of rum corked and leaded, on the highest part. We descended the mountain with cautious steps, until we came among the low spruces, and the next day at noon we reached our canoes.

It is difficult by any orthography, precisely to express the name of this mountain, and convey the nasal sound which the natives give. No-tar-dn or Ca-ta-din is as near perhaps as the powers of the letters will admit.

The Indians have a superstition respecting this mountain, that an evil spirit, whom they call *Pamola,* inhabits it, at least in the winter, and flies off in the spring with tremendous rumbling noises. They have a tradition, that no person, i.e. native, who has attempted to ascend it, has lived to return. They allege, that many moons ago, seven Indians resolutely ascended the mountain, and that they were never heard of afterwards, having been undoubtedly killed by Pamola in the mountain. The two Indians, whom we hired to pilot and assist us in ascending the mountain, cautioned us not to proceed if we should hear any uncommon noise; and when we came to the cold part of the mountain, they refused to proceed ahead — however, when they found that we were determined to proceed, even without them, they again went forward courageously, and seemed ambitious to be first on the summit. On our return to Indian Old Town, it was with difficulty that we could convince the natives that we had been upon the top of Mount Catardin, nor should we have been able to satisfy them of the fact, so superstitious were they, had it not been for the Indians who had accompanied us.

Zebulon Pike Attempts
Pikes Peak, 1806

Z EBULON MONTGOMERY PIKE made two notable explorations in the American West. The first, in 1805, took him to the headwaters of the Mississippi River, and the second, the following year, in search of the sources of the Arkansas and Red rivers – and also, in collusion with James Wilkinson, a Spanish double agent linked with Aaron Burr, to find a route for invading the Spanish territory of New Mexico. Neither expedition was completely successful. On the first, Pike incorrectly identified a lake in Minnesota as the fountain of the Mississippi, and on the second, after struggling across the rugged Sangre de Cristo mountains to the upper Rio Grande, his party was arrested by Spanish forces. The wayward explorers were not released until the summer of 1807.

It was while traveling up the Arkansas River in late 1806 that Pike first glimpsed the 14,110-foot mountain that now bears his name. The distant peak appeared at first "like a small blue cloud" on the horizon; after approaching to within what he thought was a day's march away, he set out with a few men to climb it. He seriously underestimated the distances involved, and never got within miles of the top. His failure is certainly understandable, for with the exception of the members of the recently returned Lewis and Clark expedition, no other Americans had even *seen* the Rocky Mountains, and Pike and his men were certainly the first whites to try to climb them. Today, when thousands of tourists annually drive or ride to the summit of Pikes Peak, it is easy to laugh at Pike's claim that "no human being could have ascended to its pinical." But few of us would want to try what he tried: the first ascent, from its base on the prairie and in cold, wintry conditions, of a mountain almost eight thousand feet higher than any hitherto attempted in the nation.

The selection below is taken from *The Journals of Zebulon Montgomery Pike*, first published in 1810.

15th November, Saturday. — Marched early. Passed two deep creeks and many high points of the rocks; also, large herds of buffalo. At two o'clock in the afternoon I thought I could distinguish a mountain to our right, which appeared like a small blue cloud; viewed it with the spy glass, and was still more confirmed in my conjecture, yet only communicated it to doctor Robinson, who was in front with me, but in half an hour, they appeared in full view before us. When our small party arrived on the hill they with one accord gave three *cheers* to *the Mexican mountains*. The appearance can easily be imagined by those who have crossed the Alleghany; but their sides were whiter, as if covered with snow, or a white stone. Those were a *spur* of the grand western chain of

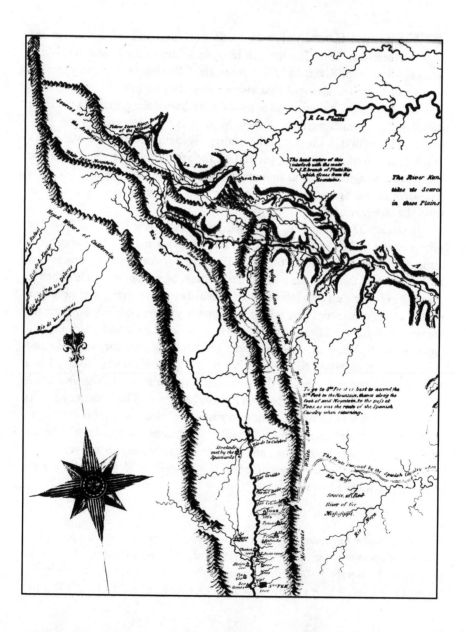

mountains, which divide the waters of the Pacific from those of the Atlantic oceans, and it divided the waters which empty into the bay of the Holy Spirit, from those of the Mississippi, as the Alleghany does, those which discharge themselves into the latter river and the Atlantic. They appear to present a natural boundary between the province of Louisiana and New Mexico and would be a defined and natural boundary.

▲

24th November, Monday. — Early in the morning cut down fourteen logs, and put up a breast work, five feet high on three sides and the other was thrown on the river. After giving the necessary orders for their government, during my absence, in case of our not returning. We marched at one o'clock with an idea of arriving at the foot of the mountain; but found ourselves obliged to take up our nights lodging under a single cedar, which we found in the prairie, without water and extremely cold. Our party besides myself consisted of doctor Robinson, privates Miller and Brown. Distance 12 miles.

25th November, Tuesday. — Marched early, with an expectation of ascending the mountain, but was only able to encamp at its base, after passing over many small hills covered with cedars and pitch pines. Our encampment was on a creek where we found no water for several miles from the mountain, but near its base, found springs sufficient. Took a meridional observation, and the altitude of the mountain. Killed two buffalo. Distance 22 miles.

26th November, Wednesday. — Expecting to return to our camp that evening, we left all our blankets and provisions at the foot of the mountain. Killed a deer of a new species, and hung his skin on a tree with some meat. We commenced ascending, found it very difficult, being obliged to climb up rocks, sometimes almost perpendicular; and after marching all day, we encamped in a cave, without blankets, victuals or water. We had a fine clear sky, whilst it was snowing at the bottom. On the side of the mountain, we found only yellow and pitch pine. Some distance up we found buffalo, higher still the new species of deer and pheasants.

27th November, Thursday. — Arose hungry, dry, and extremely sore, from the inequality of the rocks, on which we had lain all night, but were amply compensated for toil by the sublimity of the prospects below. The unbounded prairie was overhung with clouds, which appeared like the ocean in a storm, wave piled on wave and foaming, whilst the sky was perfectly clear where we were. Commenced our march up the mountain, and in about one hour arrived at the summit of this chain: here we found the snow middle deep; no sign of beast or bird inhabiting this region. The thermometer which stood at 9° above 0 [Centigrade; about 52° Fahrenheit] at the foot of the mountain, here fell to 4° below 0 [22° Fahrenheit]. The summit of the Grand Peak, which was entirely bare of vegetation and covered with snow, now appeared at a distance of 15 or 16 miles from us, and as high again as what we had ascended, and would have taken a whole day's march to have arrived at its base, when I believe no human being could have ascended to its pinical. This with the condition of my soldiers who had light overalls on, and no stockings, and every way ill provided to endure the inclemency of the region; the bad prospect of killing any thing to subsist on, with the further detention of two or three days, which it must occasion, determined us to return. The clouds from below had now ascended the mountain and entirely enveloped the summit on which rests eternal snows. We descended by a long deep ravine with much less difficulty than contemplated. Found all our baggage safe, but the provisions all destroyed. It began to snow, and we sought shelter under the side of a projecting rock, where we, all four, made a meal on one partridge, and a piece of deer's ribs, the ravens had left us, being the first we had eaten in that 48 hours.

Edwin James Climbs
Pikes Peak, 1820

EDWIN JAMES WAS born in Vermont in 1797 and educated in both medicine and the natural sciences. In 1819, when he was just twenty-two years old, James was chosen to serve as botanist, geologist, and surgeon to the expedition of Major Stephen H. Long, which set out the following spring to explore the western plains and to measure the height of the "Grand Peak" attempted by Pike fourteen years earlier. The expedition moved up the Platte River and then its south branch, reaching the base of the Rockies in July. A prominent mountain visible to the west was at first thought to be Pikes Peak, but was in fact today's Longs Peak; when the explorers realized their mistake they turned south and soon sighted the true Pikes Peak. James, along with two other men, climbed the mountain over two long days, reaching the top on July 14, 1820.

James wrote about the ascent for his *Account of an Expedition from Pitts-burgh to the Rocky Mountains,* first published in 1822. His account reflects his training as a scientist but is also highly sensitive to the novelty and grandeur of the peak, particularly the flower-sprinkled tundra above timberline, which he called "a region of astonishing beauty." The ascent itself, though not technically difficult, was a genuine venture into the unknown, and James writes with quiet understatement about the hardships and uncertainties faced by the party: they ran out of food, bivouacked at high altitude, and finally returned to find their camp destroyed by fire. In addition they found them-selves in a typical mountaineering dilemma: high on the peak, with the afternoon growing late, unsure whether they would be able to reach the summit and return by nightfall. To their credit, they continued the climb, thereby completing the first recorded ascent of a 14,000-foot peak in the United States.

At an early hour on the morning of the 13th [July 13, 1820], Lieutenant Swift, accompanied by the guide, was despatched from camp, to measure a base near the peak, and to make there a part of the observations requisite for calculating its elevation. Dr. James, being furnished with four men, two to be left at the foot of the mountain to take care of the horses, and two to accompany him in the proposed ascent to the summit of the peak, set off at the same time. [James wrote this section himself. He switches to first person below.]

This detachment left the camp before sunrise, and taking the most direct route across the plains, arrived at eleven o'clock at the base of the mountain. Here Lieutenant Swift found a place suited to his purpose; where, also, was a convenient spot for those who were to ascend the mountain to leave their horses. At this place was a narrow, woodless valley, dividing transversely several sandstone ridges, and extending westward to the base of the peak.

After establishing their horse-camp, the detachment moved up the valley on foot, arriving about noon at the boiling spring, where they dined on a saddle of venison, and some bison ribs they had brought ready-cooked from camp.

——————— ▲ ———————

After we had dined, and hung up some provisions in a large red cedar-tree near the spring, intending it for a supply on our return, we took leave of Lieutenant Swift, and began to ascend the mountain. We carried with us each a small blanket, ten or twelve pounds of bison meat, three gills of parched corn meal, and a small kettle.

The sandstone extends westward from the springs, about three hundred yards, rising rapidly upon the base of the mountain; it is of a deep red colour, for the most part compact and fine, but sometimes embracing angular fragments of petrosilex and other siliceous stones, with a few organic impressions. The granite which succeeds to this is coarse, and of a deep red colour; some loose fragments of gneiss were seen lying about the surface, but none in place. The granite at the base of the mountain contains a large proportion of felspar, of the rose-coloured variety, in imperfect cubic crystals. The mass appears to be rapidly disintegrating, under the operation of frost and other causes, crumbling into small masses of half an ounce weight, or less.

The ascending party found the surface in many places covered with such quantities of this loose and crumbled granite, rolling from under their feet, as rendered the ascent extremely difficult. We now began to credit the assertions of the guide, who had conducted us to the foot of the peak, and there left us, with the assurance that the whole of the mountain to its summit was covered with sand and gravel; so that, though many attempts had been made by the Indians and by hunters to ascend it, none had ever proved successful. We passed several of these tracts, not without some apprehension for our lives, as there was danger, when the foothold was once lost, of sliding down, and being thrown over precipices. After labouring with extreme fatigue over about two miles, in which several of these dangerous places occurred, we halted at sunset in a small cluster of fir trees. We could not, however, find a piece of even

ground large enough to lie down upon, and were under the necessity of securing ourselves from rolling into the brook near which we encamped by means of a pole placed against two trees. In this situation, we passed an uneasy night; and though the thermometer fell only to 54°, felt some inconvenience from cold.

On the morning of the 14th, as soon as daylight appeared, having suspended in a tree our blankets, all our provisions, except about three pounds of bison's flesh, and whatever articles of clothing could be dispensed with, we continued the ascent, hoping to be able to reach the summit of the peak, and return to the same camp in the evening. After passing about half a mile of rugged and difficult travelling, like that of the preceding day, we crossed a deep chasm, opening towards the bed of the small stream we had hitherto ascended; and following the summit of the ridge between these, found the way less difficult and dangerous.

Having passed a level tract of several acres covered with the aspen, poplar, a few birches, and pines, we arrived at a small stream running towards the south, nearly parallel to the base of the conic part of the mountain which forms the summit of the peak. From this spot we could distinctly see almost the whole of the peak: its lower half thinly clad with pines, junipers, and other evergreen trees; the upper, a naked conic pile of yellowish rocks, surmounted here and there with broad patches of snow. But the summit appeared so distant, and the ascent so steep, that we began to despair of accomplishing the ascent and returning on the same day.

About the small stream before mentioned, we saw an undescribed white-flowered species of caltha, some pediculariae, the shrubby cinque-foil (potentilla fruticosa, Ph.) and many alpine plants. At this point a change is observed in the character of the rock, all that which constitutes the peak beyond containing to mica. It is a compact, fine-grained aggregate of quartz, felspar, and hornblende; the latter in small proportion, and sometimes wholly wanting.

The day was bright, and the air nearly calm. As we ascended rapidly, we could perceive a manifest change of temperature; and before we reached the outskirts of the timber, a little wind was felt from the northeast. On this part of the mountain is frequently seen the yellow-flowered stone-crop (sedum steno-petalum, Ph.), almost the only herbaceous plant which occurs in the most closely wooded parts of the mountain. We found the trees of a smaller size, and more scattered in proportion to the elevation at which they grew; and arrived at about twelve o'clock at the limit above which none are found. This is a defined line, encircling the peak in a part which, when seen from the plain, appeared near the summit; but when we arrived at it, a greater part of the whole elevation of the mountain seemed still before us. Above the timber the ascent is steeper, but less difficult than below; the surface being so highly inclined that the large masses, when loosened, roll down, meeting no obstruction until they arrive at the commencement of the timber. The red cedar, and the flexile pine, are the trees which appear at the greatest elevation. These are small, having thick and extremely rigid trunks; and near the commencement of the naked part of the mountain, they have neither limbs nor bark on that side which is exposed to the descending masses of rocks. It may appear a contradiction to assert, that trees have grown in a situation so exposed as to be unable to produce or retain bark or limbs on one side; yet of the fact that they are now standing and living in such a situation there can be no doubt. It is, perhaps, probable the timber may formerly have extended to a greater elevation on the sides of this peak than at present, so that those trees which are now of the outskirts of the forest were formerly protected by their more exposed neighbours.

A few trees were seen above the commencement of snow; but these are very small, and entirely procumbent, being sheltered in the crevices and fissures of the rock. There are also the roots of trees to be seen at some distance above the part where any are now standing.

A little above the point where the timber disappears entirely, commences a region of astonishing beauty, and of great interest on account of its productions. The intervals of soil are sometimes extensive, and covered with a carpet of low but brilliantly-flowering alpine plants. Most of these have either matted procumbent stems, or such as, including the flower, rarely rise more than an inch in height. In many of them the flower is the most conspicuous and the largest part of the plant, and in all the colouring is astonishingly brilliant.

A deep blue is the prevailing colour among these flowers; and the pentemon erianthera, the mountain columbine (aquilegia coerulea), and other plants common to less elevated districts, were much more intensely coloured than in ordinary situations. It cannot be doubted, that the peculiar brilliancy of colouring observed in alpine plants, inhabiting near the utmost limits of phaenogamous vegetation, depends principally upon the intensity of the light transmitted from the bright and unobscured atmosphere of those regions, and increased by reflection from the immense impending masses of snow. May the deep cerulean tint of the sky have an influence in producing the corresponding colour so prevalent in the flowers of these alpine plants? At about two o'clock we found ourselves so much exhausted as to render a halt necessary. Mr. Wilson, who had accompanied us as a volunteer, had been left behind some time since, and could not now be seen in any direction. As we felt some anxiety on his account, we halted, and endeavoured to apprize him of our situation; but repeated calls, and the discharging of the rifleman's piece, produced no answer. We therefore determined to wait some time to rest, and to eat the provision we had bought, hoping, in the meantime, he would overtake us.

We halted at a place about a mile above the edge of the timber. The stream by which we were sitting we could perceive to fall immediately from a large body of snow, which filled a deep ravine on the south-eastern side of the peak. Below us, on the right, were two or three extensive patches of snow; and ice could be seen everywhere in the crevices of the rocks.

Here, as we were sitting at our dinner, we observed several small animals, nearly of the size of the common gray squirrel; but shorter, and more clumsily built. They were of a dark gray colour, inclining to brown, with a short thick head, and erect rounded ears. In habits and appearance, they resemble the prairie dog, and are believed to be a species of the same genus. The mouth of their burrow is usually placed under the projection of a rock; and near these the party afterwards saw several of the little animals watching their approach, and uttering all the time a shrill note, somewhat like that of the ground squirrel. Several attempts were made to procure a specimen of this animal, but always without success, as we had no guns but such as carried a heavy ball.

After sitting about half an hour, we found ourselves somewhat refreshed, but much benumbed with cold. We now found it would be impossible to reach the summit of the mountain, and return to our camp of the preceding night, during that part of the day which remained; but as we could not persuade ourselves to turn back, after having so nearly accomplished the ascent, we resolved to take our chance of spending the night on whatever part of the mountain it might overtake us. Wilson had not yet been seen; but as no time could be lost, we resolved to go as soon as possible to the top of the peak, and look for him on our return. We met, as we proceeded, such numbers of unknown and interesting plants, as to occasion much delay in collection; and were under the mortifying necessity of passing by numbers we saw in situations difficult of access.

As we approached the summit, these [plants] became less frequent, and at length ceased entirely. Few cryptogamous plants are seen about any part of the mountain; and neither these nor any others occur frequently on the top of the peak. There is an area of ten or fifteen acres forming the summit, which is nearly level; and on this part scarce a lichen was to be seen. It is covered to great depth with large splintery fragments of a rock entirely similar to that found at the base of the peak, except perhaps a little more compact in its structure. By removing a few of these fragments, they were found to rest upon a bed of ice, which is of great thickness and may, perhaps, be as permanent as the rocks with which it occurs.

It was about 4 o'clock P.M. when the party arrived on the summit. In our way we had attempted to cross a large field of snow, which occupied a deep ravine, extending down about half a mile from the top, on the south-eastern side of the peak. This was, however, found impassable, being covered with a thin ice, not sufficiently strong to bear the weight of a man. We had not been long on the summit when we were rejoined by the man who had separated from us, near the outskirts of the timber. He had turned aside and lain down to rest, and afterwards pursued his journey by a different route.

From the summit of the peak, the view towards the north-west and south-west is diversified with innumerable mountains, all white with snow; and on some of the more distant it appears to extend down to their bases. Immediately under our feet, on the west, lay the narrow valley of the Arkansa, which we could trace running towards the north-west, probably more than sixty miles.

On the north side of the peak was an immense mass of snow and ice. The ravine in which it lay terminated in a woodless and apparently fertile valley, lying west of the first great ridge, and extending far towards the north. This valley must undoubtedly contain a considerable branch of the Platte. In a part of it, distant probably thirty miles, the smoke of a large fire was distinctly seen, supposed to indicate the encampment of a party of Indians.

To the east lay the great plain, rising as it receded, until in the distant horizon it appeared to mingle with the sky. A little want of transparency in the atmosphere, added to the great elevation from which we saw the plain, prevented our distinguishing the small inequalities of the surface. The Arkansa, with several of its tributaries, and some of the branches of the Platte, could be distinctly traced as on a map, by the lines of timber along their courses.

On the south the mountain is continued, having another summit, (supposed to be that ascended by Captain Pike,) at the distance of eight or ten miles. This, however, falls much below the high peak in point of elevation, being wooded quite to its top. Between the two lies a small lake, apparently a mile long, and half a mile wide, discharging eastward into the Boiling-spring creek. A few miles farther towards the south, the range containing these two peaks terminates abruptly.

The weather was calm and clear while the detachment remained on the peak; but we were surprised to observe the air in every direction filled with such clouds of grasshoppers, as partially to obscure the day. They had been seen in vast numbers about all the higher parts of the mountain, and many had fallen upon the snow and perished. It is, perhaps, difficult to assign the cause which induces these insects to ascend to those highly elevated regions of the atmosphere. Possibly they may have undertaken migrations to some remote district; but there appears not the least uniformity in the direction of their movements. They extended upwards from the summit of the mountain to the utmost limit of vision; and as the sun shone brightly, they could be seen by the glittering of their wings, at a very considerable distance.

About all the woodless parts of the mountain, and particularly on the summit, numerous tracks were seen, resembling those of the common deer, but most probably have been those of the animal called the big horn. The skulls and horns of these animals we had repeatedly seen near the licks and saline springs at the foot of the mountain, but they are known to resort principally about the most elevated and inaccessible places.

The party remained on the summit only about half an hour; in this time the mercury fell to 42°, the thermometer hanging against the side of a rock, which in all the early part of the day had been exposed to the direct rays of the sun. At the encampment of the main body in the plains, a corresponding thermometer stood in the middle of the day at 96°, and did not fall below 80° until a late hour in the evening.

Great uniformity was observed in the character of the rock about the upper part of the mountain. It is a compact, indestructible aggregate of quartz and felspar, with a little hornblende, in very small particles. Its fracture is fine, granular, or even; and the rock exhibits a tendency to divide when broken into long, somewhat splintery fragments. It is of a yellowish brown colour, which does not perceptibly change by long exposure to the air. It is undoubtedly owing to the close texture and the impenetrable firmness of this rock that so few lichens are found upon it. For the same reason it is little subject to disintegration by the action of frost. It is not improbable that the splintery fragments, which occur in such quantities on all the higher parts of the peak, may owe their present form to the agency of lightning. No other cause seems adequate to the production of so great an effect.

Near the summit some large detached crystals of felspar, of a pea-green colour, were collected; also large fragments of transparent, white and smoky quartz, and an aggregate of opaque white quartz, with crystals of hornblende.

At about five in the afternoon the party began to descend, and a little before sunset arrived at the commencement of the timber; but before we reached the small stream at the bottom of the first descent, we perceived we had missed our way. It was now become so dark as to render an attempt to proceed extremely hazardous; and as the only alternative, we kindled a fire, and laid ourselves down upon the first spot of level ground we could find. We had neither provisions nor blankets; and our clothing was by no means suitable for passing the night in so bleak and inhospitable a situation. We could not, however, proceed without imminent danger from precipices; and by the aid of a good fire, and no ordinary degree of fatigue, found ourselves able to sleep during a greater part of the night.

15th. At day break on the following morning, the thermometer stood at 38°. As we had few comforts to leave, we quitted our camp as soon as the light was sufficient to enable us to proceed. We had travelled about three hours when we discovered a dense column of smoke rising from a deep ravine on the left hand. As we concluded this could be no other than the smoke of the encampment where we had left our blankets and provisions, we descended directly towards it. The fire had spread and burnt extensively among the leaves, dry grass, and small timber, and was now raging over an extent of several acres. This created some apprehension, lest the smoke might attract the notice of any Indians who should be at that time in the neighbourhood, and who might be tempted by the weakness of the party to offer some molestation. But we soon discovered a less equivocal cause of regret in the loss of our *cache* of provisions, blankets, clothing, &c. which had not escaped the conflagration. Most of our baggage was destroyed; but out of the ruins we collected a beggarly breakfast, which we ate, notwithstanding its meanness, with sufficient appetite.

An Anonymous Ascent
of Mount Washington, 1825

B Y 1825 THE ascent of Mount Washington had become *de rigueur* for the serious botanist. Jacob Bigelow, Francis Boott, and Edward Tuckerman, among other botanical luminaries, visited the peak during the early part of the nineteenth century and were subsequently commemorated by place names familiar to today's climbers. Even the renowned Thomas Nuttall, perhaps the most prolific of botanists, made the pilgrimage, though it is not clear that he ever reached the summit.

The written legacy of this scientific army, though interesting in its own way, is generally pretty sober stuff, heavily freighted with Latinate detail and maintaining a serious tone in keeping with its subject. But the following account, gleaned from the October 1825 issue of the *Worcester Magazine and Historical Journal*, is refreshingly different. Its anonymous author was obviously impressed by Mount Washington, but didn't let an excess of awe overburden his prose, which is light and playful where it is not downright scurrilous. He gently lampoons the pretensions of science and readily admits that his climb was made purely for pleasure. Here is a delightfully written record of what surely was one of the first solely recreational mountain ascents in America.

From the period of the first settlement of New England down to the present time, the giant heights then called the "Crystal Hills," and since denominated the White Mountains, have attracted the attention, and tempted the visits of many a curious and inquisitive traveller. They have now become the resort of the idle wanderers who pursue pleasure even on their barren summits, or of the scientific enquirers, who explore their rocky sides with unbounded industry, who consider themselves happy, and their toils rewarded, if, perchance, they discover some quaint moss or obscure lichen, invisible to common observers and unknown to former learned strollers. The crowds of visitors of the colossal piles, plunder nothing but a few perishing flowers, withered grasses, or mineral fragments: they leave to every new climber, the severe labors of ascending, the sublime views from the summits, and all the novelty and grandeur of mountain scenery.

The White Mountains are indeed most interesting objects. Standing as they do in a rude and wild region, not remarkable for towering elevations, they are distinguished for their lofty height. Mount Washington, the tallest of the brothers, is said to exceed in altitude the Alleghanies of the South, and the Green Mountains of the North, by nearly 2,500 feet. He even rises above the more celebrated peaks of other more romantic lands: Olympus, connected as he is with so many classic recollections, is only of equal stature. [Mount Olympus, at 9,570 feet, is actually more than three thousand feet higher than Mount Washington.] Ben Nevis, the most elevated land in the island of Great Britain, and Snowdon, the king of the Welsh Hills, are lower by more than 2,000 feet.

It was in the pleasant season of spring, that the writer, in company with an intelligent friend, set forth on the excursion which has furnished the materials for the narrative in the following pages. Believing that every speck of the soil of our country is interesting to its inhabitants, he is induced to suppose, that the description of the most massive of its piles of earth and stone, will be amusing to some.

Our journey had been along the Eastern side of the range and upon the banks of the rapid, but beautiful, stream of the Androscoggin. This noble river, issuing from a series of solitary lakes, embosomed in the forest, and dignified with Indian names, almost as formidable as the red warriors themselves, pours Westward seeking an outlet among the ridges of hills that encompass it about. At length, it does escape through an opening in the mountain barrier, and rushes through the vallies at its base, with a hurried motion, as if the favourable opportunity might be lost by any delay; but after journeying to the South for a few miles, it is again obstructed by an opposing ridge, and wanders on to the East, in quest of a channel to convey its waters to the sea. It does not, however, take the direct course to the ocean, until it has traversed fifty miles between parallel hills, of so firm structure as to resist every attempt of their prisoner to break from its confinement. Then it goes on with a clear and tranquil motion, scattering fertility along its banks, till it meets with other obstructions. At Rumford a precipice is stretched across the bed of the waters: They are not precipitated in one broad sheet from its edge, but tumbling from cliff to cliff, are dashed into foam. The spray, tinged with all the bright colors of the rainbow, rises from their commotion and is painted by the sun-beams. The thunder of this miniature cataract is heard from a distance, and the earth, either in reality or imagination, trembles with the heavy falling. The descent is estimated at seventy feet. After dashing over the rock, the river spreads out in a broad basin, and seems resting to recover power before it rushes over a second ledge, which opposes its passage about a fourth of a mile below. It leaps over this smaller bar, and frets along another quarter of a mile, and again plunges down a declivity, about fifteen feet in height. An island at the foot of the last rapid, covered with fair trees, rests placidly amid the uproar, as if smiling on the turmoil around it. The snowy whiteness of the stream is beautifully contrasted with the green and waving foliage.

All the difficulties are not yet surmounted. The Pejypscot rocks sturdily spread themselves across the path and the river descends about eighty feet: at Brunswick it goes down among saw mills and broken masses of stone fifty feet more. At length it joins itself to the Kenebeck, a lazy and sluggish stream, in Merry-meeting Bay, a very appropriate name: for if the Androscoggin could be supposed to be an intelligent and animated being, it might well rejoice on coming within sight of the broad Atlantic. Indeed, it owes no gratitude to the earth for mingling its waters with its indolent partner and afterwards with the broad ocean: for, from the moment of its rising among the Northern Hills, until its arrival at the place of destination, it receives no favors, but forces its way along by violence; encountering and subduing all possible difficulties, and often scooping out for itself a channel through the solid rock.

This river has scenery singularly wild and elegant. I have been floated over its current where it steals out from the Lakes, in those bright days which gladden the declining year, when departing summer lingers with its warmest smile upon the lap of autumn. The Fish-Hawk screamed from the dry branches of some stately tree, and smoothed his feathers, or plunged in the water for his prey. The stream glided on calmly through green recesses, overshadowed by majestic pines, as if pausing to enjoy the cool shade. There was scarcely a sound, except the voluptuous humming of the bees, plundering from the flowers that bent over the clear expanse, their sweets. The Squirrel, that merry little Aristocrat, sat up and gnawed his nutshell with a most princely air, and looked down upon the small birds, fluttering and pecking beneath, with supreme contempt, till tired with his feast, he bounded away and frolicked among the branches with light hearted joy. The Bittern crept along the sands, and the Wild Ducks swam down in fleets, till, frightened by the dashing of our oars, they took flight, with loud but not unmusical cries. Sometimes the stream gushed through narrow passes where the eternal hills closed down on either hand upon its path, and then there were the broken murmurs of the rapids. The forests stained by the early frosts had put on their robes of many colors. Rich dyes were on the leaves, crimson and yellow, purple and gold. The Maples dressed in deep red, looked like warriors sprinkled with blood; and as the drapery, so peculiar to our seasons and climate, spread along the hills, it appeared like a Persian carpet let down from the summits and floating along the sides.

Reserving a general description of the Mountains and a narration of the interesting facts gathered from the observations of others or the results of personal experience, to be placed, as important matters commonly are, in a Postscript, we would now invite the reader to join our little party and clamber with us over the rocks.

Leaving, with regret, the smooth and level road along the intervale of the Androscoggin, we turned Westward into the forest, and pursued our journey through highways hollowed out from the woods, and carried over the little streams and meadows on most uncomfortable structures, formed by placing the trunks of trees parallel with each other, and very happily named "gridiron bridges," from their close resemblance to the separated bars and rough surface of that instrument, till we arrived at a cottage built of squared and jointed logs. The interstices between the timbers were closely filled with moss, so as to shut out wind and rain, and the building, wainscotted on the interior with broad strips of Hemlock bark, had an air of great neatness and substantial usefulness. In the front, uprose the majestic height; the sides clothed with the deep green covering of Firs and Pines, except where dark furrows marked the path of the headlong torrents, fed from the snows above: and the bare summit, grey and bald with age.

Having procured an addition to our party, not in the capacity of a guide, but of a baggage waggon, to transport our moveables, we set forward. The inventory of our goods and chattels was not swelled with the list of philosophical instruments, the incumbrances of learned travellers. It was the noon of a sultry June day, and we succeeded in ascertaining, with tolerable accuracy, that it was hot, without the aid of a thermometer; we were equally fortunate, after a few hours toil, in the discovery that we were climbing up-hill, without the assistance of a barometer. Having no felonious design upon the stones, and little acquaintance with the profound science of minerals, so abounding with barbarous names, that the uninitiated are compelled to wonder, that words so stupendous should ever have been invented, and admire even more, that they can be recollected, we were not even provided with a hammer. Not intending to enter into any speculations on heights or distances, we had not brought in memory, sines, or angles, or tangents, figures which it is a wo to see, and a misery to hear named.

An easy walk of about two miles through a field of stately Maples, brought us to the foot of the mountain, on the North-East of the range, and we began to ascend the banks of a stream which conveys its tribute of the Androscoggin. Beneath the Pines and Firs, the earth was covered with a thick and luxuriant growth of bushes, peculiar to the woods of Northern regions. As we advanced, the way, if so it may be said, where way there was none, became more difficult. Fallen and decaying trunks, prostrated by the storms, obstructed the passage. Sometimes rocks were piled upon rocks, presenting abrupt precipices along which we rose, resting on some feeble foothold, and leaping from one moss-grown crag to another, with great labor and some little peril. Had a branch broken, a root drawn from its slender fastening, or a stone overturned, the reader might have been amused with the pleasant addition of a catalogue of broken bones. The hosts of vexatious insects who find shelter among the evergreens, swarmed round us in such multitudes that it seemed as if intelligence must have been communicated by telegraphic dispatches of our arrival, to collect such legions in so short a space. The Musquito sounded his shrill horn, the little Gnat answered the signal with his trumpet, and the Black Flies joining their forces, they all commenced a most active attack upon our veins, continuing operations without mercy. They fixed their stings in every point of surface exposed without covering; where the protecting dress was thin, they settled and drank with great satisfaction of the blood below; where it was loose, they used no ceremony in procuring their repast. If fatigue forced us to yawn, they very freely entered our mouths, and with great impertinence intruded themselves along with the prospects, into our eyes. The Crocodile, notorious all over the world for his hypocrisy, is said to feign sleep, and spread open his enormous jaws, to secure a repast upon the prey collected in this manner: if the feast were not more agreeable to him, than it proved to us, he would not easily be persuaded to try the same trick a second time. Not a breath of air stirred among the leaves. The dense foliage shut out the views above, below, and around.

Six hours of severe labor had brought us about five miles upon our way, when the shades of evening came silently and calmly upon the forest. Upon the margin of a rivulet we found a suitable place for repose and there we kindled our fire to prepare our simple meal, to fright away the wild beasts, and to stifle with its smoke the legions of tormentors. Our tent was of easy construction. Clearing a little spot before the blaze, two forked sticks were erected, support-ing a pole laid across horizontally; rafters rested on this beam, sloping towards the ground after the most approved architectural rules for the inclination of roofs. A thatch of Hemlock branches covered these timbers and the same material inclosed the sides. Small twigs of the Fir tree, spread under this shelter, made a fragrant and pleasant bed. The preparations for supper were of no trifling importance to those who had gained a keen appetite from severe exercise. Hunger wonderfully quickens invention, and we were soon supplied with a culinary apparatus, which Count Rumford might have envied for its simplicity and perfection. With a split stick for spit, strips of Birch bark for plates, fingers and teeth for knives and forks, and a mountain relish for food, we contrived to make a sumptuous repast of our roasted pork, and sweetened the princely feast with pure water from the spring, by way of dessert. These preliminaries being satisfactorily adjusted, we stretched ourselves on the per-fumed couches so easily prepared, and diligently invited sleep. Our winged enemies had no intention of concluding an armistice, or of ceasing hostilities, to permit the enjoyment of such refreshment; the only intervals of slumber were, when the thick smoke of the huge fire, blazing in front, fell upon the house and obliged these busy antagonists to decamp. Once, the impatience under their incessant provocation had nearly produced serious inconvenience. In a moment of great indignation, I seized on one of the main pillars of the building with a degree of strength, compared with the frail structure, even as that of him of old, who moved the columns of the temple to and fro till they fell and crushed the flower of the Philistines, their best and noblest, on the day of their solemn festival: the results were almost similar: we were half buried beneath the ruins drawn down on the buzzing disturbers of the peace.

With the first light of returning day we struck our tent, and took up the line of march, to finish the remaining four miles. The trees became more dwarfish and diminutive in stature and the carpet of moss thicker and deeper. At length we emerged from among the taller plants and entered a zone of different character where the stunted Pines, short Spruces, and low Firs, were matted and twisted together. These natives of the highlands, perhaps planted in the solitude in the days of Adam, have scarcely reached a height equal to that of the degenerate descendants from the Father of the Human Race. The trunks are stout and firmly rooted, shooting out strong horizontal branches, closely interwoven, and forming an almost impenetrable barrier. At about the distance of a mile from the summit, the thicket terminated, and a barren region commenced, covered with moss to the depth of a foot, and without trees. Rocks were piled together, in separate fragments of all varieties of shape and size, yet so firmly wedged and fixed as to afford a firm and solid foothold for the tread of the passer. The ascent was made toilsome by the steep declivity, and vexatious from the structure of the sterile waste. One peak, standing directly before other and higher elevations, intercepted the view from below, and seemed the termination of what had become a very weary journey for pleasure; but after clambering up the rocky side, another steep presented itself rising beyond, raising the same hope that it was the last, to end in the same disappointment. At length we did reach the last, and stood on one of the highest summits of the most elevated land in North America.

Benjamin Bonneville in the Wind River Range, 1833

B
ENJAMIN LOUIS EULALIE de Bonneville was born in France in 1796, the son of a highly educated mother and a radical father. For a time another noted radical, Thomas Paine, lived in the Bonneville household. When Paine left the country to escape the persecution of Napoleon Bonaparte, Mme. Bonneville and the children followed him to America. Benjamin enrolled at West Point, graduating in 1815, and after several years of service in the East was transferred to Fort Smith, Arkansas, there beginning what was to be a long association with the American frontier.

In 1832, having secured the backing of a number of investors, including Jacob Astor, Bonneville requested a two-year leave of absence from the Army in order to explore the fur-rich Green River country of Wyoming. He left in May with a hundred and ten men and spent more than three years in the mountains. The expedition was in many respects unsuccessful; Bonneville's army of trappers was unable to compete with the many others already operating in the area, and his explorations added little to what was already known of the region. In addition, he had overstayed his leave, and upon returning to civilization found he'd been discharged from the Army. (He was eventually reinstated and went on to serve admirably in the Mexican and Civil wars.)

Bonneville's Green River exploration is important to the history of mountaineering for two reasons. First, Bonneville was responsible for sending out the party that, under the direction of Joseph Reddeford Walker, made the first recorded crossing of the High Sierra – a difficult exploit recounted in the selection after this one. Second, Bonneville himself climbed a high peak in the Wind River range. Today it is impossible to be sure, but some evidence indicates that Bonneville reached the summit of 13,804-foot Gannett Peak, the highest point in Wyoming. If so, it was the first recorded climb of a glacier-clad peak in the United States.

Working from Bonneville's journals, the writer Washington Irving (better known today for such stories as "Rip Van Winkle" and "The Legend of Sleepy Hollow") wrote a somewhat glamorized book called *The Adventures of Capt. Bonneville USA*, from which the following excerpt is taken. First published in 1837, the book proved quite popular and helped establish a reputation for Bonneville that he may not have deserved. As mentioned above, most of

Bonneville's explorations were unoriginal, and his motives were more capital-istic than altruistic. On the other hand, Bonneville was known to be ahead of his time in his dealings with the Indians, with whom he was generally honest and humane, and he was a capable leader who never, in a military career spanning fifty years and two wars, lost a single man under his command. And even though Gannett Peak is hardly "the loftiest point of the North American continent," much less "twenty-five thousand feet above the level of the sea," Bonneville can probably be credited with making an ascent whose overall difficulty would not be exceeded for decades.

Having forded Wind River a little above its mouth, Captain Bonneville and his three companions proceeded across a gravelly plain, until they fell upon the Popo Agie, up the left bank of which they held their course, nearly in a southerly direction. Here they came upon numerous droves of buffalo, and halted for the purpose of procuring a supply of beef. As the hunters were stealing cautiously to get within shot of the game, two small white bears suddenly presented themselves in their path, and, rising upon their hind legs, contemplated them for some time with a whimsically solemn gaze. The

hunters remained motionless; whereupon the bears, having apparently satisfied their curiosity, lowered themselves upon all fours, and began to withdraw. The hunters now advanced, upon which the bears turned, rose again upon their haunches, and repeated their serio-comic examination. This was repeated several times, until the hunters, piqued at their unmannerly staring, rebuked it with a discharge of their rifles. The bears made an awkward bound or two, as if wounded, and then walked off with great gravity, seeming to commune together, and every now and then turning to take another look at the hunters. It was well for the latter that the bears were but half grown, and had not yet acquired the ferocity of their kind.

The buffalo were somewhat startled at the report of the firearms; but the hunters succeeded in killing a couple of fine cows, and, having secured the best of the meat, continued forward until some time after dark, when, encamping in a large thicket of willows, they made a great fire, roasted buffalo beef enough for half a score, disposed of the whole of it with keen relish and high glee, and then "turned in" for the night and slept soundly, like weary and well fed hunters.

At daylight they were in the saddle again, and skirted along the river, passing through fresh grassy meadows, and a succession of beautiful groves of willows and cotton-wood. Toward evening, Captain Bonneville observed a smoke at a distance rising from among hills, directly in the route he was pursuing. Apprehensive of some hostile band, he concealed the horses in a thicket, and, accompanied by one of his men, crawled cautiously up a height, from which he could overlook the scene of danger. Here, with a spy-glass, he reconnoitred the surrounding country, but not a lodge nor fire, not a man, horse, nor dog, was to be discovered; in short, the smoke which had caused such alarm proved to be the vapor from several warm, or rather hot springs of considerable magnitude, pouring forth streams in every direction over a bottom of white clay. One of the springs was about twenty five yards in diameter, and so deep that the water was of a bright green color.

They were now advancing diagonally upon the chain of the Wind River Mountains, which lay between them and Green River valley. To coast round their southern points would be a wide circuit; whereas, could they force their way through them, they might proceed in a straight line. The mountains were lofty, with snowy peaks and cragged sides; it was hoped, however, that some practicable defile might be found. They attempted, accordingly, to penetrate the mountains by following up one of the branches of the Popo Agie, but soon found themselves in the midst of stupendous crags and precipices that barred all progress. Retracing their steps, and falling back upon the river, they consulted where to make another attempt. They were too close beneath the mountains to scan them generally, but now recollected having noticed, from the plain, a beautiful slope rising, at an angle of about thirty degrees, and apparently without any break, until it reached the snowy region. Seeking this gentle acclivity, they began to ascend it with alacrity, trusting to find at the top one of those elevated plains which prevail among the Rocky Mountains. The slope was covered with coarse gravel, interspersed with plates of freestone. They attained the summit with some toil, but found, instead of a level, or rather undulating plain, that they were on the brink of a deep and precipitous ravine, from the bottom of which rose a second slope, similar to the one they had just ascended. Down into this profound ravine they made their way by a rugged path, or rather fissure of the rocks, and then labored up the second slope. They gained the summit only to find themselves on another ravine, and now perceived that this vast mountain, which had presented such a sloping and even side to the distant beholder on the plain, was shagged by frightful precipices, and seamed with longitudinal chasms, deep and dangerous.

In one of these wild dells they passed the night, and slept soundly and sweetly after their fatigues. Two days more of arduous climbing and scrambling only served to admit them into the heart of this mountainous and awful solitude; where difficulties increased as they proceeded. Sometimes they scrambled from rock to rock, up the bed of some mountain stream, dashing its bright way down to the plains; sometimes they availed themselves of the paths made by the deer and the mountain sheep, which, however, often took them to the brinks of fearful precipices, or led to rugged defiles, impassable for their horses. At one place, they were obliged to slide their horses down the face of a rock, in which attempt some of the poor animals lost their footing, rolled to the bottom and came near being dashed to pieces.

In the afternoon of the second day, the travellers attained one of the elevated valleys locked up in this singular bed of mountains. Here were two bright and beautiful little lakes, set like mirrors in the midst of stern and rocky heights, and surrounded by grassy meadows, inexpressibly refreshing to the eye. These probably were among the source of those mighty streams which take their rise among these mountains, and wander hundreds of miles through the plains.

In the green pasture bordering upon these lakes, the travellers halted to repose, and to give their weary horses time to crop the sweet and tender herbage. They had now ascended to a great height above the level of the plains, yet they beheld huge crags of granite piled one upon another, and beetling like battlements far above them. While two of the men remained in the camp with the horses, Captain Bonneville, accompanied by the other man, set out to climb a neighboring height, hoping to gain a commanding prospect, and discern some practicable route through this stupendous labyrinth. After much toil, he reached the summit of a lofty cliff, but it was only to behold gigantic

peaks rising all around, and towering far into the snowy regions of the atmosphere. Selecting one which appeared to be the highest, he crossed a narrow
intervening valley, and began to scale it. He soon found that he had undertaken a tremendous task; but the pride of man is never more obstinate than
when climbing mountains. The ascent was so steep and rugged that he and his
companion were frequently obliged to clamber on hands and knees, with their
guns slung upon their backs. Frequently, exhausted with fatigue, and dripping
with perspiration, they threw themselves upon the snow, and took handfuls of
it to allay their parching thirst. At one place, they even stripped off their coats
and hung them upon the bushes, and thus lightly clad, proceeded to scramble
over these eternal snows. As they ascended still higher, there were cool breezes
that refreshed and braced them, and springing with new ardor to their task,
they at length attained the summit.

Here a scene burst upon the view of Captain Bonneville, that for a time
astonished and overwhelmed him with its immensity. He stood, in fact, upon
that dividing ridge which Indians regard as the crest of the world; and on each
side of which the landscape may be said to decline to the two cardinal oceans of
the globe. Whichever way he turned his eye, it was confounded by the vastness
and variety of objects. Beneath him, the Rocky Mountains seemed to open all
their secret recesses: deep, solemn valleys; treasured lakes; dreary passes;
rugged defiles, and foaming torrents; while beyond their savage precincts, the
eye was lost in an almost immeasurable landscape, stretching on every side
into dim and hazy distance, like the expanse of a summer's sea. Whichever way
he looked, he beheld vast plains glimmering with reflected sunshine, mighty
streams wandering on their shining course toward either ocean, and snowy
mountains, chain beyond chain, and peak beyond peak, till they melted like
clouds into the horizon. For a time, the Indian fable seemed realized: he had
attained that height from which the Blackfoot warrior, after death, first catches
a view of the land of souls, and beholds the happy hunting grounds spread out
below him, brightening with the abodes of the free and generous spirits. The
captain stood for a long while gazing upon this scene, lost in a crowd of vague
and indefinite ideas and sensations. A long-drawn inspiration at length relieved him from this enthrallment of the mind, and he began to analyze the
parts of this vast panorama. A simple enumeration of a few of its features may
give some idea of its collective grandeur and magnificence.

The peak on which the captain had taken his stand commanded the whole
Wind River chain; which, in fact, may rather be considered one immense
mountain, broken into snowy peaks and lateral spurs, and seamed with narrow valleys. Some of these valleys glittered with silver lakes and gushing
streams; the fountain heads, as it were, of the mighty tributaries to the Atlantic
and Pacific Oceans. Beyond the snowy peaks, to the south, and far, far below

the mountain range, the gentle river, called the Sweet Water, was seen pursuing its tranquil way through the rugged regions of the Black Hills. In the east, the headwaters of Wind River wandered through a plain, until, mingling in one powerful current, they forced their way through the range of Horn Mountains, and were lost to view. To the north were caught glimpses of the upper streams of the Yellowstone, that great tributary of the Missouri. In another direction were to be seen some of the sources of the Oregon, or Columbia, flowing to the northwest, past those towering landmarks the Three Tetons, and pouring down into the great lava plain; while, almost at the captain's feet, the Green River, or Colorado of the West, set forth on its wandering pilgrimage to the Gulf of California; at first a mere mountain torrent, dashing northward over a crag and precipice, in a succession of cascades, and tumbling into the plain where, expanding into an ample river, it circled away to the south, and after alternately shining out and disappearing in the mazes of the vast landscape, was finally lost in a horizon of mountains. The day was calm and cloudless, and the atmosphere so pure that objects were discernible at an astonishing distance. The whole of this immense area was inclosed by an outer range of shadowy peaks, some of them faintly marked on the horizon, which seemed to wall it in from the rest of the earth.

It is to be regretted that Captain Bonneville had no instruments with him with which to ascertain the altitude of this peak. He gives it as his opinion that it is the loftiest point of the North American continent; but of this we have no satisfactory proof. It is certain that the Rocky Mountains are of an altitude vastly superior to what was formerly supposed. We rather incline to the opinion that the highest peak is further to the northward, and is the same measured by Mr. Thompson, surveyor to the Northwest Company; who, by the joint means of the barometer and trigonometric measurement, ascertained it to be twenty-five thousand feet above the level of the sea, an elevation only inferior to that of the Himalayas.

For a long time, Captain Bonneville remained gazing around him with wonder and enthusiasm; at length the chill and wintry winds, whirling about the snow-clad height, admonished him to descend. He soon regained the spot where he and his companion had thrown off their coats, which were now gladly resumed, and, retracing their course down the peak, they safely rejoined their companions on the border of the lake.

Zenas Leonard Crosses
the Sierra Nevada, 1833

I N THE SUMMER of 1833, at a "rendezvous" on the Green River, the
Bonneville Expedition took on a twenty-four-year-old trapper named
Zenas Leonard. Leonard was placed under the command of Joseph
Reddeford Walker, with whom he set out that July with some sixty other men
to explore the Great Basin region and discover a route to the Pacific. By mid-
October they were camped at the eastern base of the Sierra Nevada, a tremendous mountain barrier that had never been crossed by whites. The party
quickly reached the top of the range, but was bogged down for more than a
week among the snowbound peaks and cirques of the range's broad western
slope. The descent was agonizingly slow; the party suffered from the cold and
was forced to slaughter horses to stay alive. Their route took them along the
rugged divide between Yosemite and Hetch Hetchy valleys, along one stretch
of which Leonard saw high waterfalls that would "precipitate themselves from
one lofty precipice to another, until they are exhausted in rain below," and
cliffs that seemed "to be more than a mile high" – possibly a reference to
Hetch Hetchy, but more likely to Yosemite Valley, which Walker's party is
generally credited with discovering.

Leonard did not climb any peaks, but his writing nonetheless warrants a
place in this collection. The selection below, first published in 1839 in the
Narrative of the Adventures of Zenas Leonard, not only includes the first written description of the High Sierra and Yosemite Valley – it is also an unembel-
lished, harrowing tale of suffering and deliverance.

In the morning we despatched hunters to the mountain in search of game
and also to look out for a pass over the mountain, as our provisions were
getting scarce – our dried buffalo meat being almost done. After prowling
about all day, our hunters returned in the evening, bringing the unwelcome
tidings that they had not seen any signs of game in all their ramblings, and
what was equally discouraging, that they had seen no practicable place for
crossing the mountain. . . . [The next] evening the balance of our scouting
parties returned, but none of them had killed any game. One of them had
found an Indian path, which they thought led over the mountain – whereupon

it was resolved that in the morning we would take this path, as it seemed to be our only prospect of preservation. Accordingly, at an early hour the next morning we started on our journey along the foot of the mountain in search of the path discovered the previous day, and found it. On examination we found that horses traveled it, and must of course come from the west. This gave us great encouragement, as we were very fearful we would not be able to get our horses over at all. Here we encamped for the night. In the morning we started on our toilsome journey. Ascending the mountain we found to be very difficult from the rocks and its steepness. This day we made but poor speed, and encamped on the side of the mountain.

October 16. Continued our course until in the afternoon, when we arrived at what we took for the top, where we again encamped, but without anything to eat for our horses, as the ground was covered with a deep snow, which from appearance, lays on the north side of the peaks the whole year around. These peaks are generally covered with rocks and sand, totally incapable of vegetation; except on the south side, where grows a kind of juniper or gin shrub, bearing a berry tasting similar to gin. Here we passed the night without anything to eat except these gin berries, and some of the insects from the lake described above, which our men had got from the Indians. We had not suffered much from cold for several months previous to this; but this night, surrounded as we were with the everlasting snows on the summit of this mountain, the cold was felt with three-fold severity.

———————— ▲ ————————

The next morning it was with no cheerful prospect that each man prepared himself for traveling, as we had nothing to eat worth mentioning. As we advanced, in the hollows sometimes we would encounter prodigious quantities of snow. When we would come to such places, a certain portion of the men would be appointed alternately to go forward and break the road, to enable our horses to get through; and if any of the horses would get swamped, these same men were to get them out. In this tedious and tiresome manner we spent the whole day without getting more than eight or ten miles. In some of these ravines where the snow is drifted from the peaks, it never entirely melts, and may be found at this season of the year from ten to one hundred feet deep. From appearance it never melts on the top, but in warm weather the heap sinks by that part melting which lays next the ground. This day's travel was very severe on our horses, as they had not a particle to eat. They began to grow stupid and stiff, and we began to despair of getting them over the mountain. We encamped this night on the south side of one of these peaks or ridges without anything to eat, and almost without fire. To add to the troubles and fatigues which we encountered in the day time, in getting over the rocks and

through the snow, we had the mortification this evening to find that some of our men had become almost unmanageable, and were desirous of turning back and retracing our steps to the buffalo country! The voice of the majority, which always directs the movements of such a company, would not pacify them; nor had the earnest appeals of our captain any effect. The distance was too great for them to undertake without being well provided, and the only way they could be prevented, was by not letting them have any of the horses or ammunition. Two of our horses were so much reduced that it was thought they would not be able to travel in the morning at all, whereupon it was agreed that they should be butchered for the use of the men. This gave our men fresh courage, and we went to bed this night in better spirits than we had done for a long time. Some of the men had fasted so long, and were so much in want of nourishment, that they did not know when they had satisfied the demands of nature, and eat as much and as eagerly of this black, tough, lean, horse flesh, as if it had been the choicest piece of beef steak.

In the morning, after freely partaking of the horse meat, and sharing the remainder to each man, we renewed our journey, now and then coming onto an Indian path, but as they did not lead in the direction we were going, we did not follow them—but the most of the distance we this day traveled, we had to encounter hills, rocks and deep snows. The snow in most of the hollows we this day passed through, looks as if it had remained here all summer, as eight or ten inches from the top it was packed close and firm—the top being loose and light, having fell only a day or two previous. About the middle of the afternoon we arrived at a small lake or pond, where we concluded to encamp, as at this pond we found a small quantity of very indifferent grass, but which our horses cropped off with great eagerness. Here we spent the night, having yet seen nothing to create a hope that we had arrived near the opposite side of the mountain—and what was equally as melancholy, having yet discovered no signs of game.

The next morning we resumed our labor, fortunately finding less snow and more timber, besides a number of small lakes, and some prospect of getting into a country that produced some kind of vegetation. The timber is principally pine, cedar, and red wood, mostly of a scrubby and knotty quality. After traveling a few miles further, however, than any other day since we had reached the top of the mountain, we again encamped on the margin of another small lake, where we also had the good fortune to find some pasture for our horses. This evening it was again decided to kill three more of our horses which had grown entirely worthless from severe traveling and little food. The next morning several parties were despatched in search of a pass over the mountain, and to make search for game; but they all returned in the evening without finding either. The prospect at this time began to grow somewhat gloomy and threaten us with hard times again. We were at a complete stand. No one was acquainted with the country, nor no person knew how wide the summit of this mountain was. We had traveled for five days since we arrived at what we supposed to be the summit—we were now still surrounded with snow and rugged peaks—the vigor of every man almost exhausted—nothing to give our poor horses, which were no longer any assistance to us in traveling, but a burthen, for we had to help the most of them along as we would an old and feeble man.

This mountain must be near as high as the main chain of the Rocky Mountains—at least a person would judge so from the vast quantity of snow with which it is covered, and the coldness of the air. The descent from the Rocky Mountains to this is but trifling, and supposed by all the company not to be greater than we had ascended this mountain from the plain—though we had no means of ascertaining the fact. It is true, however, that the vast plain through which we had traveled was almost perfectly level, on part of which the water gradually descended to the west, and on the other towards the east.

Our situation was growing more distressing every hour, and all we now thought of was to extricate ourselves from this inhospitable region; and, as we were perfectly aware, that to travel on foot was the only way of succeeding, we spent no time in idleness—scarcely stopping in our journey to view an occasional specimen of the wonders of nature's handiwork. We traveled a few miles every day, still on the top of the mountain, and our course continually obstructed with snow, hills and rocks. Here we began to encounter in our path, many small streams which would shoot out from under these high snowbanks, and after running a short distance in deep chasms which they have through ages cut in the rocks, precipitate themselves from one lofty precipice to another, until they are exhausted in rain below. Some of these precipices appeared to us to be more than a mile high. Some of the men thought that if we could succeed in descending one of these precipices to the bottom, we might thus work our way into the valley below — but on making several attempts we found it utterly impossible for a man to descend, to say nothing of our horses. We were then obliged to keep along the top of the dividing ridge between two of these chasms which seemed to lead pretty near in the direction we were going — which was west — in passing over the mountain, supposing it to run north and south. In this manner we continued until the 25th without any particular occurrence, except that of our horses dying daily — the flesh of which we preserved for food. Our course was very rough and tiresome, having to encounter one hill of snow and one ledge of rocks after another. On the 25th every man appeared to be more discouraged and down-spirited than ever, and I thought that our situation would soon be beyond hope if no prospect of getting from the mountain would now be discovered. This day we sent out several parties on discoveries, who returned in the evening without bringing the least good news, except one man, who was last coming, having separated from his companions, brought a basket full of acorns to camp. These were the first acorns we had seen since we left the state of Missouri. These nuts our hunter had got from an Indian who had them on his back traveling as though he was on a journey across the mountain, to the east side. When the Indian seen our hunter he dropped his basket of provision and run for life. These nuts caused no little rejoicing in our camp, not only on account of their value as food, but because they gave us the gratifying evidence that a country mild and salubrious enough to produce acorns was not far distant, which must be vastly different from any we had passed through for a long time. We now felt agreeably surprised that we had succeeded so far and so prosperously, in a region of many miles in extent where a native Indian could find nothing to eat in traversing the same route, but acorns. These nuts are quite different from those in Missouri — being much larger and more palatable. They are from one and one-half to three inches in length, and about three-fourths in diameter, and when roasted in the ashes or broiled, are superior to any chesnuts I ever eat — (though a person subsisting upon very lean horse meat for several days is hardly capable of judging with precision in a case of this kind.)

The next morning we resumed our journey somewhat revived with the strong expectation that after a few days more tedious traveling, we would find ourselves in a country producing some kind of game by which we might recruit our languid frames, and pasture to resuscitate the famished condition of our

horses. We still found snow in abundance, but our course was not so much obstructed with rocks as formerly. In two or three days we arrived at the brink of the mountain. This at first was a happy sight, but when we approached close, it seemed to be so near perpendicular that it would be folly to attempt a descent. In looking on the plain below with the naked eye, you have one of the most singular prospects in nature; from the great height of the mountain the plain presents a dim yellow appearance; but on taking a view with the spy glass we found it to be a beautiful plain stretched out towards the west until the horizon presents a barrier to the sight. From the spot where we stood to the plain beneath, must at least be a distance of three miles, as it is almost perpendicular, a person cannot look down without feeling as if he was wafted to and fro in the air, from the giddy height. A great many were the surmises as to the distance and direction to the nearest point of the Pacific. Captain Walker, who was a man well acquainted with geography, was of the opinion that it was not much further than we could see with the aid of our glass, as the plain had the appearance of a sea shore. Here we encamped for the night, and sent men out to discover some convenient passage down towards the plain — who returned after an absence of a few hours and reported that they had discovered a pass or Indian trail which they thought would answer our pur-pose, and also some signs of deer and bear, which was equally as joyful news — as we longed to have a taste of some palatable food. The next morning after pursuing our course a few miles along the edge of the mountain top we arrived at the path discovered by our men, and immediately commenced the descent, gladly leaving the cold and famished region of snow behind.

Elisha Mitchell Climbs
Mount Mitchell, 1835

Elisha Mitchell, born in 1793 in Connecticut, studied the sciences at Yale and graduated at the head of his class in 1813. Four years later he was appointed to a professorship at the University of North Carolina in Chapel Hill. Though he primarily taught mathematics, he was also interested in botany and made a number of botanical excursions throughout the state, some of which took him into the Great Smokies and the Blue Ridge. In 1835 he climbed and measured the height of what is now known as Mount Mitchell, at 6,684 feet the highest point in the United States east of the Rockies. Some years later the North Carolina congressman and booster Thomas L. Clingman disputed Mitchell's claim of having been the first to reach this highest point, prompting Mitchell to return to the mountain in 1857 to prove his claim. While traveling alone on this expedition he was caught out by a storm, and on steep, slick terrain he slipped into a creek and drowned.

Mitchell was before all else a scientist, and the account below, which appeared in 1838 as an article in *The American Journal of Science and Arts*, is primarily about measuring mountains rather than climbing them. But, like the outline of a high peak emerging from a Great Smokies mist, Mitchell's appreciation of the mountains' beauty shows through his recitation of heights and distances.

The younger Michaux, on his way from the Valley of the Mississippi, in the fall of 1802, passed through the counties of Yancy and Burke, and in the small volume, containing an account of his travels, that was published soon after his return to Paris, the opinion is expressed, that in these counties, the Alleghany Mountains attain their greatest elevation. He mentions, in evidence that this belief is well founded, that his father found trees and plants growing upon them which he did not meet with again before reaching Canada.

The geology of these counties has some peculiar features. They were visited during the last summer, for the purpose of tracing the boundaries of their rock formations, and along with other collateral objects, provision was made for measuring the heights of their principal mountains, with their bearings and distances from each other. Prof. Mitchell in a letter to the editor, dated University of North Carolina, May 12, 1838, remarks that the results transmitted were obtained by himself. He adds —

"In their general accuracy I placed a confidence at the time which has been increased by the publication of the Report of the Surveys made by the engineers employed by the Charleston and Louisville Rail Road Company. For the height of Mount Washington I trusted to Worcester as the best authority within my reach. The difference in elevation between the northern and southern mountains is probably not considerable; in point of beauty there is in some instances a decided superiority on the side of the latter. Mount Washington, according to his measurement, is not so high as the highest peak of the Black Mountain."

One barometer he observed was stationed at Morganton, and a record kept of its movements by Mr. Pearson of that place. This served as a standard. The observations made at the same time (nearly,) upon the tops of the mountains and at Morganton, furnished the data for calculating their elevations above that village, and the mean of ten observations, on successive days, gave what is probably a near approximation to the height of Morganton above the level of the sea — nine hundred and sixty eight feet. Deducting from this the descent to the bed of the Catawba, there remains only about eight hundred feet of fall between the ford leading over Linville and the sea.

North of the point where the James River leaves the mountains, the first high ridge of the Alleghanies is called the Blue Ridge. In North Carolina, this name is applied to the range that separates the eastern and western waters. This is commonly the first high mountain, but not always. The *Table Mountain,* which forms so fine and striking a feature in the scenery about Morganton, is not a part of the Blue Ridge, but a spur or outlier. It seems, when seen from Morganton, to be a round tower, rising perpendicularly from the summit of the first range of the Alleghanies. It is, in fact, a narrow ridge, affording a very fine prospect of the fertile valley of the Catawba and its tributaries on the southeast and east, and of nature in her wildest dress where the Linville pours over the rocks along a deep ravine, wholly untenanted and uncultivated, and of a vast extent of mountain peaks and ranges on the northeast. Its top is two thousand four hundred and fifty three feet above Morganton, and a little more than fifteen miles distant in a right line.

The Grandfather, seventeen miles from the Table, and twenty eight from Morganton, has hitherto been generally supposed the highest mountain in North Carolina. But this proves to be a mistake, as may be seen in the following table. There is a mountain not far off called the Grandmother; from being crowned with the balsam of fir it is conjectured that the elevation may be twenty six hundred feet.

The *Roan Mountain* is fifteen miles from the Grandfather, and thirty five northwest from Morganton, lying directly over or beyond the Hawksbill. It touches the Tennessee line, but the highest peaks are in North Carolina. This is the easiest of access, the most beautiful, and will best repay the labor of ascending it of all our high mountains. With the exception of a body of rocks looking like the ruins of an old castle, near its southwestern extremity, the top of the Roan may be described as a vast meadow, without a tree to obstruct the prospect; where a person may gallop his horse for a mile or two, with Carolina at his feet on one side, and Tennessee on the other, and a green ocean of mountains raised into tremendous billows immediately about him. It is the elysium of a southern botanist, as a number of plants are found growing in this cold and humid atmosphere, which are not seen again till we have gone some hundreds of miles farther north. It is the pasture ground for the young horses of the whole country about it during the summer. We found the strawberry here in the greatest abundance and of the finest quality, in regard to both size and flavor, on the 30th of July.

The *Black Mountain* is a long ridge, at a medium distance of about thirty miles from Morganton. It has some peaks of greater elevation than any point that has hitherto been measured in North America, east of the Rocky Mountains, and is believed to be the highest mountain in the United States. The Black Mountain cost nearly a week's labor in fixing upon the peak to be measured and the measurement. For the sake of comparison the following heights are given. The first five are copied from Worcester's Gazetteer:

Mount Washington in New Hampshire, hitherto accounted the highest mountain in the United States — highest peak,	6,234
Mansfield Mountain, Vermont,	4,279
Saddle Mountain, Massachusetts,	4,000
Round Top, highest of the Catskills,	3,804
Peaks of Otter, Virginia,	3,955
Table Mountain, Burke, North Carolina,	3,421
Grandfather,	5,556
Yeates' Knob,	5,895
Black, at Thomas Young's,	5,946

Roan,	6,038
Highest peak of the Black,	6,476

There are other high mountains at no great distance from those that were measured; as the Bald Mountain in the western part of Yancy, and the White Top in Virginia, which are nearly if not quite as high as the Roan. In the southeastern part of Haywood county, near the South Carolina line, there is a tremendous pile, and between the counties of Haywood and Macon and the State of Tennessee, the Unikee Mountain swells to a great elevation. But these appear to the eye to be lower than the Black.

The Pilot Mountain, which has heretofore enjoyed great celebrity, is much lower than several others. The ascent of the Black Mountain is very difficult on account of the thick laurels which are so closely set, and their strong branches so interwoven, that a path cannot be forced by pushing them aside; and the hunters have no method of advancing, when they happen to fall in with the worst of them, but that of crawling along their tops. The bear, in passing up and down the mountain, finds it wisest to keep [to] the ridges, and trampling down the young laurels as they spring up, breaking the limbs from the old ones and pushing them aside, he forms at last a sort of burrow above ground, through this bed of vegetation, along which he passes without difficulty. This is a bear trail. The top is covered with the balsam fir, from the dark and sombre shade of whose foliage it doubtless received the name of the Black Mountain. The growth of the tree is such on these high summits, that it is easy to climb to the top and taking hold of the highest branch look abroad upon the prospect. At the time of our visit, the mountain was enveloped in mist, which prevented our seeing more than a couple of hundred yards, and we were so uncomfortable from cold, that some of the company urged a return with the least possible delay.

William Redfield Climbs
Mount Marcy, 1837

B Y THE 1830s, genuinely unexplored wilderness was becoming scarce in the Northeast. Mount Katahdin, though remote, had already been ascended at least five times, and three separate trails had been built to accommodate the ever-increasing number of visitors to Mount Washington. But the Adirondacks were still a blank on the map when, in 1836, New York Secretary of State James Dix proposed a systematic survey of the state's natural resources. Dix's proposal was enthusiastically received by the legislature, and the resulting fieldwork occupied the next five years. Among the many prominent scientists involved with the survey were Ebenezer Emmons, in charge of the district encompassing the highest part of the Adirondacks, the botanist John Torrey, and the geologist James Hall. Accompanying them, but not officially attached to the survey, was William Redfield, an accomplished amateur scientist who had done pioneering work in meteorology and would go on to become the first president of the American Association for the Advancement of Science.

It was Redfield, accompanied by Hall, who got the first close look at Mount Marcy, the highest point in New York. In August 1836 the pair had hiked in from the McIntyre Iron Works, up the Opalescent River – then called the East Branch of the Hudson – and past Lake Colden. From a high point beyond the lake they got a clear enough view of the 5,344-foot mountain to realize it was significantly higher than any in the Catskills, then thought to be the highest ground in the state. After this first foray Redfield returned to civilization, but Hall remained behind, joining up with Emmons for the first ascent of 4,867-foot Whiteface Mountain, which also afforded a good view of Marcy.

All three explorers returned the following year for a go at what Redfield termed "the high peak of Essex," accompanied by Torrey, John Cheney, Harvey Holt, Emmons's son Ebenezer Jr., the artist Charles C. Ingham and, probably, three guides. The ascent from the McIntyre Mine took three days. Hall wrote a brief firsthand account of the climb that was published in the *Albany Daily Advertiser* on August 15, 1837, and Emmons touched on the ascent in his official report to the New York State Assembly. But the most detailed account of the climb was written by Redfield and published first as letters to the *New York Journal of Commerce,* then as an article in the *American Journal of Science and Arts.* The latter was reprinted in 1838 in *The Family Magazine,* from which the selection below is excerpted.

Notwithstanding the increase of population, and the rapid extension of our settlements since the peace of 1783, there is still found, in the northern part of the state of New York, an uninhabited region of considerable extent, which presents all the rugged characters and picturesque features of a primeval wilderness. This region constitutes the most elevated portion of the great triangular district, which is situated between the line of the St. Lawrence, the Mohawk, and Lake Champlain. That portion of it which claims our notice in the following sketches, lies mainly within the county of Essex, and the contiguous parts Hamilton and Franklin, and comprises the head waters of the principal rivers in the northern division of the state.

In the summer of 1836, the writer had occasion to visit the new settlement at McIntyre, in Essex county, in company with the proprietors of that settlement, and other gentlemen who had been invited to join the expedition. Our party consisted of the Hon. Archibald McIntyre of Albany, the late Judge McMartin of Broadalbin, Montgomery county, and David Henderson, Esq. of Jersey City, proprietors, together with David C. Colden, Esq. of Jersey City, and Mr. James Hall, assistant state geologist for the northern district.

It has been noticed that the north branch of the Hudson, after its exit from Lake Sanford, joins the main branch of the river, about seven miles below the settlement at McIntyre. Having prepared for an exploration up the latter stream, we left McIntyre on the 17th of July, with three assistants, and the necessary equipage for encampment. Leaving the north branch, we proceeded through the woods in a southeasterly direction, passing two small lakes, till, at the distance of three or four miles from the settlement, we reached the southern point of one of the mountains, and assuming here a more easterly course, we came, about noon, to the main branch of the river. Traces of wolves and deer were frequently seen, and we discovered also the recent tracks of a moose, *Cervus Alces, L.* We had also noticed on the 16th, at the inlet of Lake Sanford, the fresh and yet undried footstep of a panther, which apparently had just crossed the inlet.

------------ ▲ ------------

The great ascent which we had made from our first encampment, and the apparent altitude of the mountain peaks before us, together with the naked condition of their summits, rendered it obvious that the elevation of this mountain group had been greatly underrated; and we were led to regret our want of means for a barometrical measurement. The height of our present encampment above Lake Sanford was estimated to be from ten to twelve hundred feet, and the height of Lake Colden, above tide, at from one thousand eight hundred, to two thousand feet, the elevation of Lake Sanford being assumed from such information as we could obtain, to be about eight hundred feet. The elevation of the peaks on either side of Lake Colden, were estimated from two thousand, to two thousand five hundred feet above the lake. These conclusions were entered in our notes, and are since proved to have been tolerably correct, except as they were founded on the supposed elevation of Lake Sanford, which had been very much underrated.

August 19th. The rain had fallen heavily during the night, and weather was still such as to preclude the advance of the party. But the ardor of individuals was hardly to be restrained by the storm; and during the forenoon, Mr. Henderson, with John Cheney, our huntsman, made the circuit of Lake Colden, having in their course beaten up the quarters of a family of panthers, to the great discomfiture of Cheney's valorous dog. At noon, the weather being more favorable, Messrs. McIntyre, McMartin and Hall, went up the border of the lake to examine the valley which extends beyond it in a N.N.E. and N.E. direction, while the writer, with Mr. Henderson, resumed the ascent of the main stream of the Hudson. Notwithstanding the wet, and the swollen state of the stream, we succeeded in ascending more than two miles in a southeasterly and southerly direction, over a constant succession of falls and rapids of an interesting character. In one instance, the river has assumed the bed of a displaced trap dyke, by which the rock has been intersected, thus forming a chasm or sluice of great depth, with perpendicular walls, in which the river is precipitated in a cascade of fifty feet.

Before returning to camp, the writer ascended a neighboring ridge for the purpose of obtaining a view of the remarkably elevated valley from which the Hudson here issues. From this point a mountain peak was discovered, which obviously exceeded in elevation the peaks which had hitherto engaged our attention. Having taken the compass bearing of this peak, further progress was relinquished, in hope of resuming the exploration of this unknown region on the morrow.

On returning to our camp, we met the portion of our party which had penetrated the valley north of the lake, and who had there discovered another lake of nearly equal extent, which discharges by an outlet that falls into Lake Colden. On the two sides of this lake, the mountains rise so precipitously as to preclude any passage through the gorge, except by water. The scenery was described as very imposing, and some fine specimens of the opalescent rock were brought from this locality. Immense slides or avalanches had been precipitated into this lake from the steep face of the mountain, which induced the party to bestow upon it the name of Avalanche lake.

Another night was passed at this camp, and the morning of the 20th opened with thick mists and rain, by which our progress was further delayed. It was at last determined, in view of the bad state of the weather and our short stock of provisions, to abandon any further exploration at this time, and to return to the settlement.

──────── ▲ ────────

At a later period of this year, Professor Emmons, in the execution of his geological survey, and accompanied by Mr. Hall, his assistant, ascended the Whiteface mountain, a solitary peak of different formation, which rises in the north part of the county. From this point, Prof. E. distinctly recognised as the highest of the group, the peak on which the writer's attention had been fastened at the termination of our ascent of the Hudson, and which he describes as situated about sixteen miles south of Whiteface. Prof. E. then proceeded southward through the remarkable Notch, or pass, which is described in his Report, and which is situated about five miles north from McIntyre. The Wallface mountain, which forms the west side of the pass, was ascended by him on this occasion, and the height of its perpendicular part was ascertained to be about twelve hundred feet, as may be seen by reference to the geological Report which was published in February last, by order of the Legislature. It appears by the barometrical observations made by Prof. Emmons, that the elevation of the tableland which constitutes the base of these mountains at McIntyre, is much greater than from the result of our inquiries we had been led to suppose.

The interest excited in our party by the short exploration which has been described, was not likely to fail till its objects were more fully accomplished. Another visit to this alpine region was accordingly made in the summer of the present year. Our party on this occasion consisted of Messrs. McIntyre, Henderson and Hall, (the latter at this time geologist of the western district of the state,) together with Prof. Torrey, Prof. Emmons, Messrs. Ingham and Strong of New York, Miller of Princeton, and Emmons, Jr. of Williamstown.

----------- ▲ -----------

We reached our old camp at Lake Colden at 5 P.M. [August 3, 1837] where we prepared our quarters for the night. The mountain peak which rises on the eastern side of this lake and separates it from the upper valley of the main stream of the Hudson, has received the name of Mount McMartin, in honor of one now deceased, who led the party of last year, and whose spirit of enterprise and persevering labors contributed to establishing the settlement at the great Ore Beds, as well as other improvements advantageous to this section of the state.

On the 4th, we once more resumed the ascent of the main stream, proceeding first in an easterly direction, and then to the south, over falls and rapids, till we arrived at the head of the great Dyke Falls. Calcedony was found by Prof. Emmons near the foot of these falls. Continuing our course on a more gradual rise, we soon entered upon unexplored ground, and about three miles from camp, arrived at the South Elbow, where the bed of the main stream changes to a northeasterly direction, at the point where it receives a tributary which enters from south-southwest. Following the former course, we had now fairly entered the High Valley which separates Mount McMartin from the High Peak on the southeast, but so enveloped were we in the deep growth of the forest, that no sight of the peaks could be obtained. About a mile from the South Elbow we found another tributary entering from south-southeast, apparently from a mountain ravine which borders the High Peak on the west. Some beautifully opalescent specimens of the labradorite were found in the bed of this stream.

Another mile of our course brought us to a smaller tributary from the north, which from the alluvial character of the land near its entrance is called the High Meadow fork. This portion of our route is in the centre of this mountain valley, and has the extraordinary elevation of three thousand and seven hundred feet above tide. We continued the same general course for another mile, with our route frequently crossed by small falls and cascades, when we emerged from the broader part of the valley and our course now became east-southeast and southeast, with a steeper ascent and higher and more frequent falls in the Stream. The declivity of the mountain which encloses the valley on the north and that of the great peak, here approximate closely to each other, and the valley assumes more nearly the character of a ravine or pass between two mountains, with an increasing ascent, and maintains its course for two or three miles, to the summit of the pass. Having accomplished more than half the ascent of this pass we made our camp for the night, which threatened to be uncommonly cold and caused our axemen to place in requisition some venerable specimens of the white birch which surrounded our encampment.

A portion of the deep and narrow valley in which we were now encamped, is occupied by a longitudinal ridge consisting of boulders and other *debris,* the materials, evidently, of a tremendous slide or avalanche, which at some unknown period has descended from the mountain; the momentum of the mass in its descent having accumulated and pushed forward the ridge, after the manner of the late slide at Troy, beyond the centre of the valley or gorge into which it is discharged. It appears indeed that the local configuration of surface in these mountain valleys, except where the rock is in place, ought to be ascribed chiefly to such causes. It seems apparent also, that the Hudson, at the termination of its descent from the High Valley, once discharged itself into Lake Colden, the latter extending southward at that period to the outlet of the Still Water, which has been noticed in our account of the former exploration. This portion of the ancient bed of the lake has not only been filled, and the bed of the stream as well as the remaining surface of the lake raised above the former level, but a portion of the finer *debris* brought down by the main stream, has flowed northwardly into the present lake and filled all its southern portions with a solid and extensive shoal, which is now fordable at a low stage of the water. The fall of heavy slides from the mountains appears also to have separated Avalanche Lake from Lake Colden, of which it once formed a part, and so vast is the deposit from these slides as to have raised the former lake about eighty feet above the surface of the latter. In cases where these slides have been extensive, and rapid in their descent, large hillocks or protuberances are formed in the valleys; and the denudation from above, together with the accumulation below, tends gradually to diminish the extent and frequency of their occurrence. But the slides still recur, and their pathway may often be perceived in the glitter of the naked rock, which is laid bare in their course from the summit of the mountain toward its base, and these traces constitute one of the most striking features in the mountain scenery of this region.

On the morning of the fifth, we found that ice had formed in exposed situations. At an early hour we resumed our ascending course to the southeast, the stream rapidly diminishing and at length becoming partially concealed under the grass-covered boulders. At 8:40 A.M. we arrived at the head of the stream on the summit of this elevated pass, which here forms a beautiful and open mountain meadow, with the ridges of the two adjacent mountains rising in an easy slope from its sides. From this little meadow, which lies within the present limits of the town of Keene, the main branch of the Hudson and a fork of the east branch of the Au Sable commence their descending course in opposite directions, for different and far distant points of the Atlantic Ocean. The elevation of this spot proves by our observations to be more than four thousand seven hundred feet above tide water; being more than nine hundred feet above the highest point of the Catskill mountains, which have so long been considered the highest in this state.

The descent of the Au Sable from this point is most remarkable. In its comparative course to Lake Champlain, which probably does not exceed forty miles, its fall is more than four thousand six hundred feet! This, according to our present knowledge, is more than twice the descent of the Mississippi proper, from its source to the ocean. Waterfalls of the most striking and magnificent character are known to abound on the course of the stream.

Our ascent to the source of the Hudson had brought us to an elevated portion of the highest mountain peak which was also a pricipal object of our exploration, and its ascent now promised to be of easy accomplishment by proceeding along its ridge, in a W.S.W. direction. On emerging from the pass, however, we immediately found ourselves entangled in the zone of dwarfish pines and spruces, which with their numerous horizontal branches interwoven with each other, surround the mountain at this elevation. These gradually decreased in height, till we reached the open surface of the mountain, covered only with mosses and small alpine plants, and at 10 A.M. the summit of the High Peak of Essex was beneath our feet.

The aspect of the morning was truly splendid and delightful, and the air on the mountain-top was found to be cold and bracing. Around us lay scattered in irregular profusion, mountain masses of various magnitudes and elevations, like to a vast sea of broken and pointed billows. In the distance lay the great valley or plain of the St. Lawrence, the shining surface of Lake Champlain, and the extensive mountain range of Vermont. The nearer portions of the scene were variegated with the white glare of recent mountain slides as seen on the sides of various peaks, and with the glistening of the beautiful lakes which are so common throughout this region. To complete the scene, from one of the nearest settlements a vast volume of smoke soon rose in majestic splendor, from a fire of sixty acres of forest clearing, which had been prepared for the "burning," and exhibiting in the vapor which it imbodied, a gorgeous array of the prismatic colors, crowned with the dazzling beams of the mid-day sun.

The summit, as well as the mass of the mountain, was found to consist entirely of the labradoritic rock, which has been mentioned as constituting the rocks of this region, and a few small specimens of hypersthene were also procured here. On some small deposits of water, ice was found at noon, half an inch in thickness. The source of the Hudson, at the head of the High Pass, bears N. 70° E. from the summit of this mountain, distant one and a quarter miles, and the descent of the mountain is here more gradual than in any other direction. Before our departure we had the unexpected satisfaction to discover, through a depression in the Green mountains, a range of distant mountains in nearly an east direction, and situated apparently beyond the valley of the Connecticut; but whether the range thus seen, be the White mountains of New Hampshire, or that portion of the range known as the mountains of Franconia, near the head of the Merrimack, does not fully appear. Our barometrical observations on this summit show an elevation of five thousand four hundred and sixty-seven feet. This exceeds by about six hundred feet, the elevation of the Whiteface mountain, as given by Prof. Emmons; and is more than sixteen hundred and fifty feet above the highest point of the Catskill mountains.

John Charles Frémont
Climbs Frémont Peak, 1842

J OHN CHARLES FRÉMONT, born in 1813 in Savannah, Georgia, was one of America's most fascinating and wide-ranging explorers. Soon after finishing college he joined the United States Topographical Corps, under whose auspices he helped unravel the maze of mountain country along the Tennessee-North Carolina border. In 1838, at the behest of the War Department, he helped map the upper reaches of the Missouri River. Two years later he was in Washington, D.C., where he met and secretly married Jessie Benton, the sixteen-year-old daughter of Senator Thomas Hart Benton of Missouri. Benton, though at first indignant over the hasty marriage, quickly came to appreciate Frémont and used his influence to place him in command of the next government expedition to explore the far West.

Frémont made a total of five western expeditions. Traveling at times with the famed guide Kit Carson, he explored the Missouri, the Columbia, and the Rio Grande rivers, and also crossed the Great Basin and the Sierra Nevada. He was one of the first whites to see the Great Salt Lake in Utah, forwarding a report on that region that led eventually to the decision of the Mormons to settle there. He and his party nearly froze to death crossing the Sierra in winter; several of his men *did* freeze to death while attempting to cross the San Juan Mountains of Colorado. Elsewhere he lost men to Indian attacks, and all too frequently his men wound up eating their horses to stay alive. He became famous as stories about such incredible scrapes circulated widely. Many Easterners considered Frémont a genius for guiding his men through so many crises, though a few thought him a blunderer for getting into them in the first place.

In 1855, his exploring days over, Frémont moved to New York. The following year, the recently formed Republican Party nominated him for president; he ran against James Buchanan, the Democratic Party candidate, polling 1,341,000 votes to Buchanan's 1,838,000. During the Civil War he served in Missouri, where in 1861, a year before Abraham Lincoln's Emancipation Proclamation, he issued an order freeing the slaves of that state. Later he fought in the "mountain district" of Virginia, Kentucky, and Tennessee, where he was frustrated by the superior generalship of Stonewall Jackson. His early emancipation order had greatly pleased the abolitionists, and in 1864 their radical wing of the Republican Party nominated him for a second presidential attempt. When it became clear that his candidacy would only result in a victory for the Democrats over Lincoln, Frémont decided to withdraw. His political career went downhill from there, though he did serve for several years as territorial governor of Arizona before his death in 1890.

It was on Frémont's first western expedition, to Wyoming's South Pass region in 1842, that he decided to climb a prominent peak in the Wind River Range. Following the ascent Frémont claimed to have reached the highest point in the Rockies, but in fact he had not even gotten to the top of the Wind Rivers. If, as is generally supposed, he reached what is today called Frémont Peak, 13,780 feet, he was still lower than nearby 13,804-foot Gannett Peak. He may have been lower still – the historian Francis Farquhar thinks he actually climbed a less prominent point called Mount Chauvenet.

After this first expedition, Frémont returned to Washington and – with considerable help from his gifted wife, whose literary ability supported the family when Frémont couldn't – wrote an account of his experiences. In that account, first published in 1845, Frémont was careful to place himself in the best light possible, even when things were going badly. In the excerpt that follows, he mentions only briefly the unnecessary hardships and dissensions that marked the climb, preferring, as he wrote, to avoid "dwelling upon trifling incidents not connected with the objects of the expedition." Frémont's version of the climb is well written and perfectly truthful in all matters not touching upon his own leadership, but to get a balanced view of the expedition, it is necessary to read also the account that follows it, written by his topographer, Charles Preuss.

10th. [August 10, 1842] – The air at sunrise is clear and pure, and the morning extremely cold, but beautiful. A lofty snowy peak of the mountain is glittering in the first rays of the sun, which have not yet reached us. The long mountain wall to the east, rising two thousand feet abruptly from the plain, behind which we see the peaks, is still dark, and cuts clear against the glowing sky. A fog, just risen from the river, lies along the base of the mountain. A little before sunrise, the thermometer was at 35°, and at sunrise 33°. Water froze last night, and fires are very comfortable. The scenery becomes hourly more interesting and grand, and the view here is truly magnificent; but, indeed, it needs something to repay the long prairie journey of a thousand miles. The sun has shot above the wall, and makes a magical change. The whole valley is glowing and bright, and all the mountain peaks are gleaming like silver. Though these snow mountains are not the Alps, they have their own character

John Charles Frémont

of grandeur and magnificence, and doubtless will find pens and pencils to do them justice. . . . We were now approaching the loftiest part of the Wind River chain; and I left the valley a few miles from our encampment, intending to penetrate the mountains as far as possible with the whole party. We were soon involved in very broken ground, among long ridges covered with fragments of granite. Winding our way up a long ravine, we came unexpectedly in view of a most beautiful lake, set like a gem in the mountains. The sheet of water lay transversely across the direction we had been pursuing; and, descending the steep, rocky ridge, where it was necessary to lead our horses, we followed its banks to the southern extremity. Here a view of the utmost magnificence and grandeur burst upon our eyes. With nothing between us and their feet to lessen the effect of the whole height, a grand bed of snow-capped mountains rose before us, pile upon pile, glowing in the bright light of an August day. Immediately below them lay the lake, between two ridges, covered with dark pines, which swept down from the main chain to the spot where we stood. Here, where the lake glittered in the open sunlight, its banks of yellow sand and the light foliage of aspen groves contrasted well with the gloomy pines. "Never before," said Mr. Preuss, "in this country or in Europe, have I seen such grand, magnificent rocks." I was so much pleased with the beauty of the place, that I determined to make the main camp here, where our animals would find good pasturage, and explore the mountains with a small party of men.

━━━━━━━━ ▲ ━━━━━━━━

12th. — Early in the morning we left the camp, fifteen in number, well armed, of course, and mounted on our best mules. A pack-animal carried our provisions, with a coffeepot and kettle, and three or four tin cups. Every man had a blanket strapped over his saddle, to serve for his bed, and the instruments were carried by turns on their backs. We entered directly on rough and rocky ground; and, just after crossing the ridge, had the good fortune to shoot an antelope. We heard the roar, and had a glimpse of a waterfall as we rode along, and, crossing in our way two fine streams, tributary to the Colorado, in about two hours' ride we reached the top of the first row or range of the mountains. Here, again, a view of the most romantic beauty met our eyes. It seemed as if, from the vast expanse of uninteresting prairie we had passed over, Nature had collected all her beauties together in one chosen place. We were overlooking a deep valley, which was entirely occupied by three lakes, and from the brink to the surrounding ridges rose precipitously five hundred and a thousand feet, covered with the dark green of the balsam pine, relieved on the border of the lake with the light foliage of the aspen. They all communicated with each other, and the green of the waters, common to mountain lakes of great depth, showed that it would be impossible to cross them. The surprise manifested by our guides when these impassable obstacles suddenly barred our progress, proved that they were among the hidden treasures of the place, unknown even to the wandering trappers of the region. Descending the hill, we proceeded to make our way along the margin to the southern extremity. A narrow strip of angular fragments of rock sometimes afforded a rough pathway for our mules, but generally we rode along the shelving side, occasionally scrambling up, at a considerable risk of tumbling back into the lakes.

―――――――― ▲ ――――――――

We had reached a very elevated point, and in the valley below, and among the hills, were a number of lakes of different levels; some two or three hundred feet above others, with which they communicated by foaming torrents. Even to our great height the roar of the cataracts came up, and we could see them leaping down in lines of snowy foam. From this scene of busy waters, we turned abruptly into the stillness of a forest, where we rode among the open bolls of the pines, over a lawn of verdant grass, having strikingly the air of cultivated grounds. This led us, after a time, among masses of rock which had no vegetable earth but in hollows and crevices though still the pine forest continued. Towards evening we reached a defile, or rather a hole in the mountains, entirely shut in by dark pine-covered rocks.

A small stream, with scarcely perceptible current, flowed through a level bottom of perhaps eighty yards width, where the grass was saturated with water. Into this the mules were turned, and were neither hobbled nor picketed during the night, as the fine pasturage took away all temptation to stray; and we made our bivouac in the pines. The surrounding masses were all of granite. While supper was being prepared, I set out on an excursion in the neighborhood, accompanied by one of my men. We wandered about among the crags and ravines until dark, richly repaid for our walk by a fine collection of plants, many of them in full bloom. Ascending a peak to find the place of our camp, we saw that the little defile in which we lay communicated with the long green valley of some stream, which, here locked up in the mountains, far away to the south, found its way in a dense forest to the plains.

Looking along its upward course, it seemed to conduct, by a smooth gradual slope, directly towards the peak, which, from long consultation as we approached the mountain, we had decided to be the highest of the range. Pleased with the discovery of so fine a road for the next day, we hastened down to the camp, where we arrived just in time for supper. Our table-service was rather scant; and we held the meat in our hands, and clean rocks made good plates, on which we spread our macaroni. Among all the strange places on which we had occasion to encamp during our long journey, none have left so vivid an impression on my mind as the camp of this evening. The disorder of the masses which surrounded us—the little hole through which we saw the stars over head — the dark pines where we slept — and the rocks lit up with the glow of our fires, made a night-picture of very wild beauty.

13th. — The morning was bright and pleasant, just cool enough to make exercise agreeable, and we soon entered the defile I had seen the preceding day. It was smoothly carpeted with soft grass, and scattered over with groups of flowers, of which yellow was the predominant color. Sometimes we were forced, by an occasional difficult pass, to pick our way on a narrow ledge along the side of the defile, and the mules were frequently on their knees; but these obstructions were rare, and we journeyed on in the sweet morning air, delighted at our good fortune in having found such a beautiful entrance to the mountains. This road continued for about three miles, when we suddenly reached its termination in one of the grand views which, at every turn, meet the traveler in this magnificent region. Here the defile up which we had traveled opened out into a small lawn, where, in a little lake, the stream had its source.

There were some fine *asters* in bloom, but all the flowering plants appeared to seek the shelter of the rocks, and to be of lower growth than below, as if they loved the warmth of the soil, and kept out of the way of the winds. Immediately at our feet, a precipitous descent led to a confusion of defiles, and before us rose the mountains, as we have represented them in the annexed view. It is not by the splendor of far-off views, which have lent such a glory to the Alps, that these impress the mind; but by a gigantic disorder of enormous masses, and a savage sublimity of naked rock, in wonderful contrast with innumerable green of a rich floral beauty, shut up in their stern recesses. Their wildness seems well suited to the character of the people who inhabit the country.

I determined to leave our animals here, and make the rest of our way on foot. The peak appeared so near, that there was no doubt of our returning before night; and a few men were left in charge of the mules, with our provisions and blankets. We took with us nothing but our arms and instruments, and, as the day had become warm, the greater part left our coats. Having made an early dinner, we started again. We were soon involved in the most ragged precipices, nearing the central chain very slowly, and rising but little. The first ridge hid a succession of others; and when, with great fatigue and difficulty, we had climbed up five hundred feet, it was but to make an equal descent on the other side; all these intervening places were filled with small deep lakes, which met the eye in every direction, descending from one level to another, sometimes under bridges formed by huge fragments of granite, beneath which was heard the roar of the water. These constantly obstructed our path, forcing us to make long *détours*; frequently obliged to retrace our steps, and frequently falling among the rocks. Maxwell was precipitated towards the

face of a precipice, and saved himself from going over by throwing himself flat on the ground. We clambered on, always expecting, with every ridge that we crossed, to reach the foot of the peaks, and always disappointed, until about four o'clock, when, pretty well worn out, we reached the shore of a little lake, in which was a rocky island. We remained here a short time to rest, and continued on around the lake, which had in some places a beach of white sand, and in others was bound with rocks, over which the way was difficult and dangerous, as the water from innumerable springs made them very slippery.

By the time we had reached the further side of the lake, we found ourselves all exceedingly fatigued, and, to the satisfaction of the whole party, we encamped. The spot we had chosen was a broad flat rock, in some measure protected from the winds by the surrounding crags, and the trunks of fallen pines afforded us bright fires. Near by was a foaming torrent, which tumbled into the little lake about one hundred and fifty feet below us, and which, by way of distinction, we have called Island lake. We had reached the upper limit of the piney region; as, above this point, no tree was to be seen, and patches of snow lay everywhere around us, on the cold sides of the rocks. The flora of the region we had traversed since leaving our mules was extremely rich, and, among the characteristic plants, the scarlet flowers of the *dodecatheon dentatum* everywhere met the eye, in great abundance. A small green ravine, on the edge of which we were encamped, was filled with a profusion of alpine plants, in brilliant bloom. From barometrical observations, made during our three days' sojourn at this place, its elevation above the Gulf of Mexico is 10,000 feet. During the day, we had seen no sign of animal life; but among the rocks here, we heard what was supposed to be the bleat of a young goat, which we searched for with hungry activity, and found to proceed from a small animal of a gray color, with short ears and no tail—probably the Siberian squirrel. We saw a considerable number of them, and, with exception of a small bird like a sparrow, it is the only inhabitant of this elevated part of the mountains. On our return, we saw, below this lake, large flocks of the mountain-goat. We had nothing to eat to-night. Lajeunesse, with several others, took their guns, and sallied out in search of a goat; but returned unsuccessful. At sunset, the barometer stood at 20.522; the attached thermometer 50°. Here we had the misfortune to break our thermometer, having now only that attached to the barometer. I was taken ill shortly after we had encamped, and continued so until late in the night, with violent headache and vomiting. This was probably caused by the excessive fatigue I had undergone, and want of food, and perhaps, also, in some measure, by the rarity of the air. The night was cold, as a violent gale from the north had sprung up at sunset, which entirely blew away the heat of the fires. The cold, and our granite beds, had not been favorable to sleep, and we were glad to see the face of the sun in the morning. Not being delayed by any preparation for breakfast, we set out immediately.

On every side, as we advanced, was heard the roar of waters, and of a torrent, which we followed up a short distance, until it expanded into a lake about one mile in length. On the northern side of the lake was a bank of ice, or rather of snow covered with a crust of ice. Carson had been our guide into the mountains, and, agreeably to his advice, we left this little valley, and took to the ridges again, which we found extremely broken, and where we were again involved among precipices. Here were ice-fields; among which we were all dispersed, seeking each the best path to ascend the peak. Mr. Preuss attempted to walk along the upper edge of one of these fields, which sloped away at an angle of about twenty degrees; but his feet slipped from under him, and he went plunging down the plain. A few hundred feet below, at the bottom, were some fragments of sharp rock, on which he landed; and, though he turned a couple of somersets, fortunately received no injury beyond a few bruises. Two of the men, Clement Lambert and Descoteaux, had been taken ill, and lay down on the rocks, a short distance below; and at this point I was attacked with headache and giddiness, accompanied by vomiting, as on the day before. Finding myself unable to proceed, I sent the barometer over to Mr. Preuss, who was in a gap two or three hundred yards distant, desiring him to reach the peak if possible, and take an observation there. He found himself unable to proceed further in that direction, and took an observation, where the barometer stood at 19.401; attached thermometer 50°, in the gap. Carson, who had gone over to him, succeeded in reaching one of the snowy summits of the main ridge, whence he saw the peak towards which all our efforts had been directed, towering eight or ten hundred feet into the air above him. In the mean time, finding myself grow rather worse than better, and doubtful how far my strength would carry me, I sent Basil Lajeunesse, with four men, back to the place where the mules had been left.

We were now better acquainted with the topography of the country, and I directed him to bring back with him, if it were in any way possible, four or five mules, with provisions and blankets. With me were Maxwell and Ayer; and after we had remained nearly an hour on the rock, it became so unpleasantly cold, though the day was bright, that we set out on our return to the camp, at which we all arrived safely, straggling in one after the other. I continued ill during the afternoon, but became better towards sundown, when my recovery was completed by the appearance of Basil and four men, all mounted. The men who had gone with him had been too much fatigued to return, and were relieved by those in charge of the horses; but in his powers of endurance Basil resembled more a mountain-goat than a man. They brought blankets and provisions, and we enjoyed well our dried meat and a cup of good coffee. We rolled ourselves up in our blankets, and, with our feet turned to a blazing fire, slept soundly until morning.

15th. — It had been supposed that we had finished with the mountains; and the evening before it had been arranged that Carson should set out at daylight, and return to breakfast at the Camp of the Mules, taking with him all but four or five men, who were to stay with me and bring back the mules and instruments. Accordingly, at the break of day they set out. With Mr. Preuss and myself remained Basil Lajeunesse, Clement Lambert, Janisse, and Descoteaux. When we had secured strength for the day by a hearty breakfast, we covered what remained, which was enough for one meal, with rocks, in order that it might be safe from any marauding bird, and, saddling our mules, turned our faces once more towards the peaks. This time we determined to proceed quietly and cautiously, deliberately resolved to accomplish our object if it were within the compass of human means. We were of opinion that a long defile which lay to the left of yesterday's route would lead us to the foot of the main peak. Our mules had been refreshed by the fine grass in the little ravine at the Island camp, and we intended to ride up the defile as far as possible, in order to husband our strength for the main ascent. Though this was a fine passage, still it was a defile of the most rugged mountains known, and we had many a rough and steep slippery place to cross before reaching the end. In this place the sun rarely shone; snow lay along the border of the small stream which flowed through it, and occasional icy passages made the footing of the mules very insecure, and the rocks and ground were moist with the trickling waters in this spring of mighty rivers. We soon had the satisfaction to find ourselves riding along the huge wall which forms the central summits of the chain. There at last it rose by our sides, a nearly perpendicular wall of granite, terminating 2,000 to 3,000 feet above our heads in a serrated line of broken, jagged cones. We rode on until we came almost immediately below the main peak, which I denominated the Snow peak, as it exhibited more snow to the eye than any of the neighboring summits. Here were three small lakes of a green color, each, perhaps, of a thousand yards in diameter, and apparently very deep. These lay in a kind of chasm; and, according to the barometer, we had attained but a few hundred feet above the Island lake. The barometer here stood at 20.450, attached thermometer 70°.

We managed to get our mules up to a little bench about a hundred feet above the lakes, where there was a patch of good grass, and turned them loose to graze. During our rough ride to this place, they had exhibited a wonderful surefootedness. Parts of the defile were filled with angular, sharp fragments of rock, three or four and eight or ten feet cube; and among these they had worked their way, leaping from one narrow point to another, rarely making a false step, and giving us no occasion to dismount. Having divested ourselves of every unnecessary encumbrance, we commenced the ascent. This time, like experienced travelers, we did not press ourselves, but climbed leisurely, sitting down so soon as we found breath beginning to fail. At intervals we reached places where a number of springs gushed from the rocks, and about 1800 feet above the lakes came to the snow line. From this point our progress was uninterrupted climbing. Hitherto I had worn a pair of thick moccasins, with soles of *parflèche,* but here I put on a light, thin pair, which I had brought for the purpose, as now the use of our toes became necessary to a further advance. I availed myself of a sort of comb of the mountain, which stood against the wall like a buttress, and which the wind and the solar radiation, joined to the steepness of the smooth rock, had kept almost entirely free from snow. Up this I made my way rapidly. Our cautious method of advancing at the outset had spared my strength; and, with the exception of a slight disposition to headache, I felt no remains of yesterday's illness. In a few minutes we reached a point where the buttress was overhanging, and there was no other way of surmounting the difficulty than by passing around one side of it, which was the face of a vertical precipice of several hundred feet.

Putting hands and feet in the crevices between the blocks, I succeeded in getting over it, and, when I reached the top, found my companions in a small valley below. Descending to them, we continued climbing, and in a short time reached the crest. I sprang upon the summit, and another step would have precipitated me into an immense snow-field five hundred feet below. To the edge of this field was a sheer icy precipice; and then, with gradual fall, the field sloped off for about a mile, until it struck the foot of another lower ridge. I stood on a narrow crest, about three feet in width, with an inclination of about

20°N. 51°E. As soon as I had gratified the first feelings of curiosity, I descended, and each man ascended in his turn; for I would only allow one at a time to mount the unstable and precarious slab, which it seemed a breath would hurl into the abyss below. We mounted the barometer in the snow of the summit, and, fixing a ramrod in a crevice, unfurled the national flag to wave in the breeze where never flag waved before. During our morning's ascent, we had met no sign of animal life, except the small sparrow-like bird already mentioned. A stillness the most profound and a terrible solitude forced themselves constantly on the mind as the great features of the place. Here, on the summit, where the stillness was absolute, unbroken by any sound, and solitude complete, we thought ourselves beyond the region of animated life; but while we were sitting on the rock, a solitary bee (*bromus, the humble-bee*) came winging his flight from the eastern valley, and lit on the knee of one of the men.

It was a strange place, the icy rock and the highest peak of the Rocky mountains, for a lover of warm sunshine and flowers; and we pleased ourselves with the idea that he was the first of his species to cross the mountain barrier — a solitary pioneer to foretell the advance of civilization. I believe that a moment's thought would have made us let him continue his way unharmed; but we carried out the law of this country, where all animated nature seems at war; and, seizing him immediately, put him in at least a fit place — in the leaves of a large book, among the flowers we had collected on our way. The barometer stood at 18.293, the attached thermometer at 44°; giving for the elevation of this summit 13,570 feet above the Gulf of Mexico, which may be called the highest flight of the bee. It is certainly the highest known flight of that insect. From the description given by Mackenzie of the mountains where he crossed them, with that of a French officer still farther to the north, and Colonel Long's measurements to the south, joined to the opinion of the oldest traders of the country, it is presumed that this is the highest peak of the Rocky Mountains. The day was sunny and bright, but a slight shining mist hung over the lower plains, which interfered with our view of the surrounding country. On one side we overlooked innumerable lakes and streams, the spring of the Colorado of the Gulf of California; and on the other was the Wind River valley, where were the heads of the Yellowstone branch of the Missouri; far to the north, we could just discover the snowy heads of the *Trois Tétons,* where were the sources of the Missouri and Columbia rivers; and at the southern extremity of the ridge, the peaks were plainly visible, among which were some of the Nebraska or Platte river. Around us, the whole scene had one main, striking feature, which was that of terrible convulsion. Parallel to its length, the ridge was split into chasms and fissures; between which rose the thin lofty walls, terminated with slender minarets and columns. According to the barometer, the little crest of the wall on which we stood was three thousand five hundred and seventy feet above that place, and two thousand seven hundred and eighty above the little lakes at the bottom, immediately at our feet. Our camp at the Two Hills (an astronomical station) bore south 3° east, which, with a bearing afterwards obtained from a fixed position, enabled us to locate the peak. The bearing of the *Trois Tétons* was north 50° west, and the direction of the central ridge of the Wind River mountains south 39° east. The summit rock was gneiss, succeeded by sienite gneiss. Sienitic and feldspar succeeded in our descent to the snow line, where we found a feldspathic granite. I had remarked that the noise produced by the explosion of our pistols had the usual degree of loudness, but was not in the least prolonged, expiring almost instantaneously.

Having now made what observations our means afforded, we proceeded to descend. We had accomplished an object of laudable ambition, and beyond the strict order of our instructions. We had climbed the loftiest peak of the Rocky mountains, and looked down upon the snow a thousand feet below; and, standing where never human foot had stood before, felt the exultation of first explorers. It was about two o'clock when we left the summit, and when we reached the bottom, the sun had already sunk behind the wall, and the day was drawing to a close. It would have been pleasant to have lingered here and on the summit longer; but we hurried away as rapidly as the ground would permit, for it was an object to regain our party as soon as possible, not knowing what accident the next hour might bring forth.

We reached our deposite of provisions at nightfall. Here was not the inn which awaits the tired traveler on his return from Mont Blanc, or orange groves of South America, with their refreshing juices and soft fragrant air; but we found our little *cache* of dried meat and coffee undisturbed. Though the moon was bright, the road was full of precipices, and the fatigue of the day had been great. We therefore abandoned the idea of rejoining our friends, and lay down on the rock, and, in spite of the cold, slept soundly.

Charles Preuss on
Frémont Peak, 1842

ACCOMPANYING FRÉMONT ON his ascent of Frémont Peak was Charles Preuss, who served as cartographer on several western expeditions. Preuss was born in Hohscheid, Germany, in 1803 and in college studied the emerging science of geodesy. In 1834 he emigrated to the United States, where he made maps for the U.S. Coast Survey. Later he worked as a mining engineer in Britain. Upon returning to America he hoped to get his old job back, but found that Congress had reduced funding for the survey. He was referred to Frémont, who was then assembling his first expedition. Preuss, by this time hard up for work, agreed to serve as the expedition's cartographer. If his diaries are any indication, he did not greatly enjoy the experience, but he nonetheless accompanied Frémont on several other expeditions.

Preuss's diaries, written on the scene in his native German and never intended to be published, gave him an outlet for feelings he probably could not have expressed openly in the field. They are brutally honest and provide an alternative to Frémont's sanitized writings. In the latter, in one typical passage, Frémont credits Preuss with a "cheerful philosophy which often brightened dark situations," but that cheer is rarely evident in the diaries. What actually characterizes the journal is Preuss's chronic dissatisfaction – not to mention his dour, cryptic personality and his low opinion of Frémont:

June 4, 1842 – Weather good. Food Bad.

June 5 – Slept in the tent, one blanket underneath, another blanket on top; damned hard.

Weather good. In the afternoon went to Kansas. Had a drink. Shot a pigeon and ate it.

June 6 – The way I feel today, I wish with all my heart that I had stayed in Washington. Not because of the hardships, but because of that simpleton Frémont.

June 7 – Murky weather, melancholy mood.

The diary continues in this cryptic vein for some time. But eventually, perhaps under the influence of the open prairie life and the constantly changing scenery, Preuss begins to open up. The entries become longer and, particularly after the mountains come into view, he takes great interest in the landscape. For Preuss the Rockies could never compare to the glacier-clad Alps of his homeland, but after his experiences in the Wind Rivers he was at least willing to concede that America's mountains had charms of their own, and he wrote at considerable length about the Frémont Peak climb – partly because of its innate interest, and partly, no doubt, for the opportunity it gave of remarking on Frémont's ineptitude. In so doing, he produced a delightfully idiosyncratic climbing story, the first unabashedly subjective mountaineering account in our literature.

By all rights, Preuss should have enjoyed a long and successful career following the Frémont expeditions. He was a genuinely skilled cartographer, and his western maps (one of which was the first to show the California goldfields) were considered the best of their day. But in 1854, after returning to the East Coast, he became ill. A few weeks later – perhaps, as Jessie Frémont put it, aware that his days in the open wilderness were over – he killed himself. His diaries went with his other personal effects back to Germany, where they remained in obscurity for a century before being translated and published in 1958 under the title *Exploring with Frémont*.

August 2 (Tuesday)

Yesterday afternoon and this morning Frémont set up his daguerreotype to photograph the rocks; he spoiled five plates that way. Not a thing was to be seen on them. That's the way it often is with these Americans. They know everything, they can do everything, and when they are put to a test, they fail miserably. . . .

A small thunderstorm is coming up, with big raindrops. How carefully they cover the newly collected buffalo chips with the tablecloth [i.e., a buffalo hide].

Oh, strange and miserable prairie life!

We are now about five days travel distance from the mountains. Since there is more country *beyond* those mountains, probably ten to fifteen days will pass before we shall turn our faces eastward again.

August 4 (Thursday)

Today we had the mountains before us all day. Even yesterday afternoon we had a glimpse of them. Whoever has seen Switzerland and expects something similar here is bound for a great disappointment. An American has measured them to be as high as 25,000 feet. I'll be hanged if they are half as high, yea, if they are 8,000 feet high. A little snow on their peaks; that is all, as far as I can see now, that distinguishes them from other high mountains.

I am reminded of the day when I walked from Liestal to Solothurn. When I came around a corner of rocks which reached right up to the road, I saw in front of me the entire range of the Alps from Mont Blanc to the Alps of Tirol. Overjoyed, I threw off my knapsack and jumped around like a fool! Then I started running fast to reach the peaks before sundown—the magnificent glaciers looked that close in the sunshine. Now, if I compare that view with the one I see today, it is as though I were to turn my eyes from the face of a lovely girl to the wrinkled face of an old woman.

Our honest, or rather reputedly dishonest native German bird, the magpie, I saw today for the first time in America. I was as pleased with the sight as if I had seen a piece of Germany.

Alas, I shall probably never become an American, no matter how well I may fare in this country. I shall long for Germany as long as I live. To be sure, when I am at home, enjoying the company of my wife and child, I do not realize the difference so much. Thank God I see at least the end of the expedition. How glad I shall be when the bugle is sounded for the return march.

August 5 (Friday)

This morning we got a thorough soaking. So far we have been mighty lucky with the weather. This is only the second time that we really got wet, and now, at noon, the sun is drying everything.

Our flour and our coffee will soon be exhausted. The bread ration is damnably small. For the time being we have plenty of grass and buffalo, although famine has been prophesied for us and the horses.

The mountains are today even less impressive than yesterday. Tomorrow we shall probably reach the foot of the mountains.

We no longer think of the danger from Indians. We met the traces of the "big party." They say that there were about 1,000 lodges or tents, hence at least 5,000 persons. I am glad that they went back home.

We caught two abandoned or stray horses and a dog. We took them along. One of the horses mentioned above found its owner in Fort Bissonet.

I saw beautiful wild ducks today. . . .

Frémont is roaming through the mountains collecting rocks and is keeping us waiting for lunch. I am hungry as a wolf. That fellow knows nothing about mineralogy or botany. Yet he collects every trifle in order to have it interpreted later in Washington and to brag about it in his report. Let him collect as much as he wants—if he would only not make us wait for our meal.

Today he said the air up here is too thin; that is the reason his daguerreo-type was a failure. Old boy, you don't understand the thing, that is it.

August 8 (Monday)

This is now the fourth day on which we are tormented by rain. This is the last straw! I have had to crawl into his tent. There is no other shelter for me since the Sioux lodge was so foolishly cut up.

On account of the rain we have made only short journeys. Now we camp at Little Sandy Creek, the first water which takes its course to the west, toward the Pacific Ocean. It is a small arm of the Green River, which empties into the Gulf of California.

Yesterday we passed an old beaver colony. How these fellows can work! It is nothing for them to saw with their teeth through trees one to one and one-half feet in diameter. I should like to see an inhabited village. But there is little hope. The poor fellows are so pursued that one finds them only sporadically in this region.

As I said, these Rocky Mountains are no Swiss Alps. But it is true that they are magnificent, strangely shaped rocks. In a few days I shall be able to say more about them.

Our fare is getting worse and worse. No thought of bread any longer. Ham and bacon are likewise gone. Dried buffalo meat, hard as wood, and antelope prepared in buffalo fat — that is all. How glad we would be if we only had the pork which we buried at the Platte.

August 9 (Tuesday)

I see that I have to write daily; otherwise I may forget important things. Thus I have not recorded that I found here our German hare and ate it, too. Our aunt in Detmold and Ernestine in the Alverd district, to be sure, prepare it more to my taste than our cooks.

For several days now I feel dizzy when I bend down and want to straighten up again. Could it be caused by eating meat without bread? How-ever, I shall not take any pills or salt. Nature will cure it all right.

In climbing mountains I realize that I have become somewhat older. In 1829 in Switzerland I was so much more active. Of course, there is a great difference between the ages of twenty-six and thirty-nine.

This noon we camp at Big Sandy Creek; tonight we shall reach the New Fork. Both empty into the above-mentioned Green River.

I had imagined the Rocky Mountains entirely different, namely as a divide between eastern and western America, somewhat like the Apennine Range, broken only by some valleys and ravines. But these are individual mountain ranges, separated by plateaus, fifty to one hundred miles wide.

August 10 (Wednesday)

Yesterday afternoon we had a hard hailstorm. Finally, the sky seems to have cleared again; it is clear and bright, but terribly cold. Now, five o'clock in the morning, the thermometer shows thirty-three degrees, and the cook's washrags are frozen stiff.

We are here at the New Fork, a pretty, rushing creek. The mountains are about ten miles distant — a nice long chain with strangely shaped peaks, all snow covered. I got up early this morning to walk to an isolated butte, from which one must have a beautiful view of the range. But the water was so cold and deep that I turned back and now look at the view from the fire. Day after tomorrow we shall probably climb the peak, and then we shall move eastward as rapidly as possible toward our dear home.

Noon. We camp here at a lovely little lake at the foot of the mountains. The shores are covered with aspen and fir. The finest trout swim in the crystal clear water; I wish we had them in the frying pan. In the foreground are cliffs about seven hundred feet high, with the more distant snow peaks towering beyond.

Wild garlic grows here, too, and, luckily, we shall soon eat it with our antelope meat.

I was forced to take a cold bath. The river (the third "New Fork") which empties into the lake was too rocky to risk crossing on the back of a stumbling horse. I therefore walked through, the water up to my belly, holding the reins.

August 11 (Thursday)

Last night, just when we were observing, the chief again caused a great commotion. He thought he had heard a rifle crack, called the watch — and then the fun started.

Our leader had repeatedly assured us that there is no danger at all here, but he advised Frémont — out of politeness, I believe — not to sleep in the tent because this would be too good an aim for the Indians. I could not make up my mind to leave the tent, and today that brought about a certain tension, not only between Frémont and myself, but also between me and the rest of the people. Only, of course, because I want to be smarter than the others.

This was the second incident of this nature. When the horses got scared by the lanterns and caused a commotion, I remained lying in my spot, although the others moved to find a safer place. I was too much convinced of the real cause because it had all happened before.

To be sure, I believe I should change my attitude and make myself more agreeable here in the distant prairie. This is not the East, where I can move away when people seem too foolish.

Today Frémont again wanted to take pictures. But the same as before, nothing was produced. This time it was really too bad, because the view was magnificent.

The last barometer, with which we wanted to measure the mountains tomorrow, was broken when we unpacked it. Fortunately it could be repaired.

Otherwise we would not have climbed the mountains. No one would have waited just for me.

Oh, I wish I were home again!

August 12 (Friday)

Indeed, I must call it good luck that the barometer was repaired. Today we traveled through wonderful regions with our mules; with horses we could not have undertaken *such* a task. But the mosquitoes!

We left ten men in the camp, and fifteen of us, all on mules, started this morning to survey the mountains. Right from the beginning it was confoundedly rough and rocky, but that was nothing compared to what was ahead of us. After a ride of about two hours we reached the spur of a low mountain chain of the Rocky Mountains. Before our eyes there unfolded a lovely landscape, with three mountain lakes surrounded by cliffs. — Oh these mosquitoes! — The mountains were partly covered by spruce and fir; in the valley only aspen can be seen.

We moved on, but the route became so rocky that I dismounted when we moved along the shore of one of the lakes and led my animal. Twice the low branches brushed off my cap in spite of all my stooping and turning. After about an hour of such hardship I was able to mount the mule again. But only for fifteen minutes was the route better. Then, again, rock upon rock — and so steep that I felt sorry for my poor mule. However, I did not dismount again; my bones do not enjoy climbing very much.

On the north side of the lake we halted for lunch, which was prepared in a somewhat informal manner; kitchen utensils could not very well be taken along on such a trip. Soon we started again and moved through more of the same terrain as before. When we found a good plot of grass and water among the rocks, we camped there for the night.

Tomorrow we shall continue in the same way until we come to the point where we shall probably have to make the final ascent to the peak on foot. One thing I can mark down right now. As interesting as the mountains are, they cannot at all be compared to the Alps of Switzerland. No glaciers, ice lakes, avalanches, or waterfalls are to be seen. A little snow on the peak — that is all.

August 17 (Wednesday)

I have to catch up with quite a bit. Only last night we returned from the mountains to our main camp at the lake, which we had reached on the tenth.

On the morning of the twelfth, we, fifteen of us, left this camp among the rocks and rode on our mules about two or three miles until we found grass and water again. The mountain trails became still rougher and steeper, and we did not know if and when we should find grass again — there is nowhere any lack of water. Hence we thought it best to leave our animals under the guard of three men and continue on foot. The mountains appeared to us so close now and the highest peak, which we had selected for climbing, looked so easy that we firmly believed that we could be back to our mules and our provisions before nightfall. Hence we did not take along anything; only I, a more experienced mountaineer, stuck a piece of dried buffalo meat in my pocket.

It was a terrible climb over rocks and through water. The actual height which we had to climb we were forced to repeat at least two or three times because we had to go downhill again and again, from one mountain to the other. The leader, Carson, walked too fast. This caused some exchange of words. Frémont got excited, as usual, and designated a young chap to take the lead — he could not serve as a guide, of course. Frémont developed a headache, and as a result we stopped soon afterwards, about eleven o'clock. He decided to climb the peak the next morning, with renewed strength and cooler blood. We went back some one hundred steps, where we had found the last pine trees, so that we could have a fire for the night — only for warmth, of course, since we had nothing to cook. In the course of the afternoon the quarrel was smoothed over. One claimed he had not meant it as the other had assumed, and the headache was relieved. The night was very cold, the wind violent, and, as always, the best spots were already taken by others. There was nothing with which to cover oneself, and I can truthfully say that I did not sleep a single minute. I lay down, was forced up again by the smoke of the fire, smoked a pipe, tried again, became frightened because a burning piece of wood fell close to my feet, turned around because my back was all cold — and thus the night passed.

How glad I was when dawn came and we started out. The hike was disagreeable all around. No supper, no breakfast, little or no sleep — who can enjoy climbing a mountain under these circumstances? Moreover, all the men, with perhaps two exceptions, would have much preferred to stay in camp. What possible interest do these fellows have in such an undertaking? In addition, the party soon split up; some remained behind, others tried to find another route, and some sat down, maintaining complete inability to move on. I soon found myself completely isolated; because of the chaotic jumble of rocks, one soon loses sight of another, although separated by only a few paces. Snow covered the less slopy surfaces where the wind could not drive it away — it was soft where the sun shines, covered with an icy crust in the shade. I took my course over one of these surfaces. With the first steps I could dig my heels into the snow; then it became harder, I slipped, sat down on my pants, and slid downhill at a great speed. Although I made all efforts to hold back by trying to dig my fingers into the icy crust, I slid down about two hundred feet, until the bare rocks stopped me again. Fortunately I could see that the rock toward which I was sailing was not very sharp. When I arrived, I rolled over twice and got away with two light bruises, one on my right arm and one on my arse. The pain made me sit still for a few minutes; then I dragged myself to my feet, found my book, and climbed on slowly. After about half an hour I had climbed so high that I could look over all the lower peaks. On one of them I saw a part of the company sitting down, among them Frémont. I began to shout, and they recognized me. Now I was happy to have gained such a lead, because this way I could reach the goal slowly and comfortably. The peak was still about 1,000 feet above me. I tried to discover the easiest route as far as I could look ahead, and started out again. I walked fifty steps; then I rested and looked for the others, who remained, to my surprise, on the same spot. Finally I noticed two moving in my direction, but I saw nothing of the others. I started up again in order to be the first on top, ahead of all the others. But how easily one can be fooled. It did not take long until I could no longer go forward. Nothing but vertical rocks, which naturally looked low to me from below but which were so steep that it was impossible to climb them. You can imagine how vexed I was: the peak just a few hundred feet above me, and all that hard, perilous work for nothing. I had to retrace my steps, and in the meantime the others had probably reached the peak by an easier route. Disgruntled, I climbed back to a spot where I could turn either right or left. Which route had the others taken? I began to halloo, but got no answer. I went on a little farther and found footprints in the snow which led to the right. These I ought to follow. Yet I was so tired that for some time I was uncertain whether I should follow them at all. But to think that Frémont might be on top while I had the book and the compass, and with all the work ahead of me: to take the bearings in all directions (such nonsense!) and to record the rivers and mountains. What sort of a look would I receive from Frémont! And then the disgrace; no, no, my old legs would have to try it again. . . .

I had regained about five hundred feet when I met Johny with the barometer. Now I heard that Frémont had become sick and had returned with all of them except Johny and Kit Carson, whom he sent ahead to meet me on the peak and to tell me that I should do what I could. Johny found so much hard snow on the other side that he did not want to chance carrying the barometer. Carson, he said, had gone on.

This changed the situation; all ambition left me. I turned back with the barometer to the snow line, took the altitude there, 19.421, and had Johny fire his gun to inform Kit. Then I turned back, no longer concerned about the old mountaineer; if he could not find me, he would surely turn back.

Quite exhausted, I reached the pine trees, reported the meager result, and we were all rather dissatisfied. I could not keep from remarking that in such an undertaking some preparations for sleeping, eating, and drinking would not be altogether amiss and might indeed be conducive to better success.

In the meantime several men had been dispatched to bring up, if possible, some mules, with victuals, for further service. They reappeared in a surprisingly short time; they had found a better route. Seldom has a supper tasted better to me, although it consisted only of coffee and dried buffalo meat. We now had woolen blankets also, which promised a better night's rest.

But what about the mountain? I did not wish to suggest anything. It finally looked as if Frémont would be satisfied with the altitude I had established and would add five or six hundred feet in order to fix the assumed highest point.

Before we lay down to sleep, he arranged with Kit that the latter should return with some of the people to the mules and that we should follow with the five animals that had been brought up and eat breakfast there.

I did not learn anything about this arrangement. When we awoke early in the morning, Kit and several others had already left. "Well, Mr. Preuss," said Frémont, "I hope we shall, after all, empty a glass on top of the mountain." We had taken along some brandy expressly for this purpose, as well as an American flag (Star-spangled Banner).

Then he explained further that we should try to get to the base of the next highest peak with the mules and then start once more, but slowly, from there. Whoever did not want to come along could remain behind. We were six men with five mules. Frémont, I, and Basil, the new guide in Kit's place, were the three who would, of course, go under any circumstances. Likewise Johny, the carrier of the barometer, who, as a mulatto, had no privilege to choose. Clément, as one could see, joined reluctantly, and de Couteau did not want to be alone guarding the fire. Coffee and meat were still sufficient for a breakfast and a supper. We quickly ate breakfast and then mounted the mules. Basil, as the guide, went on foot. I certainly felt quite different from the previous morning. Well rested, enough to eat and to drink, and a strong mule under one's arse — that is something entirely different. I never knew what these animals can accomplish. Half a year ago I would not have believed that I could have dared to cross such ground on such a beast. Everything progressed without danger. Basil led us to the right side of the mountain, where he thought he was sure to find a possibility of climbing up. And he was right. At a small lake where quite a bit of grass still grew, just below the last ascent, we dismounted and started our undertaking. They had become wiser and followed my advice not to climb long enough to get out of breath, but to rest every time one of the party could not keep up. Thus we went on slowly, but surely, until we came to some flat, smooth stretches of rock. For those with short legs it was impossible to cross these because one could not get a sure footing. De Couteau and Clément were across. The former extended to us a ramrod, which he had taken along, and thus pulled us over this place. However, now the going became worse and worse. Thus far we had crawled over bare rocks; the rocks close to us were covered with snow, from which only single points protruded. . . .

Someone hit upon the idea of trying to cross the snow that was quite soft, and then everything proceeded without danger. The leader, de Couteau, tried every step, carefully, and each of us followed in his tracks. Thus we continued, carefully and slowly, and soon we reached the summit. The highest rock was so small that only one after the other could stand on it. Pistols were fired, the flag unfurled, and we shouted "hurrah" several times. Then the barometer was set up, and I observed twice. The results were 18.320 and 18.293, thermometer, 45.3° and 44°, which will probably correspond to almost 10,000 feet. As on the entire journey, Frémont allowed me only a few minutes for my work. When the time comes for me to make my map in Washington, he will more than regret this unwise haste. After about fifteen minutes we started on our return trip. Compared to the ascent it was very easy because we made use of the soft snow as much as possible. Below, at the little lake, the barometer was set up once more in order to find the actual height of the peak. The result was 20.450, thermometer, 70.5°. Then we mounted our animals and rode to the pine trees, where we consumed the rest of our provisions and, wrapped in our blankets, went to sleep around the fire.

The next morning, it was the sixteenth of August, we started even before sunrise. We wanted to have breakfast at the place where the other nine men waited with the rest of the mules. Our guide, Basil, lost the way or perhaps thought he could find a better one. For that reason we got into such a confusion of rocks and small lakes that we hardly knew how to get out of it. Twenty times we had to dismount and shove the animals by force over the rocks. We climbed after them and mounted again for a short stretch. It was almost noon when we reached the spot, which was only two miles distant as the crow flies. But instead of finding men, mules, and breakfast, we found only a piece of paper fastened to a post, on which Kit Carson informed us that he and the others had moved to the base camp at the lake. He had assumed that we, too, had gone there by a shorter route. Frémont began to rave again, wanted to dismiss everybody, go home immediately, etc., etc. The nonsense naturally ended again with a headache.

What were we to do now? The beasts had endured quite a lot, but to stay there another night without any provisions at all was not an agreeable prospect. Thus Frémont decided, to the satisfaction of all of us, to try to reach the main camp. No one knew the way; the best we could do was to follow the tracks of the others. However, we soon lost the tracks in the rocks, and this caused for some time the same difficulties we had encountered in the morning. What the poor beasts had to suffer was terrible. Blows and digs with the spurs fairly rained upon them, accompanied by constant cursing and swearing. I let the others go ahead and remained quite unruffled with my good mule. I gave her a slight stroke with the whip, and she calmly got over the worst places. After about two hours we came upon better ground, found again the tracks of the others, and reached the camp before sunset without further mishap. Clément's mule did not want to move, and he had to walk and drive it ahead of him.

Frémont had calmed down in the meantime and treated Kit much better than I should have expected. To be sure, what could we have done without him in the prairie? How could we get back if we lost our only *good* buffalo hunter? This and other small troubles and annoyances had gotten on Frémont's nerves, which is not at all surprising with a childishly passionate man like him. In consequence he decided to let this be the end of the expedition and go straightway back to the Sweet Water instead of rounding the mountains. He imparted this news to me last night, and who was happier than I? I gladly agreed to all his reasons, whether good or bad. Thus we broke camp this noon and are now in the proximity of the same spot on the first New Fork, which we had reached on the ninth. The first twelve miles homeward are behind us, there is no longer any talk of danger from Indians, and thus we shall, with God's help, come back to our families.

Henry David Thoreau
Climbs Wachusett, 1842

HENRY DAVID THOREAU, the iconoclastic writer and philosopher of Walden Pond, climbed a number of mountains during his short life. From an early age his mind had been imprinted with the images of mountains met in literature, from the Bible's Ararat to the Alps of Goethe and Wordsworth. By the age of twenty-two he'd climbed Mount Washington, and before he died of tuberculosis at forty-four he would also climb Wachusett, Monadnock, Lafayette, Greylock, Katahdin, and others, some of them several times. These trips, particularly the one to Katahdin, impressed him deeply, affecting even his dreams. He dreamed repeatedly of a mountain he imagined to be just east of Concord and that he ascended, as he once wrote in his journal,

> along a rocky ridge half clad with stinted trees, where wild beasts haunted, till I lost myself quite in the upper air and clouds, seeming to pass an imaginary line which separates a hill, mere earth heaped up, from a mountain, into a super-terranean grandeur and sublimity. What distinguishes that summit above the earthy line, is that it is unhandselled, awful, grand. It can never become familiar; you are lost the moment you set foot there. You know no path, but wander, thrilled, over the bare and pathless rock, as if it were solidified air and cloud.

This passage, from Thoreau's journal entry of October 29, 1857, is reminiscent of his actual experiences on Mount Katahdin, which he'd climbed ten years earlier.

Thoreau knew of the young and growing sport of mountaineering in Europe and of the feats of explorers such as Benjamin Bonneville and Stephen Long in the American West. Judged against such climbs, his own ascents were modest. But he made much of his small feats, and his mountain writing remains some of the most compelling in our literature. He was a transcendentalist, a word whose root means to "climb over," and just as his climbs took him literally above the scenes of ordinary life, so his writing rises above mere narrative, expressing lofty ideas through the concrete imagery of the mountain landscape.

The following account, of a climb of 2,006-foot Wachusett, a conspicuous glacial monadnock a day's walk west of Thoreau's home in Concord, is what one scholar has called a typical transcendentalist "excursion," a journey that is both actual and imaginary and that reaches its gentle climax, fittingly, on the highest ground. Thoreau made the trip with Richard Fuller, the brother of Margaret Fuller of *The Dial*, which published some of Thoreau's early work. The essay from which the following selection is excerpted was first published, not in *The Dial*, but in *The Boston Miscellany* of January 1843.

In due time we began to ascend the mountain, passing, first, through a grand sugar maple wood, which bore the marks of the auger, then a denser forest, which gradually became dwarfed, till there were no trees whatever. We at length pitched our tent on the summit. It is but nineteen hundred feet above the village of Princeton, and three thousand above the level of the sea; but by this slight elevation it is infinitely removed from the plain, and when we reached it we felt a sense of remoteness, as if we had traveled into distant regions, to Arabia Petraea, or the farthest East. A robin upon a staff was the highest object in sight. Swallows were flying about us, and the chewink and cuckoo were heard near at hand. The summit consists of a few acres, destitute of trees, covered with bare rocks, interspersed with blueberry bushes, raspberries, gooseberries, strawberries, moss, and a fine, wiry grass. The common yellow lily and dwarf cornel grow abundantly in the crevices of the rocks. This clear space, which is gently rounded, is bounded a few feet lower by a thick shrubbery of oaks, with maples, aspens, beeches, cherries, and occasionally a mountain-ash intermingled, among which we found the bright blue berries of the Solomon's-seal, and the fruit of the pyrola. From the foundation of a wooden observatory, which was formerly erected on the highest point, forming a rude, hollow structure of stone, a dozen feet in diameter, and five or six in height, we could see Monadnock, in simple grandeur, in the northwest, rising nearly a thousand feet higher, still the "far blue mountain," though with an altered profile. The first day the weather was so hazy that it was in vain we endeavored to unravel the obscurity. It was like looking into the sky again, and the patches of forest here and there seemed to flit like clouds over a lower heaven. As to voyagers of an aerial Polynesia, the earth seemed like a larger island in the ether; on every side, even as low as we, the sky shutting down, like an unfathomable deep, around it, a blue Pacific island, where who knows what islanders inhabit? and as we sail near its shores we see the waving of trees and hear the lowing of kine.

We read Virgil and Wordsworth in our tent, with new pleasure there, while waiting for a clearer atmosphere, lor did the weather prevent our appreciating the simple truth and beauty of Peter Bell:

"And he had lain beside his asses,
On lofty Cheviot Hills:

And he had trudged through Yorkshire dales,
Among the rocks and winding scars;
Where deep and low the hamlets lie
Beneath their little patch of sky
And little lots of stars."

Who knows but this hill may one day be a Helvellyn, or even a Parnassus, and the Muses haunt here, and other Homers frequent the neighboring plains?

Not unconcerned Wachusett rears his head
    Above the field, so late from nature won,
With patient brow reserved, as one who read
    New annals in the history of man.

The blueberries which the mountain afforded, added to the milk we had brought, made our frugal supper, while for entertainment the even-song of the wood thrush rang along the ridge. Our eyes rested on no painted ceiling nor carpeted hall, but on skies of Nature's painting, and hills and forests of her embroidery. Before sunset, we rambled along the ridge to the north, while a hawk soared still above us. It was a place where gods might wander, so solemn and solitary, and removed from all contagion with the plain. As the evening came on, the haze was condensed in vapor, and the landscape became more distinctly visible, and numerous sheets of water were brought to light.

"Et jam summa procul villarum culmina fumant,
Majoresque cadunt altis de montibus umbrae."
And now the tops of the villas smoke afar off,
And the shadows fall longer from the high mountains.

As we stood on the stone tower while the sun was setting, we saw the shades of night creep gradually over the valleys of the east; and the inhabitants went into their houses, and shut their doors, while the moon silently rose up, and took possession of that part. And then the same scene was repeated on the west side, as far as the Connecticut and the Green Mountains, and the sun's rays fell on us two alone, of all New England men.

It was the night but one before the full of the moon, so bright that we could see to read distinctly by moonlight, and in the evening strolled over the summit without danger. There was, by chance, a fire blazing on Monadnock that night, which lighted up the whole western horizon, and, by making us aware of a community of mountains, made our position seem less solitary. But at length the wind drove us to the shelter of our tent, and we closed its door for the night, and fell asleep.

It was thrilling to hear the wind roar over the rocks, at intervals when we waked, for it had grown quite cold and windy. The night was, in its elements, simple even to majesty in that bleak place, — a bright moonlight and a piercing wind. It was at no time darker than twilight within the tent, and we could easily see the moon through its transparent roof as we lay; for there was the moon still above us, with Jupiter and Saturn on either hand, looking down on Wachusett, and it was a satisfaction to know that they were our fellow-travelers still, as high and out of our reach as our own destiny. Truly the stars were given for a consolation to man. We should not know but our life were fated to be always groveling, but it is permitted to behold them, and surely they are deserving of a fair destiny. We see laws which never fail, of whose failure we never conceived; and their lamps burn all the night, too, as well as all day, — so rich and lavish is that nature which can afford this superfluity of light.

The morning twilight began as soon as the moon had set, and we arose and kindled our fire, whose blaze might have been seen for thirty miles around. As the daylight increased, it was remarkable how rapidly the wind went down. There was no dew on the summit, but coldness supplied its place. When the dawn had reached its prime, we enjoyed the view of distinct horizon line, and could fancy ourselves at sea, and the distant hills the waves in the horizon, as seen from the deck of a vessel. The cherry-birds flitted around us, the nuthatch and flicker were heard among the bushes, the titmouse perched within a few feet, and the song of the wood thrush again rang along the ridge. At length we saw the sun rise up out of the sea, and shine on Massachusetts; and from this moment the atmosphere grew more and more transparent till the time of our departure, and we began to realize the extent of the view, and how the earth, in some degree, answered to the heavens in the breadth, the white villages to the constellations in the sky. There was little of the sublimity and grandeur which belong to mountain scenery, but an immense landscape to ponder of a summer's day. We could see how ample and roomy is nature. As far as the eye could reach there was little life in the landscape; the few birds that flitted past did not crowd. The travelers on the remote highways, which intersect the country on every side, had no fellow-travelers for miles, before or behind. On every side, the eye ranged over successive circles of towns, rising one above another, like the terraces of a vineyard, till they were lost in the horizon. Wachusett is, in fact, the observatory of the State. There lay Massachusetts, spread out before us in its length and breadth, like a map. There was the level horizon which told of the sea on the east and south, the well-known hills of New Hampshire on the north, and the misty summits of the Hoosac and Green Mountains, first made visible to us the evening before, blue and unsubstantial, like some bank of clouds which the morning wind would dissipate, on the northwest and west. These last distant ranges, on which the eye rests unwearied, commence with an abrupt boulder in the north, beyond the Connecticut, and travel southward, with three or four peaks dimly seen. But Monadnock, rearing its masculine front in the northwest, is the grandest feature. As we beheld it, we knew that it was the height of land between the two rivers, on this side the valley of the Merrimack, on that of the Connecticut, fluctuating with their blue seas of air, — these rival vales, already teeming with Yankee men along their respective streams, born to what destiny who shall tell? Watatic and the neighboring hills, in this State and in New Hampshire, are a continuation of the same elevated range on which we were standing. But that New Hampshire bluff, — that promontory of a State, — lowering day and night of this our State of Massachusetts, will longest haunt our dreams.

We could at length realize the place mountains occupy on the land, and how they come into the general scheme of the universe. When first we climb their summits and observe their lesser irregularities, we do not give credit to the comprehensive intelligence which shaped them; but when afterward we behold their outlines in the horizon, we confess that the hand which moulded their opposite slopes, making one to balance the other, worked round a deep centre, and was privy to the plan of the universe. So is the least part of nature in its bearings referred to all space. These lesser mountain ranges, as well as the Alleghanies, run from northeast to southwest, and parallel with these mountain streams are the more fluent rivers, answering to the general direction of the coast, the bank of the great ocean stream itself. Even the clouds, with their thin bars, fall into the same direction by preference, and such even is the course of the prevailing winds, and the migration of men and birds. A mountain chain determines many things for the statesman and philosopher. The improvements of civilization rather creep along its sides than cross its summit. How often is it a barrier to prejudice and fanaticism! In passing over these heights of land, through their thin atmosphere, the follies of the plain are refined and purified; and as many species of plants do not scale their summits, so many species of folly, no doubt, do not cross the Alleghanies; it is only the hardy mountain-plant that creeps quite over the ridge, and descends into the valley beyond.

We get a dim notion of the flight of birds, especially of such as fly high in the air, by having ascended a mountain. We can now see what landmarks mountains are to their migrations; how the Catskills and Highlands have hardly sunk to them, when Wachusett and Monadnock open a passage to the northeast; how they are guided, too, in their course by the rivers and valleys; and who knows but by the stars, as well as the mountain ranges, and not by the petty landmarks which we use. The bird whose eye takes in the Green Mountains on the one side, and the ocean on the other, need not be at a loss to find its way.

Thoreau Climbs Greylock, 1844

THE TWO YEARS following the climb of Wachusett were not good ones for Thoreau. In 1843 he moved to New York to try his hand at freelance writing; he sold only two essays and less than a year later was back in Concord. In 1844 *The Dial,* the magazine most sympathetic to his work, ceased publication. Then he accidentally started a forest fire near Concord. Humiliated, he set out that summer on a walking tour that took him first to 3,165-foot Monadnock and then to 3,491-foot Saddleback, or Mount Greylock, from whose summit he viewed the stunning sunrise described in the selection below. According to the scholar William Howarth, the trip was a turning point in Thoreau's life: when he got back to Concord he found a letter from a friend proposing a walking trip in Europe, but he declined the invitation, deciding instead to remain home and continue with his writing. The following year he retired to Walden Pond and began work on both *Walden* and *A Week on the Concord and Merrimack Rivers.*

The following account, describing the ascent of Greylock, was eventually published in 1849 in the *Week,* where it appears as a digression from the main travel narrative. Its tone is less pastoral than that of the Wachusett essay. Instead of reading idyllic passages from Wordsworth and Virgil, Thoreau muses over the hard facts in the business section of a newspaper. And the essay's climax, though it, too, occurs atop the mountain, is completely opposite that on Wachusett. From the latter, Thoreau had seen Massachusetts spread beneath him "like a map," displaying its physical reality plainly and leading him to remark on how mountains fit logically into the landscape. On Greylock, however, all such reality is lost in the morning mist, and the world becomes for the writer a blank and limitless field for the play of his imagination.

I had come over the hills on foot and alone in serene summer days, plucking the raspberries by the way-side, and occasionally buying a loaf of bread at a farmer's house, with a knapsack on my back, which held a few traveller's books and a change of clothing, and a staff in my hand. I had that morning looked down from the Hoosack Mountain, where the road crosses it, on the village of North Adams in the valley, three miles away under my feet, showing how uneven the earth may sometimes be, and making it seem an accident that it should ever be level and convenient for the feet of man. Putting a little rice and sugar and a tin cup into my knapsack at this village, I began in the afternoon to ascend the mountain, whose summit is three thousand six hundred feet above the level of the sea, and was seven or eight miles distant by the path. My route lay up a long and spacious valley called the Bellows, because the winds rush up or down it with violence in storms, sloping up to the very clouds between the principal range and a lower mountain. There were a few farms scattered along at different elevations, each commanding a fine prospect of the mountains to the north, and a stream ran down the middle of the valley, on which near the head there was a mill. It seemed a road for the pilgrim to enter upon who would climb to the gates of heaven. Now I crossed a hay-field, and now over the brook on a slight bridge, still gradually ascending all the while, with a sort of awe, and filled with indefinite expectations as to what kind of inhabitants and what kind of nature I should come to at last. It now seemed some advantage that the earth was uneven, for one could not imagine a more noble position for a farm house than this vale afforded, further from or nearer to its head, from a glen-like seclusion overlooking the country at a great elevation between these two mountain walls.

— ▲ —

It seemed as if he must be the most singular and heavenly-minded man whose dwelling stood highest up the valley. The thunder had rumbled at my heels all the way, but the shower passed off in another direction, though if it had not, I half believed that I should get above it. I at length reached the last house but one, where the path to the summit diverged to the right, while the summit itself rose directly in front. But I determined to follow up the valley to its head, and then find my own route up the steep, as the shorter and more adventurous way. I had thoughts of returning to this house, which was well kept and so nobly placed, the next day, and perhaps remaining a week there, if I could have entertainment. Its mistress was a frank and hospitable young woman, who stood before me in a dishabille, busily and unconcernedly combing her long black hair while she talked, giving her head the necessary toss with each sweep of the comb, with lively, sparkling eyes, and full of interest in that lower world from which I had come, talking all the while as familiarly as if she had known me for years, and reminding me of a cousin of mine. She had at first taken me for a student from Williamstown, for they went by in parties, she said, either riding or walking, almost every pleasant day, and were a pretty wild set of fellows; but they never went by the way I was going. As I passed the last house, a man called out to know what I had to sell, for seeing my knapsack, he thought that I might be a peddler, who was taking this unusual route over the ridge of the valley into South Adams. He told me that it was still four or five miles to the summit by the path which I had left, though not more than two in a straight line from where I was, but that nobody ever went this way; there was no path, and I should find it as steep as the roof of a house. But I knew that I was more used to woods and mountains than he, and went along through his cowyard, while he, looking at the sun, shouted after me that I should not get to the top that night. I soon reached the head of the valley, but as I could not see the summit from this point, I ascended a low mountain of the opposite side, and took its bearing with my compass. I at once entered the woods, and began to climb the steep side of the mountain in a diagonal direction, taking the bearing of a tree every dozen rods. The ascent was by no means difficult or unpleasant, and occupied much less time than it would have taken to follow the path. Even country people, I have observed, magnify the difficulty of travelling in the forest, especially among mountains. They seem to lack their usual common sense in this. I have climbed several higher mountains without guide or path, and have found, as might be expected, that it takes only more time and patience commonly than to travel the smoothest highway. It is very rare that you meet with obstacles in this world, which the humblest man has not faculties to surmount. It is true, we may come to a perpendicular precipice, but we need not jump off, nor run our heads against it. A man may jump down his own cellar stairs, or dash his brains out against his chimney, if he is mad. So far as my experience goes, travellers generally exaggerate the difficulties of the way. Like most evil, the difficulty is imaginary; for what's the hurry? If a person lost would conclude that after all he is not lost, he is not beside himself, but standing in his own old shoes on the very spot where he is, and that for the time being he will live there; but the places that have known him, *they* are lost, — how much anxiety and danger would vanish. I am not alone if I stand by myself. Who knows where in space this globe is rolling? Yet we will not give ourselves up for lost, let it go where it will.

I made my way steadily upward in a straight line through a dense undergrowth of mountain laurel, until the trees began to have a scraggy and infernal look, as if contending with frost goblins, and at length I reached the summit, just as the sun was setting. Several acres here had been cleared, and were covered with rocks and stumps, and there was a rude observatory in the middle which overlooked the woods. I had one fair view of the country before the sun went down, but I was too thirsty to waste any light in viewing the prospect, and set out at once to find water. First, going down a well-beaten path for half a mile through the low scrubby wood, till I came to where the water stood in the tracks of the horses which had carried travellers up, I lay down flat, and drank these dry one after another, a pure, cold, spring-like water, but yet I could not fill my dipper, though I contrived little syphons of grass stems and ingenious aqueducts on a small scale; it was too slow a process. Then remembering that I had passed a moist place near the top on my way up, I returned to find it again, and here with sharp stones and my hands, in the twilight, I made a well about two feet deep, which was soon filled with pure cold water, and the birds too came and drank at it. So I filled my dipper, and making my way back to the observatory, collected some dry sticks and made a fire on some flat stones, which had been placed on the floor for that purpose, and so I soon cooked my supper of rice, having already whittled a wooden spoon to eat with.

I sat up during the evening, reading by the light of the fire the scraps of newspapers in which some party had wrapped their luncheon; the prices current in New York and Boston, the advertisements, and the singular editorials which some had seen fit to publish, not foreseeing under what critical circumstances they would be read. I read these things at a vast advantage there, and it seemed to me that the advertisements, or what is called the business part of a paper, were greatly the best, the most useful, natural, and respectable. Almost all the opinions and sentiments expressed were so little considered, so shallow and flimsy, that I thought the very texture of the paper must be weaker in that part and tear more easily. The advertisements and the prices current were more closely allied to nature, and were respectable in some measure as tide and meteorological tables are; but the reading matter, which I remembered was most prized down below, unless it was some humble record of science, or an extract from some old classic, struck me as strangely whimsical, and crude, and one-idea'd, like a school-boy's theme, such as youths write and afterward burn. The opinions were of that kind that are doomed to wear a different aspect to-morrow, like last year's fashions; as if mankind were very green indeed, and would be ashamed of themselves in a few years, when they had outgrown this verdant period. There was, moreover, a singular disposition to wit and humor, but rarely the slightest real success; and the apparent success was a terrible satire on the attempt; as if the Evil Genius of man laughed the loudest at his best jokes. The advertisements, as I have said, such as were serious, and not of the modern quack kind, suggested pleasing and poetic thoughts; for commerce is really as interesting as nature. The very names of the commodities were poetic, and as suggestive as if they had been inserted in a pleasing poem, — Lumber, Cotton, Sugar, Hides, Guano, and Logwood. Some sober, private, and original thought would have been grateful to read there, and as much in harmony with the circumstances as if it had been written on a mountain top; for it is of a fashion which never changes, and as respectable as hides and logwood, or any natural product. What an inestimable companion such a scrap of paper would have been, containing some fruit of a mature life. What a relic! What a recipe! It seemed a divine invention, by which not mere shining coin, but shining and current thoughts, could be brought up and left there.

As it was cold, I collected quite a pile of wood and lay down on a board against the side of the building, not having any blanket to cover me, with my head to the fire, that I might look after it, which is not the Indian rule. But as it grew colder towards midnight, I at length encased myself completely in boards, managing even to put a board on top of me, with a large stone on it, to keep it down, and so slept comfortably. I was reminded, it is true, of the Irish children, who inquired what their neighbors did who had no door to put over them in winter nights as they had; but I am convinced that there was nothing very strange in the inquiry. Those who have never tried it can have no idea how far a door, which keeps the single blanket down, may go toward making one comfortable. We are constituted a good deal like chickens, which taken from the hen, and put in a basket of cotton in the chimney corner, will often peep till they die nevertheless, but if you put in a book, or any thing heavy, which will press down the cotton, and feel like the hen, they go to sleep directly. My only companions were the mice, which came to pick up the crumbs that had been left in those scraps of paper; still, as every where, pensioners on man, and not unwisely improving this elevated tract for their habitation. They nibbled what was for them; I nibbled what was for me. Once or twice in the night, when I looked up, I saw a white cloud drifting through the windows, and filling the whole upper story.

This observatory was a building of considerable size, erected by the students of Williamstown College, whose buildings might be seen by daylight gleaming far down in the valley. It would be no small advantage if every college were thus located at the base of a mountain, as good at least as one well-endowed professorship. It were as well to be educated in the shadow of a mountain as in more classical shades. Some will remember, no doubt, not only that they went to the college, but that they went to the mountain. Every visit to its summit would, as it were, generalize the particular information gained below, and subject it to more catholic tests.

I was up early and perched upon the top of this tower to see the daybreak, for some time reading the names that had been engraved there before I could distinguish more distant objects. An "untameable fly" buzzed at my elbow with the same non-chalance as on a molasses hogshead at the end of Long-wharf. Even there I must attend to his stale humdrum. But now I come to the pith of this long digression. — As the light increased I discovered around me an ocean of mist, which by chance reached up exactly to the base of the tower, and shut out every vestige of the earth, while I was left floating on this fragment of the wreck of a world, on my carved plank in cloudland; a situation which required no aid from the imagination to render it impressive. As the light in the east steadily increased, it revealed to me more clearly the new world into which I had risen in the night, the new terra-firma perchance of my future life. There was not a crevice left through which the trivial places we name Massachusetts, or Vermont, or New York, could be seen, while I still inhaled the clear atmosphere of a July morning, — if it were July there. All around beneath me was spread for a hundred miles on every side, as far as the eye could reach, an undulating country of clouds, answering in the varied swell of its surface to the terrestrial world it veiled. It was such a country as we might see in dreams, with all the delights of paradise. There were immense snowy pastures, apparently smooth-shaven and firm, and shady vales between the vaporous mountains, and far in the horizon I could see where some luxurious misty timber jutted into the prairie, and trace the windings of a water course, some unimagined Amazon or Orinoko, by the misty trees on its brink. As there was wanting the symbol, so there was not the substance of impurity, no spot nor stain. It was a favor for which to be forever silent to be shown this vision.

Thoreau Attempts Katahdin, 1846

I N THE SUMMER of 1845, Thoreau read a story in a Boston newspaper about a climb of Mount Katahdin by two students at Harvard. The following year, a few weeks after spending a night behind bars – his famed act of "civil disobedience" in protest of slavery – he set off to attempt the peak himself. Accompanying him were a cousin, George Thatcher of Bangor, as well as several boatmen skilled in negotiating Maine's wild rivers. Unlike his earlier trips, this was a genuine expedition, entailing hundreds of miles of difficult travel by boat and on foot simply to reach the base of the mountain. Once on the peak itself, the party climbed via Abol Stream, then directly up toward South Peak, a subsidiary summit of Katahdin. It was not the best route, and Thoreau found the climbing difficult and dangerous, though certainly stimulating. Heavy clouds prevented him from getting higher than about four thousand feet, well below the 5,267-foot summit.

The Katahdin country was by far the wildest Thoreau had ever seen. Much of it was then unmapped and uninhabited, and his trip through it affected him profoundly. His account of the climb – published first in 1848 in *Union Magazine*, then included in *The Maine Woods*, which appeared post-humously in 1864 and from which the selection below is excerpted – differs markedly from his earlier mountain essays. Its style is leaner, devoted less to thought and allusion and more to the hard physical reality of the mountain. It is perhaps the only instance in Thoreau's writing in which he does not feel welcome in nature, in which he seems to struggle against it. Certainly no-where else do we find Thoreau comparing himself, as he does here, to the pride-driven Satan of *Paradise Lost*, struggling upward through Chaos, or speaking of nature "pilfering man of some of his divine faculty." The climb mocked Thoreau's gentle, transcendentalist view of nature as a metaphorical extension of man's own consciousness. After Katahdin he saw nature as some-thing entirely separate, with which humanity had no relation at all:

Perhaps I most fully realized that this was primeval, untamed, and forever untameable *Nature*, or whatever else men call it, while com-ing down this part of the mountain. . . . Nature was here something savage and awful, though beautiful. I looked with awe at the ground

I trod on, to see what the Powers had made there, the form and
fashion and material of their work. This was that Earth of which we
have heard, made out of Chaos and Old Night. Here was no man's
garden, but the unhandselled globe. It was not lawn, nor pasture,
nor mead, nor woodland, nor lea, nor arable, nor waste-land. It was
the fresh and natural surface of the planet Earth, as it was made
forever and ever, – to be the dwelling of man, we say, – so Nature
made it, and man may use it if he can. Man was not to be associated
with it. It was Matter, vast, terrific, – not his Mother Earth that we
have heard of, not for him to tread on, or be buried in, – no, it were
being too familiar even to let his bones lie there – the home this of
Necessity and Fate. There was there felt the presence of a force not
bound to be kind to man. It was a place for heathenism and superstitious rites, – to be inhabited by men nearer of kin to the rocks and
to wild animals than we. We walked over it with a certain awe . . .
here not even the surface had been scarred by man, but it was a
specimen of what God saw fit to make this world.

On Katahdin, Thoreau discovered a higher order of nature, one that
existed on its own terms, independent of whatever imagination or science
might make of it. It was a humbling experience.

By six o'clock, having mounted our packs and a good blanket full of trout,
ready dressed, and swung up such baggage and provision as we wished to leave
behind upon the tops of saplings, to be out of the reach of bears, we started for
the summit of the mountain, distant, as Uncle George said the boatmen called
it, about four miles, but as I judged, and as it proved, nearer fourteen. He had
never been any nearer the mountain than this, and there was not the slightest
trace of man to guide us further in this direction. At first, pushing a few rods
up the Aboljacknagesic, or "open-land stream," we fastened our batteau to a
tree, and travelled up the north side, through burnt lands, now partially
overgrown with young aspens, and other shrubbery; but soon, recrossing this
stream, where it was about fifty or sixty feet wide, upon a jam of logs and
rocks, and you could cross it by this means almost anywhere, we struck at once
for the highest peak, over a mile or more of comparatively open land still, very
gradually ascending the while. Here it fell to my lot, as the oldest mountain-
climber, to take the lead: so scanning the woody side of the mountain, which
lay still at an indefinite distance, stretched out some seven or eight miles in
length before us, we determined to steer directly for the base of the highest
peak, leaving a large slide, by which, as I have since learned, some of our

predecessors ascended, on our left. This course would lead us parallel to a dark seam in the forest, which marked the bed of a torrent, and over a slight spur, which extended southward from the main mountain, from whose bare summit we could get an outlook over the country, and climb directly up the peak, which would then be close at hand. Seen from this point, a bare ridge at the extremity of the open land, Ktaadn presented a different aspect from any mountain I have seen, there being a greater proportion of naked rock, rising abruptly from the forest; and we looked up at this blue barrier as if it were some fragment of a wall which anciently bounded the earth in that direction. Setting the compass for a north-east course, which was the bearing of the southern base of the highest peak, we were soon buried in the woods.

---------- ▲ ----------

At length we reached an elevation sufficiently bare to afford a view of the summit, still distant and blue, almost as if retreating from us. A torrent, which proved to be the same we had crossed, was seen tumbling down in front, literally from out of the clouds. But this glimpse at our whereabouts was soon lost, and we were buried in the woods again. The wood was chiefly yellow birch, spruce, fir, mountain-ash, or round-wood, as the Maine people call it, and moose-wood. It was the worst kind of travelling; sometimes like the densest scrub-oak patches with us. The cornel, or bunch-berries, were very abundant, as well as Solomon's seal and moose-berries. Blue-berries were distributed along our whole route; and in one place the bushes were drooping with the weight of the fruit still as fresh as ever. It was the seventh of September. Such patches afforded a grateful repast, and served to bait the tired party forward. When any lagged behind, the cry of "blue-berries" was most effectual to bring them up. Even at this elevation we passed through a moose-yard, formed by a large flat rock, four or five rods square, where they tread down the snow in winter. At length, fearing that if we held the direct course to the summit, we should not find any water near our camping-ground, we gradually swerved to the west, till, at four o'clock, we struck again the torrent which I have mentioned, and here, in view of the summit, the weary party decided to camp that night.

While my companions were seeking a suitable spot for this purpose, I improved the little daylight that was left in climbing the mountain alone. We were in a deep and narrow ravine, sloping up to the clouds, at an angle of nearly forty-five degrees, and hemmed in by walls of rock, which were at first covered with low trees, then with impenetrable thickets of scraggy birches and spruce-trees, and with moss, but at last bare of all vegetation but lichens, and almost continually draped in clouds. Following up the course of the torrent which occupied this—and I mean to lay some emphasis on this word *up*—

pulling myself up by the side of perpendicular falls of twenty or thirty feet, by the roots of firs and birches, and then, perhaps, walking a level rod or two in the thin stream, for it took up the whole road, ascending by huge steps, as it were, a giant's stairway, down which a river flowed, I had soon cleared the trees, and paused on the successive shelves, to look back over the country. The torrent was from fifteen to thirty feet wide, without a tributary, and seemingly not diminishing in breadth as I advanced; but still it came rushing and roaring down, with a copious tide, over and amidst masses of bare rock, from the very clouds, as though a water-spout had just burst over the mountain. Leaving this at last, I began to work my way, scarcely less arduous than Satan's anciently through Chaos, up the nearest, though not the highest peak. At first scrambling on all fours over the tops of ancient black spruce-trees (*Abies nigra*), old as the flood, from two to ten or twelve feet in height, their tops flat and spreading, and their foliage blue and nipt with cold, as if for centuries they had ceased growing upward against the bleak sky, the solid cold. I walked some good rods erect upon the tops of these trees, which were overgrown with moss and mountain-cranberries. It seemed that in the course of time they had filled up the intervals between the huge rocks, and the cold wind had uniformly levelled all over. Here the principle of vegetation was hard put to it. There was apparently a belt of this kind running quite round the mountain, though, perhaps, nowhere so remarkable as here. Once, slumping through, I looked down ten feet, into a dark and cavernous region, and saw the stem of a spruce, on whose top I stood, as on a mass of coarse basket-work, fully nine inches in diameter at the ground. These holes were bear's dens, and the bears were even then at home. This was the sort of garden I made my way *over*, for an eighth of a mile, at the risk, it is true, of treading on some of the plants, not seeing any path through it — certainly the most treacherous and porous country I ever travelled.

"— *nigh founder'd, on he fares,*
Treading the crude consistence, half on foot,
Half flying."

But nothing could exceed the toughness of the twigs, — not one snapped under my weight, for they had slowly grown. Having slumped, scrambled, rolled, bounced, and walked, by turns, over this scraggy country, I arrived upon a side-hill, or rather side-mountain, where rocks, gray, silent rocks, were the flocks and herds that pastured, chewing a rocky cud at sunset. They looked at me with hard gray eyes, without a bleat or a low. This brought me to the skirt of a cloud, and bounded my walk that night. But I had already seen that Maine country when I turned about, waving, flowing, rippling, down below.

When I returned to my companions, they had selected a camping-ground on the torrent's edge, and were resting on the ground; one was on the sick list, rolled in a blanket, on a damp shelf of rock. It was a savage and dreary scenery enough; so wildly rough, that they looked long to find a level and open space for the tent. We could not well camp higher, for want of fuel; and the trees here seemed so evergreen and sappy, that we almost doubted if they would acknowledge the influence of fire; but fire prevailed at last, and blazed here, too, like a good citizen of the world. Even at this height we met with frequent traces of moose, as well as of bears. As here was no cedar, we made our bed of coarser feathered spruce; but at any rate the feathers were plucked from the live tree. It was, perhaps, even a more grand and desolate place for a night's lodging than the summit would have been, being in the neighborhood of those wild trees, and of the torrent. Some more aerial and finer-spirited winds rushed and roared through the ravine all night, from time to time arousing our fire, and dispersing the embers about. It was as if we lay in the very nest of a young whirlwind. At midnight, one of my bedfellows, being startled in his dreams by the sudden blazing up to its top of a fir-tree, whose green boughs were dried by the heat, sprang up, with a cry, from his bed, thinking the world on fire, and drew the whole camp after him.

In the morning, after whetting our appetite on some raw pork, a wafer of hard bread, and dipper of condensed cloud or water-spout, we all together began to make our way up the falls, which I have described; this time choosing the right hand, or highest peak, which was not the one I had approached before. But soon my companions were lost to my sight behind the mountain ridge in my rear, which still seemed ever retreating before me, and I climbed alone over huge rocks, loosely poised, a mile or more, still edging toward the clouds—for though the day was clear elsewhere, the summit was concealed by mist. The mountain seemed a vast aggregation of loose rocks, as if sometime it had rained rocks, and they lay as they fell on the mountain sides, nowhere fairly at rest, but leaning on each other, all rocking-stones, with cavities between, but scarcely any soil or smoother shelf. They were the raw materials of a planet dropped from an unseen quarry, which the vast chemistry of nature would anon work up, or work down, into the smiling and verdant plains and valleys of earth. This was an undone extremity of the globe; as in lignite we see coal in the process of formation.

At length I entered within the skirts of the cloud which seemed forever drifting over the summit, and yet would never be gone, but was generated out of that pure air as fast as it flowed away; and when, a quarter of a mile further, I reached the summit of the ridge, which those who have seen in clearer weather say is about five miles long, and contains a thousand acres of table-land, I was deep within the hostile ranks of clouds, and all objects were obscured by them. Now the wind would blow me out a yard of clear sunlight, wherein I stood; then a gray, dawning light was all it could accomplish, the cloud-line ever rising and falling with the wind's intensity. Sometimes it seemed as if the summit would be cleared in a few moments and smile in sunshine: but what was gained on one side was lost on another. It was like sitting in a chimney and waiting for the smoke to blow away. It was, in fact, a cloud-factory, — these were the cloud-works, and the wind turned them off done from the cool, bare rocks. Occasionally, when the windy columns broke in to me, I caught sight of a dark, damp crag to the right or left; the mist driving ceaselessly between it and me. It reminded me of the creations of the old epic and dramatic poets, of Atlas, Vulcan, the Cyclops, and Prometheus. Such was Caucasus and the rock where Prometheus was bound. Aeschylus had no doubt visited such scenery as this. It was vast, Titanic, and such as man never inhabits. Some part of the beholder, even some vital part, seems to escape through the loose grating of his ribs as he ascends. He is more lone than you can imagine. There is less of substantial thought and fair understanding in him, than in the plains where men inhabit. His reason is dispersed and shadowy, more thin and subtle like the air. Vast, Titanic, inhuman Nature has got him at disadvantage, caught him alone, and pilfers him of some of his divine faculty. She does not smile on him as in the plains. She seems to say sternly, why came ye here before your time? This ground is not prepared for you. Is it not enough that I smile in the valleys? I have never made this soil for thy feet, this air for thy breathing, these rocks for thy neighbors. I cannot pity nor fondle thee here, but forever relentlessly drive thee hence to where I *am* kind. Why seek me where I have not called thee, and then complain because you find me but a stepmother? Shouldst thou freeze or starve, or shudder thy life away, here is no shrine, nor altar, nor any access to my ear.

"Chaos and ancient Night, I come no spy
With purpose to explore or to disturb
The secrets of your realm, but . . .
. . . as my way
Lies through your spacious empire up to light."

The tops of mountains are among the unfinished parts of the globe, whither it is a slight insult to the gods to climb and pry into their secrets, and try their effect on our humanity. Only daring and insolent men, perchance, go there. Simple races, as savages, do not climb mountains — their tops are sacred and mysterious tracts never visited by them. Pomola is always angry with those who climb to the summit of Ktaadn.

According to Jackson, who in his capacity of geological surveyor of the state, has accurately measured it — the altitude of Ktaadn is 5,300 feet, or a little more than one mile above the level of the sea — and he adds: "It is then evidently the highest point in the State of Maine, and is the most abrupt granite mountain in New England." The peculiarities of that spacious table-land on which I was standing, as well as the remarkable semicircular precipice or basin on the eastern side, were all concealed by the mist. I had brought my whole pack to the top, not knowing but I should have to make my descent to the river, and possibly to the settled portion of the state alone and by some other route, and wishing to have a complete outfit with me. But at length, fearing that my companions would be anxious to reach the river before night, and knowing that the clouds might rest on the mountain for days, I was compelled to descend. Occasionally, as I came down, the wind would blow me a vista open through which I could see the country eastward, boundless forests, and lakes, and streams, gleaming in the sun, some of them emptying into the East Branch. There were also new mountains in sight in that direction. Now and then some small bird of the sparrow family would flit away before me, unable to command its course, like a fragment of the gray rock blown off by the wind.

I found my companions where I had left them, on the side of the peak, gathering the mountain cranberries, which filled every crevice between the rocks, together with blue-berries, which had a spicier flavor the higher up they grew, but were not the less agreeable to our palates. When the country is settled and roads are made, these cranberries will perhaps become an article of commerce. From this elevation, just on the skirts of the clouds, we could overlook the country west and south for a hundred miles. There it was, the State of Maine, which we had seen on the map, but not much like that. Immeasurable forest for the sun to shine on, that eastern *stuff* we hear of in Massachusetts. No clearing, no house. It did not look as if a solitary traveller had cut so much as a walking-stick there. Countless lakes, — Moosehead in the southwest, forty miles long by ten wide, like a gleaming silver platter at the end of the table; Chesuncook, eighteen long by three wide, without an island; Millinocket, on the south, with its hundred islands; and a hundred others without a name; and mountains also, whose names, for the most part, are known only to the Indians. The forest looked like a firm grass sward, and the effect of these lakes in its midst has been well compared by one who has since visited this same spot, to that of a "mirror broken into a thousand fragments, and wildly scattered over the grass, reflecting the full blaze of the sun."

Sidney Ford Attempts
Mount Rainier, 1852

M OUNT RAINIER, AT 14,410 feet the highest of America's great north-western volcanoes, had been approached as early as 1833 by William Frasier Tolmie, a botanist connected with the Hudson's Bay Company who climbed a nearby prominence now known as Mount Pleasant. But Rainier itself was not attempted until 1852, when a party scouting a route for a trans-Cascade wagon road detoured to the peak and ascended its southern flanks to perhaps as high as fourteen thousand feet. A brief account of the climb, reprinted below in its entirety, appeared in the Olympia, Washington, *Columbian* on September 18, 1852.

Each of the three climbers mentioned in the account was an early settler in the Puget Sound area. John Edgar, credited by the historian Aubrey Haines as being the leader on the climb, had worked for years for the Hudson's Bay Company and was married to a Klickitat Indian woman. The family of Sidney S. Ford, Jr. had been one of the first to settle on the Columbia River. Robert S. Bailey lived on Whidby Island before moving to Olympia in 1852 and later became assessor of the newly organized Thurston County. Haines feels there was also a fourth member of the party, Benjamin Franklin Shaw, who is not mentioned in the account below but who claimed some fifty-four years later to have been part of the climb. Shaw was a hero of Washington's Indian war of 1855–56 and a widely respected leader in the territory. He reportedly did not "claim to have been on the highest point, [but] does say that 'no other point seemed higher than the one whereon his party stood.'" This brief, ambiguous statement forms the basis for Haines's belief that the party probably climbed quite high on the mountain but not all the way to the true summit. An 1870 climb by Hazard Stevens and Philemon Beecher van Trump is generally considered the first complete ascent of the peak, but today it is impossible to be sure. Unfortunately, the *Columbian* was more interested in road building than mountain climbing, and the account below does little to clarify the matter.

About four weeks ago, a party of young men, consisting of Messrs. R. S. Bailey, S. S. Ford, jr. and John Edgar, undertook an expedition to Mount Ranier, for the purpose of ascending that mountain as far as circumstances might warrant. Ranier, as all are aware, is situated in the main Cascade range, distant from its base to Olympia about fifty five miles. On arriving at the foot of the mountain the party secured their animals, and pursued their way upward by the back-bone ridge to the main body of the mountain, and to the heighth, as near as they could judge, of nine or ten miles — the last half mile over snow of the depth probably of fifty feet, but perfectly crusted and solid. The party were two days in reaching their highest altitude, and they describe the mountain as extremely rugged, and difficult of ascent; on the slopes and table land they found a luxuriant growth of grass, far exceeding in freshness and vigor any afforded by the prairies below. On some of these table lands they

found beautiful lakes — from a half to a mile in circumference — formed from mountain streams, and the melting of snow. The party remained at their last camp, upward, two days and nights, where they fared sumptiously on the game afforded by the mountain, which they found very numerous, in the shape of brown bear, mountain goat, deer, &c., with an endless variety of the feathered genus; the side of the mountain was literally covered with every description of berries, of the most delicious flavor.

The party had a perfect view of the Sound and surrounding country — recognising the numerous prairies with which they were familiar, to which were added in their observations, several stranger prairies, of which they had no knowledge, and which, probably, have never been explored. The evenings and mornings were extremely cold, with a wind strong and piercing — the noon-day sun oppressively warm.

They describe their view of the surrounding country and scenery as most enchanting, and consider themselves richly rewarded for their toil in procuring it. This is the first party of whites, we believe, that has ever attempted to ascend Ranier.

Not being provided with instruments for taking minute observations, and there being a constant fog and mist along the range of mountains, the party were unable to make any very satisfactory discoveries in relation to a practicable route across them; yet Mr. Ford informs us, that he noticed several passes at intervals through the mountains, which, as far as he could see, gave satisfactory evidence that a good route could be surveyed, and a road cut through with all ease.

Who can calculate the benefit that would have accrued to the Puget Sound country, had its citizens taken sufficient interest in the project to have located a road across the mountains for the ingress of this year's immigration? Instead of the main body of the present influx going into the Willamette, Umpqua, Rogue River and Shasta valleys, they would have gladly wended their way to this still more inviting territory. Hundreds of claims would already have been taken, and mechanic shops established wherever the wants of the people might have required them. Commercial, and all other interests would have received an impetus before undreamed of, and the country advanced in importance in a single year, what would take ten years, by the present tardy movements of settlement and improvement. Let the people on the Sound be true to their interests the coming year, and turn their attention as early next spring as practicable, in surveying a route and establishing a road across the Cascades, and for every dollar expended in the project, they will, in the end, receive an hundred percent interest.

T. J. Dryer Climbs
Mount Saint Helens, 1853

T HOMAS JEFFERSON DRYER, the driving force behind the first ascents of both Mount Saint Helens and Mount Hood, was one of Oregon's pioneer publishers. Hoping to establish his own newspaper somewhere in the West, Dryer left New York City for San Francisco, where he was advised to try his luck in the growing Oregon Territory. Shortly afterward he arrived in Portland, with a printing press and a few hundred dollars in capital; the first issue of *The Oregonian* appeared on December 4, 1850. Besides editing *The Oregonian*, Dryer was a politically ambitious member of the Whig party, a secret supporter for a time of the so-called "know-nothings," and an enemy of the Democrats, whom he refers to obliquely in the selection after this as supporters of "Durhamism." He was also an advocate of statehood for the territory and a member of Oregon's first state legislative assembly. In 1860 he went to Washington, D.C., carrying with him the new state's lone electoral vote for Abraham Lincoln.

Dryer's motives for climbing Mount Saint Helens were varied. He was by nature curious and energetic, and always on the lookout for interesting copy for his newspaper. He never shied away from a chance to call attention either to himself or his adopted homeland, and, though he moved in the highest circles of the territory's political and social life, he seemed genuinely to enjoy the openness and camaraderie of mountain travel. Finally, he may have viewed the ascent of Saint Helens as a sort of warmup for the more difficult climb of Mount Hood that he attempted the following year.

The account below is reprinted from the September 3, 1853, issue of *The Oregonian*.

CAMP, 40 miles north Vancouver,
August 19th, 1853.

DEAR OREGONIAN: After four days' hard traveling we have made forty miles towards mount St. Helens, upon a trail (called by some a "military road,") which we care not to travel again. This trail was recently cut by a party under the command of Capt. McClelland, U.S.A., who is engaged in exploring, with a view of ascertaining the practicability of a northern route for the

Pacific railroad. It would seem that they had taken extra pains to cut and mark their way in the shape of a ram's horn, for the purpose of crossing every fallen tree in sight.

──────────── ▲ ────────────

As yet we have seen but little good land—the country generally is not only rough but poor; and a large part of the timber has been destroyed by fire. Game is undoubtedly abundant. We have witnessed numerous signs of bear, deer, elk, and panthers; although, thus far, we have seen no game larger than grouse, partridges, &c. Last night we were serenaded by a pack of wolves on the mountain near by our camp, which gave rise to a miscellaneous discussion respecting damp and dry powder and caps—marvelous stories about grizzley bears, tigers, panthers, &c., and wonderful exploits in hunting them. Finally, all became quiet except the rain, which continued through the night pattering upon our blankets, and collecting in their folds, ready to give any one a cold bath who did not exercise the greatest care in turning over.

On the morning of the 18th, we left our encampment in a drenching rain, being compelled to do so in consequence of the scarcity of grass for our horses. The trail was through thick brush dripping wet, and our wardrobe was decidedly moist. The buckskin pantaloons of our party became so elongated as to cover the toes of our boots, presenting a novel appearance. At 11 o'clock we reached a prairie and found good grass; but had a long search for water. At last we found a fine rivulet and struck a camp. Soon a large fire and a tolerable shelter under some large fir trees cheered us; and, after a lunch upon raw bacon and crackers, Messrs. Smith, Wilson and Drew, proceeded to hunt for game to appease a mountain appetite. They soon returned with five grouse, two partridges and one pigeon, which were soon cooked, and devoured with a relish. While out, Smith rode into a flock of grouse, at which he discharged both barrels of his gun without effect. Chagrined and laughed at by his comrades, he, on looking down, discovered that his horse was standing on the foot of a fluttering member of the flock, which he secured, and rode off wringing its neck in triumph. Hereafter the horse and Smith are to be sent out for game.

20th.—The rain continued throughout the night, but this morning the weather bids fair to be pleasant. The clouds are passing away and the sun occasionally shines out brightly. We have concluded to remain in camp to-day for the purpose of resting our horses, drying our "damage" and hunting for game.—P.M. the party returned to camp with an abundant supply of game; such as grouse, partridges, &c. Mr. Wilson had a chase after a deer, but could not get a shot at him. Mount St. Helens looms up majestically, apparently only a few miles off—but probably some twenty-five or thirty. It looks much more formidable and difficult of ascent than when seen at a longer distance. The snow has fallen apparently several feet upon the mountain during the last two days, which may retard our progress in ascending it.

A party of Indians passed through the prairie to-day, but did not appear to be very communicative. They, however, told us that it is yet "four sleeps" hence to the mountain.

I expect to meet the military express to-day or tomorrow, and shall send this by it. In our next we hope to give readers of the Oregonian an extended description of this hitherto unexplored country.

August 23, '53.

. . . Towards evening we came to an old volcanic region of some three miles in extent, over which we were compelled to travel. The whole surface was of lava rock, with large fissures of considerable depth. We noticed several craters—some of them appeared like walled wells coming out of a cone-shaped protuberance from four to twenty feet high. This volcanic region appears not to have been disturbed by an eruption for a much longer time than any other we have seen. Large trees are growing among the lava rocks, which is not the case at mount St. Helens.

Soon after leaving this region we encountered another river which has its source in a northerly direction, and emptying into the one we had been ascending for some fifteen or eighteen miles. At this point St. Helens appeared much nearer than before, and as we had been informed that the "military trail" led to the base of that mountain, we were induced to continue upon it, which led up the western branch. This day we had been in the saddle continuously over eleven hours, and finding no grass, were compelled by the darkness of the night to camp and tie up our horses without food.

The next morning we started at an early hour, and continued following the military trail, which crossed the river several times, as before, to avoid the spurs of the mountains. At about twelve o'clock the trail left the river in an easterly direction, which soon brought us to the top of the main Cascade Range, apparently nearer mount Rainier than St. Helens; and retreating from, rather than approaching, the latter. We, therefore, retraced our steps, and came back to the point where we had been two days before—at the forks [of] the river. Here we left the trail, and ascended a high mountain on the north side of the river, which enabled us to get some idea of the lay of the country between us and mount St. Helens, then appearing to be about eight or ten miles off.

Our progress through the dense forest was necessarily slow and tedious. At one point, one of our pack horses rolled down a steep precipice for several rods, where it would seem impossible for an animal, in doing so, to escape instant death. But upon releasing him from his burden, and assisting him to rise, we found that he was not seriously hurt — our camp and cooking utensils appeared to suffer more injury than the horse.

On the second day, further progress with horses was found impracticable. Upon looking around we fortunately found a small patch of grass, and camped. The next morning at break of day, Messrs. Wilson, Smith, Drew and ourself, took three days' rations, together with such things as were deemed necessary to aid us in the ascent, and left camp for the summit, distant about

four miles in an air line. We found the route a continual steep ascent, with the exception of an occasional descent over a precipitant ledge of rocks. About two miles from our camp we descended a high ledge to the bed of a small stream, which we followed until we struck the lava at the foot of the bare mountain — where vegetation ceases to make its appearance. The portion of this stream which we travelled has a fall of at least one thousand feet to the mile, and a much greater one higher up.

The appearance of the mountain upon a near approach is sublimely grand, and impossible to describe. The blackened piles of lava which were thrown into ridges hundreds of feet high in every imaginary shape, with an occasional high cliff of primitive formation, seeming to lift its head above and struggle to be released from its compressed position, impress the mind of the beholder with the power of Omnipotence, and the insignificance of human power when compared with that of nature's God. Above all stands a tower of eternal rock and snow, apparently stretching its high head far above the clouds and looking down with disdain upon all beneath. The glaring sunbeams upon the 'snows of a thousand winters' serve by contrast to make the immense piles of lava appear blacker than they otherwise would.

We commenced the ascent at once on the south side by climbing up the cliffs of lava towards a small cluster of spruce trees which stand a short distance from the line of perpetual snow. After several hours' hard toil we reached this point, and finding a few sticks of dry wood, kindled a fire and made our camp for the night. We here supplied ourselves with water by melting snow.

We found the night cold and extremely uncomfortable — our party did not find much repose, and as the eastern sky commenced to show the approach of day, we left the camp and pursued our way upward. The higher we ascended, the more difficult our progress. Suffice it to say that, by constant and persevering effort, we were enabled to reach the highest pinnacle of the mountain soon after meridian. The atmosphere produced a singular affect on all the party, each face looked pale and sallow, and all complained of a strange ringing in the ears. It appeared as if there were hundreds of fine toned bells jingling all around us. Blood started from our nose, and all of us found respiration difficult. With this exception, we all felt well. It would be futile to attempt to give our readers a correct idea of the appearance of the vast extent of country visible from the top of this mountain. The ocean, distant over one hundred miles, was plainly seen. The whole Coast and Cascade ranges of mountains could be plainly traced with the naked eye. The snow covered peaks of Mts. Hood, Rainier, and two others seemed close by. These form a sort of amphitheatre on a large scale, diversified with hills and valleys.

The crater has been represented to be on the southwest side of the mountain, which is not the case. We took the bearing from the top with a compass, and found it to be on the north-east side. The smoke was continually issuing from its mouth, giving unmistakable evidence that the fire was not extinguished. There is much more snow on the north than on the south side; on the latter it is bare in spots, while on the former it is hundreds of feet deep. We examined fissures in the snow several rods across, which extended a great length along the side of the mountain; and on throwing a stone down heard it strike a long distance from us.

After spending sufficient time to see what was to be seen, and building a pyramid of loose stones on the highest spot of level earth and ashes, we commenced our descent, and reached our camp at 4 o'clock in the afternoon, tired and worn out in body and *boots*. At dark we reached the timber, and camped for the night. The next morning we left our encampment on the mountain for home, which we reached in four days.

There is but little good tillage land on the route we traversed. We passed two very good prairies of sufficient extent for several claims on each, but with these exceptions, and an occasional small tract of bottom land, we saw nothing inviting to an agriculturalist. The timber is large and stands very thick until near the mountain, where it becomes more scrubby. In cutting our names upon trees near the snow line, we found the bark on the spruce fully an inch in thickness, while in the low lands it was scarcely one-fourth as thick.

We have only to add that we are fully satisfied with our trip, and are willing hereafter to let others explore mountains; while we will devote our time to matters requiring less labor, and fraught with more of the comforts of life than we have experienced in this TRIP TO THE TOP OF MOUNT ST. HELENS!

T. J. Dryer Attempts Mount Hood, 1854

D ESPITE HIS CLAIM, made following his 1853 ascent of Mount Saint Helens, that he was "willing hereafter to let others explore mountains," Dryer was back the following summer to attempt 11,235-foot Mount Hood, which of all the Cascade volcanoes looms most dominantly above Portland. Hood is a more difficult mountain than Saint Helens, being more than a thousand feet higher and more heavily glaciated. Dryer did not actually reach the summit proper, arriving instead at the "south pinnacle," a point on the crater rim about fifty feet lower, by his estimate, than the highest peak. In the account below, Dryer writes of ascending snowslopes as steep as seventy degrees, which seems doubtful to today's climbers, most of whom would not dare venture onto such steep terrain with Dryer's primitive equipment. The party's barometer being unusable, he calculated the mountain's height by means of a complicated procedure taking into account the angle of the slope, the thickness of the snow and temperature of the air at snowline, and certain theories of the geographer, Baron von Humboldt. His final figure of 18,361 feet, not surprisingly, is more than seven thousand feet off.

As with the Saint Helens ascent, Dryer gave prominent placement to the Hood climb in his newspaper, *The Oregonian*. The Hood story is more than twice as long as the Saint Helens piece, and in it Dryer gives us a more interesting picture of both the mountain itself and his climbing companions, particularly the Indian, who climbs the peak in spite of his very evident ambivalence.

The experience affected the climbers deeply; back in high camp following the climb, their dreams are haunted by cliffs and crevasses, and in the morning they wake up sunburned and swollen. Even so, Dryer ends the story with a vow to return and climb other peaks in the region. He may well have been the first American to make repeated climbs of high peaks solely for pleasure.

We left Portland, in company with Capt. Travaillot, on Friday morning, August 4th, with the full and fixed determination of ascending this hitherto unexplored mountain. We had made arrangements to meet Wells Lake, Esq.,

165

Gen. Palmer, and Capt. Barlow, at Foster's, some twenty miles on the way. Soon after our arrival at Foster's, Messrs. Lake and Barlow arrived. The next morning we set out, at an early hour, without Gen. Palmer, he not arriving in time. We placed ourselves under the command of Capt. Barlow, who is an old mountaineer, and familiar with every hill, valley, river, spring and brook of the Cascade Range. From Foster's, for several miles, the trail or immigrant road, as it is called, is comparatively good, although we cannot say anything flattering of the land as offering inducements to agriculturalists.

For some thirty miles the ascent is gradual, except an occasional hill, which, to an inexperienced traveler in the mountains, would seem to be an insurmountable barrier to further progress.

Our guide, Capt. Barlow, however, seemed to apprehend no difficulty, and, upon approaching, would dismount and start up with as much indifference as a man would start to walk through his door-yard; the rest of the party must, of course, manifest the same indifference, and follow in the wake. After some eight hours' riding over a rough, unsettled country, in a hot sun, the most of the way destitute of water, the party began exhibiting an unusual haste to get to some place where they could allay a parching thirst. Upon attaining what appeared to be the summit of the *first* bench of Mt. Hood, and immediately on the top, Capt. Barlow turned his horse's head square to the right and galloped off at a rapid rate to a clump of fir trees near the brow of a steep hill, where he immediately dismounted, stripped his horse, and turned him loose; we had nothing to do but follow suit.

Before the pack horses were unloaded, Capt. B. had kindled a blazing fire, and, with camp kettle in hand, started down the hill; we followed, in double quick time, with bucket, coffee-pot and tin cups—our pace being accelerated by a raging thirst. A few rods below we found a fine gurgling spring of the purest water, and Capt. Barlow sitting down, quietly awaiting the filling of his camp kettle from a small stream running off from a rock above. After partaking of the cooling beverage, and filling up our vessels, we returned up the hill to camp, where our indefatigable guide, Capt. Barlow, had the coffee ready for dinner; thereby evincing that we had a *commander, guide* and *cook* all in the same person.

—————— ▲ ——————

[The next] morning we had some trouble in finding all the horses, as they had wandered a mile or more from the camp after food. However, we soon got under way, and followed the same stream, which, as we ascended, became more rapid, and the valley more narrow. Towards noon we reached the second *lift*, or bench of the mountain. Just before we got to the foot of this steep mountain, the whole party were put in a good humor by the following

dialogue between Capt. Travaillot, whose home is on the "deep, deep sea," and a Frenchman by birth, education and habits, and Capt. Barlow, *the* mountaineer.

Capt. T. "Monsieur Barlow, how far you call him to dat place where we sleep yester night?"

Capt. B. "Six miles."

Capt. T. *"Six miles,* hey? Begar, sixty such miles as dat make von d—d long degree, I tink."

So we thought, and so did all the party, except Capt. Barlow, whose experience in the mountains has induced him to estimate miles according to the route traveled.

——————— ▲ ———————

In about three hours' hard traveling, we suddenly emerged into an open plain thickly covered with grass and flowers. The lofty snow-covered mountain loomed up in sublime grandeur and magnificence, apparently not more than a mile or so distant—we, however, traveled full two hours up an ascent of about 20 degrees; which brought us to the snow—lying in fields on either side and in our front. After a short search we found water, and a small clump of trees, where we encamped for the night. Our first business was to build signal fires at different points, as high up as possible, which arrangement had been agreed upon between Judge Olney's party and ourselves, to enable us to find each other. The night passed off, however, without bringing us any intelligence from the other party.

On the morning of the 7th, our party divided and left the camp at an early hour, for different parts of the mountain to search for the judge and his party. Mr. Lake and ourself started for the eastern side, while Capts. Barlow and Travaillot went west. We found a small quantity of fuel high up on a ledge of rocks, with which we kindled a fire on the top of the highest point to which we could convey the fuel. Judge Olney and Major Hallar with their Indian were also out in search of us. They discovered the smoke from the fire we had kindled, and with the aid of a glass were enabled to see us, some two miles above them; whereupon they immediately hastened to join us. But before they could get sufficiently near to arrest our attention, we had left to prosecute our search, and had got out of sight of them.

About this time, black clouds began to gather around the base of the mountain far below us, it soon commenced to thunder and lighten, and the wind to blow a severe gale from the west. Judge Olney and Maj. Hallar after much difficulty discovered our camp, and came in presenting anything but a judicial or military appearance. The Judge had lost his *hat*, by the wind lifting it from his head, and carrying it far down the mountain side. The Major had made several rents in his apparel, which required the immediate service of a tailor to make him look fit for a military or dress review. They were, withal, blessed with a good appetite, having been on short allowance for two days, as was evinced by the justice done to our tub of bacon and bread. After they had stowed away enough provender to convince us that they would do to live in the mountains without making *rye* faces at mountain fare; and after washing it down with a little ———— and snow-water, it was decided to pack up and move into a more sheltered position from the wind, and threatening weather. The horses were soon brought up and packed, whereupon we got under way towards the S.E. side of the mountain. On the route our *hat* suddenly left and went whirling down the mountain side after the Judge's, leaving our cranium exposed to the weather. However, as it had become *judicially fashionable* to go bare-headed, we did not complain; besides our Indian guide went without covering on the head and so did his Honor the Judge, therefore it was "ordered by the court," and "fully sustained by the press," that any man could either wear a hat (provided he had one) or go without, as his fancy or circumstances might make it convenient or agreeable.

Upon reaching the camp on the S.E. side where Judge Olney, Maj. Hallar, and the Indian had left their animals, we found it entirely too much exposed to the driving wind to remain there; the whole party retreated down the side of the mountain for some three miles, where we found a deep, grass-covered canyon, completely sheltered from the wind, and encamped by the side of a large spring of the purest water. As soon as the horses were picketed, coffee made, bacon fried, and other little *et ceteras* attended to; Capt. Travaillot and Maj. Hallar went out in search of sights. They soon returned with two camp-kettles full of fine strawberries of good size and fine flavor which were fully appreciated 'by the press,' and pronounced A. No. 1, by the Judge, Mr. Lake and Capt. Barlow. The Indian went out after game, but returned late, "*halo tenas moose-a-moose*" or other game. Therefore, we fell back upon our bacon, which if not particularly relished as the choicest and most delicate dish, it has a wonderful tendency to satisfy hunger and make men good natured after a long weary day's travel up and down mountains. For dessert we enjoyed a dozen fine ripe apples, presented to us by Mr. Kelly of Clackamas county, to whom, all the party expressed their hearty thanks for the delicious luxury.

About sunset, the wind abated and the clouds below disappeared. The moon rose, (having filled "her horns,") and shone with unusual brightness — and the night was beautiful, although the weather was quite cold. Before 12 o'clock the thermometer fell to the freezing point, and in the morning when we emerged from our frost-covered blankets, we found our tin cups about one-third full of ice, from the water left in them over night.

We should have mentioned that in our explorations and careful examinations from the west, around by the south to the north-east side, some two or three miles above the snow line, parties having been detached in every direction for the purpose of examination, it was decided that there was but one point, viz: on the south-east by east side where it appeared possible to make the ascent. Just as the sun was shedding his last setting rays on the mountain top, Judge Olney who was carefully examining the summit with a telescope, announced that he distinctly saw smoke ascending from the extreme top. This announcement was received with doubt by the party; but on each one taking a close and scrutinizing view, it was conceded that if there was not smoke ascending, there was something very much like it.

This discovery increased our determination to make the ascent at all hazards. We believe it has not generally been supposed, that Mt. Hood at this time was volcanic. Our route had been fully determined upon, and was in full view.

On the morning of the 8th, at the peep of day, all hands were up and breakfasted before "Old Sol" had shone his head above the eastern horizon. The horses were brought up and packed, for the purpose of moving our encampment as far up the mountain as possible. The whole party left camp with joyous mirth, vigorous spirits, rested limbs, and with a full and settled determination to make the summit. The animals were pushed at double-quick time up the side of the mountain, as far as it was safe or practicable to take them, where they were quickly stripped of their burdens and picketed. Capt. Barlow volunteered to remain behind to look after the camp and watch with a telescope our ascent. In a few minutes all were off for the top, each took some provisions and were provided with well made creepers, iron socket mountain staffs with hooks, ropes, &c., &c., — the same kind that we used in ascending Mt. St. Helens last year, and which we found indispensable for climbing snow-covered mountains.

We commenced the ascent upon the south-east side, by first traversing a sharp narrow ridge between the head waters of Dog River on our right and a tributary of the De Chutes on the left. This ridge was attained by first crossing a chasm of about 500 feet in depth, formed by the water of the last named stream. Four of the party started at once on foot to make the ascent, whilst the Judge, with his Indian guide, took a circuitous route on horseback, with a view to obtain a point of considerable elevation which we had marked as the first point to be attained as a rendezvous.

At the outstart, the party became considerably separated, each believing he could make the point of view easiest by different routes; but about two hours' hard climbing brought all together, having already experienced sufficient difficulty to satisfy all, that concert of action, by keeping together to lend encouragement and mutual assistance in times of need, could only insure success to the hazardous undertaking before us. After a few moments rest, and regaling ourselves with refreshments and by eating snow, which lay in extensive fields on either side of us, with staffs in hand and our creeper[s] now lashed firmly upon our feet, we continued the ascent with more system and deliberation than when first setting out. But a little distance, and our naked ridge was lost in the mantle of snow which now lay spread out before and on either side of us.

After attaining a high altitude, we found the snow laying in waves similar to a "chopped sea." Therefore, we had to raise at almost every step, from six inches to *two, three,* and sometimes *four feet*! The sun had softened the top of the snow sufficiently to make a slight indentation by the boot. It was decided that we should go ahead, Mr. Lake, Judge Olney, Capt. Travaillot, Maj. Hallar, and the Indian guide, in rotation as named. Thus we continued to ascend for several thousand feet at an angle of almost 50 degrees, when the rarefied atmosphere began to exhibit its effects upon *all,* but more especially upon Judge Olney, Maj. Hallar, and Capt. Travaillot. Soon Maj. H. could go no further, in consequence of dizziness in the head, which affected him seriously. After a while, Capt. T. found the blood starting from the surface and was also attacked with a like dizziness, when he prudently declined going further. After a few rods further up, the ascent became more steep—by theodolite 70-1/2 degrees—where Judge Olney was reluctantly compelled to halt, in consequence of the singular effect of the air upon him. From this point, we were compelled to make steps by kicking the toes of our boots several times into the snow. By following close to the edge of a large ledge of rocks lying perpendicular with the mountain, where the sun's reflection from the ledge had softened the snow, enabled us to get comparatively a good foot hold. Our friend Lake followed close upon our heels. The Indian, who had now a good pair of creepers and a good mountain staff, seemed determined to go as far up as the "Bostons" could; although he could not be induced to lead the way or even to go between us. For nearly two hours there was nothing said, except an occasional word of warning from us to Mr. Lake to *"close nannage,"* and the response of—"all right!"—"go ahead!"—"we'll come it!"

Finally, at 2-1/2 o'clock P.M. we attained the summit on the south-east side. We found the top similar to that of Mt. St. Helens—extremely narrow, laying in a crescent shape. Mt. St. Helens facing the north-west by a crescent, while Mt. Hood faces the south-west.—The sharp ridge on top runs from the south-west to the north, making a sharp turn to the west at the north end. The main ridge is formed of decomposed volcanic substances of a light reddish color, with cones from 20 to 50 feet high at intervals of a few rods. These cones or rocks are full of cracks or fissures, as if they had been rent by some convulsion of nature at a remote period.—Between these cones there are numerous holes, varying from the size of a common water bucket down to two or three inches in diameter. Through these *breathing holes*—as we shall call them—and through the crevices in the rocks there is constantly escaping hot smoke or gas of a strong sulphuric odor. In passing over the ridge for near half a mile we discovered a large number of these breathing holes; through some the heat was more intense than in others.

We did not carry up a thermometer; therefore, we could not get the exact degree of the heat; but from holding our hand over several of them, we have no doubt that the thermometer would have shown "boiling heat" in some of them. As soon as the Indian discovered, by holding his hand over one of these "breathem holes," the existence of fire beneath, he immediately retreated as far as he dare go down the mountain slope. The smoke or gas was very offensive to the nostrils, as well as irritating to the eyes. We attempted to look into several of them, but were prevented from getting more than a momentary glance, for the reason above mentioned. We, however, rolled stones into them, and could hear them descend for a considerable distance. We could distinctly see Mts. Jefferson, Three Sisters, McLaughlin, St. Helens, Rainier and Adams, besides two other snow peaks, whose names, if they have any, we are unacquainted with; also, Frémont's Peak and Shasta Butte mountain in California.

These last mentioned peaks must be nearly or quite five hundred miles from Mt. Hood. The vast extent of country over which the eye could reach would be received as incredible by any but those who have been upon these towering mountains on a clear day, and in an Oregon atmosphere. There appeared to be a bank of fog hanging over the ocean, which precluded us from seeing it distinctly. There was also a dark cloud or bank of smoke laying off to the north-east, very low down, which shut out a small portion of the country in that direction from our view. Aside from this, the whole country for hundreds of miles was in plain view before us. In the distance, on either side, could be traced the different ranges of the well known great coast range on the west, the Sierra Nevada on the south and south-east, the Siskiyou on the south-west, and the Blue and Rocky mountains on the east, besides the great bend of the Cascades to the north. These, together with the thousand smaller ranges, with their innumerable crests and indentations, present to the eye a perfect forest of mountains. Bearing south 15 degrees east, at a distance of perhaps about 40 miles, we discovered a lake, surrounded by a large prairie or open country. This lake, so far as we could learn, was entirely unknown. We have no doubt, from appearances, that there is a large tract of fine country in this direction, well adapted to agricultural purposes. Had it not been for the loss of three of our horses, we should have gone to the lake before we returned; as it was, we were reluctantly compelled to postpone an examination to a future time.

While on the top of the mountain we were startled by a tremendous crushing, rumbling noise below. At first we anticipated it to be an earthquake or something of that sort. Judge Olney and those below heard it also, and accounted for it on our return. It was caused by an avalanche of rock under the immense bodies of snow which lay in large fields hundreds and perhaps a thousand feet in depth. We examined some chasms in the snow of very near or quite a thousand feet in depth, and two or three hundred feet across, extending horizontally with the mountain for a great distance.

The late hour of the day, together with the visible increase of cold, forced us to retrace our steps down much sooner than we desired. Our descent was much more rapid than our ascent, although a portion of the way apparently more dangerous.

At four o'clock Mr. Lake and ourself left the summit by the same route we went up. We found the Indian awaiting our return at the commencement of the steep grade where we had encountered so much difficulty in ascending. The same order and precision was necessary in coming down that we practiced in going up. In two hours we arrived at the foot of the most difficult portion of our descent. Here we found Capt. Travaillot, Major Hallar and Judge Olney, who had been employed in making observations, triangulations and distances for the purpose of ascertaining the height of the mountain.

It being impossible to use the barometer, which Gov. Ogden, of the Hudson's Bay Company, had kindly loaned us for the occasion, the calculations were made by taking the table of the line of perpetual snow on the principal mountains of the globe, as laid down by Baron de Humboldt. By keeping a rigorous account of both the latitude, (44 deg., 30 min.,) the temperature given by thermometer, and the exposition of the side by which we made our ascent, we took as the height of our encampment, 11,250 feet; the snow at the edges of the snow-fields being twenty-eight inches within thirty feet of our camp, and the meltage only three hours in the afternoon. From that basis Capt. Travaillot and Mr. Lake took several distances, and obtained by calculation 15,442 feet, or two miles and a half to ascend under an angle of 35 degrees to reach the pinnacle; which distance gave the height of 7,111 feet, which, added to the basis, makes a total of 18,361 feet as the height of the mountain; the side north-west being approximately 500 feet lower than the principal north pinnacle, which is about fifty feet superior to the south pinnacle, which we ascended. The craters exist on both sides.

---------------- ▲ ----------------

In descending from a rarefied to a dense atmosphere, those who had not been seriously affected by the ascent came in for their share of the general debility and difficulty in breathing. We had our full share and were for a time entirely unable to travel more than a few rods at a time, without laying down on the snow or ground to rest.

Upon reaching our camp after night, being materially aided by a full moon, the reflection of which upon the snow made it light as noon-day, we were cordially received by our old friend, Capt. Barlow, and congratulated upon the success of the hazardous undertaking. The Captain had anticipated our wants and had kindly provided, ready for immediate use, all the comforts and delicacies of the camp. He had watched our ascent, aided by a good telescope, with much interest and expressed regret that he did not accompany the party. The lateness of the hour of our return, prevented the removal of our camp further down the mountain side, for the night. — Therefore, we spread our blankets as best we could and sought rest and refreshment by sleep, to dream of steep declivities, perpendicular cliffs, yawning chasms, avalanches, volcanoes, &c; by which we were awakened several times during the night. The weather was cold and uncomfortable. However, in the morning we arose stiff, sore and well-nigh worn-out. Several of the party's faces looked as if they had been in close proximity to yellow jackets' nests, badly swollen.

As soon as breakfast could be prepared and dispatched, the whole party packed up, preparatory for leaving for home. We bade adieu to Judge Olney and Maj. Hallar, who returned to the Dalles; while the residue of the party descended the mountain *en route* for home. On our return we took a different route from the one by which we approached the mountain. Capt. Barlow led us by a good route into the immigrant trail, some two or three miles east of the summit prairie. After a few miles' travel on that trail homeward, we found our old friend Mr. Rycraft, who has a trading post there. He received and welcomed us heartily. We obtained of him some vegetables and other luxuries which were very acceptable. We spent the night at this place. The next morning we left everything that would impede our progress, and by hard traveling arrived at Foster's, at sundown. The next day, Friday 11th, we arrived safely at home; improved in health, ready to resume our laboring oar, to aid and assist in guiding the frail barque of "Oregon" safely through the rocks, quick sands, and maelstroms of Durhamism and party monstrosities with which we are beset on every side.

We are now fully satisfied from looking over this whole country from the highest pinnacles of Mt. St. Helens and Hood, that Oregon is *some pumpkins* in the way of hills, dales, mountains, rivers, brooks, plains, prairies, forests, &c., and therefore we are content to remain at our post until next summer; when we intend to visit Mts. Jefferson, Three Sisters, &c.

A. C. Isaacs Attempts
Mount Shasta, 1856

I N THE SPRING of 1856, two years after its first ascent, A. C. Isaacs made an attempt on the glacier-clad, 14,162-foot volcano Mount Shasta with several companions from the San Francisco area. Even in the best of conditions, Shasta is not a trivial climb, and in early spring it can be quite hazardous, as in fact it was for Isaacs, who encountered single-digit temperatures and tremendous winds during his own attempt. The climbers reached Shasta's summit plateau but wisely decided to turn back short of the actual high point, which was still some distance away. Isaacs wrote an account of the climb that was published April 9, 1856, in the *California Daily Chronicle* and again later that month in the *Weekly Chronicle*. Unfortunately, he was not a skilled enough writer to convey the danger and intensity of the climb – particularly the fierce weather – without resorting to hyperbole. The account below is hopelessly purple prose, but through the exaggeration and flowery phrasing we sense the genuine struggle of a serious climb undertaken in serious conditions.

Up we start, and prepare ourselves once more to ascend. We leave everything at our camping place below, with the exception of our iron-pointed and hooked staves. I put on a pair of boots furnished with small spikes to prevent my slipping on the snow. For a coat I substitute a gray woolen overshirt. A few crackers are our provision. At six o'clock A.M. on the third day we commence clambering up the to-all-appearance inaccessible snow- and ice-armed ramparts of the mountain. The air is clear and brilliant, with a stiff breeze blowing and the thermometer just at freezing point. Soon we pass the last remains of the timber on each side, and scarcely a sign of vegetation checkers our path. Silently, in file, we plod along. My staff I find of very little service; it is too small, and offers little or no support in climbing the steep snow walls. The spikes in my boots are much more useful. One, two, three bluffs, and as many ravines, are surmounted. The ridges on each hand begin to show their nature and formation much more distinctly. The scene at present is somewhat like this: – A vast hollow, reaching from the now receding timber below to the very crest of the mountain – smaller snow mountains or bluffs fill in this general and vast concavity — bare and black masses of rock here and there intersperse themselves over and diversify the otherwise colorless face of the great gulf — towering above us, and at a considerable distance on each side, run the irregular outlines of the ridges that bound this immense gap — the furrows of these ridges are horrent with enormous indentations and pinnacles of igneous rock — their curves continually approximate as they near the top, till, in the vicinity of the Red Bluffs, they seem to approach pretty closely together. In the center of this waste, howling wilderness are three moving specks, that with slow and painful step still clamber on and upward towards the mountain's top. Three hours have already glided by since we started. Our hearts are somewhat cheered by observing that the yet distant and now still more acclivitous looking Red Bluffs are more distinct in feature than they were. We see that the color is not red, but an ochre or deep yellow.

My companions begin to forge ahead of me. The wind comes in portentous and powerful gusts from clefts in the eastern or right-hand ridge. Frequently our guide had expressed a fear that we should find trouble from the wind in the upper regions of the mountain. Its continually increasing velocity — the diminishing temperature of our bodies, arising both from the increasing rarity of the atmosphere and the accelerated motion of the wind, made it needful to move briskly in order not to suffer too severely from the cold, which was already beginning to nip and pinch us a good deal — hence, my brother clamberers moved on ahead. In addition to the inadequacy of my staff, I labored under the superadded difficulty arising out of a fall from a horse a day or two before. The animal had succeeded, by a double stumble and a sudden twist, in pitching me out of the saddle and into the road, and I came down almost dead square upon what an anatomist would perhaps describe as "the inferior and caudal extremity of the spinal column." It may easily be imagined how a hurt so received would operate to my prejudice in a climb like the one before me. Away, therefore, go my companions; in a while they are out of sight; I struggle on alone. This wall of snow is soon reached. *Can* I ascend it? Let us try. The top is neared — a few more crawls (it is hands and knees for it now) and it will be overcome! My footing gives way; down I slide to the bottom! O the time and strength uselessly consumed! I lie on the snow to recruit a little; then, wistfully eyeing the top, I start again. Carefully, and clutching at every knob and protruberance within my grasp, I drag my body up, up, up once more. The place from which the slip was made is attained, passed, and lo! exhausted I throw myself down on the top of the hardly won top of this snow steep. Once more, my longing eyes look upward. Gathering up my now very tired limbs, (six hours we have been working up our weary way), I advance again. Will that black fork just below the Bluffs ever be reached? Doubtful. Another still more precipitous ascent presents its face, mocking me with its glittering smile, while it dares me to attempt it. Cautiously I move over the slippery surface; down I go — down, down to the bottom! The spikes on my boots, being now bent and curved, are becoming a decided hindrance to me. It begins to look quite doubtful whether the Bluffs and I will ever, literally I may say, *scrape* a closer acquaintance together. Lying here, at any rate, will never effect it, so, at it again! This effort brings me finally to the ledge of rocks lying immediately beneath the Bluffs. On to the right I go, and O! gladness, there moving right before me, are my two companions! Roman moves on and higher, English stays to go on with me. . . .

Shall we look around and behold the mountain world below and environing us on so many sides? No! No! let us first try to go higher. Now we buckle to our armor, for our last opponent rises before us. Up the rough but almost perpendicular faces of these crags — away we clamber and scramble over icicles and frozen snow. Look not down below you, nor think thereon — only keep firm your footing. Tread lightly on these little protruberances. Spring from point to point. Clutch at the projections, be they ever so small. Your fingers freeze — well, keep them and your toes moving, moving! Ah! this last opening

above us once passed through, and we are out on the world above, and close under the first great summit! But how *shall* we scale this perpendicular breast-work! Plant your toes on any small knob you can find on its surface—feel, if possible, light as thistle-down—grasp as high up as you are able—never mind thinking how far down you may fall should you leap short. Now spring! Ah ha! through it you are! The Rubicon is passed, the goal is reached! But, O how piercingly cold and swift comes the howling blast over this southern and eastern ridge! See the summit just above us! The drift snow is being whirled about in eddying clouds in the wildest excitement! Let us on!

The cold becomes intense. We make way now as fast as our much exhausted limbs will let us, up the rocky side of the first summit. On the center of this side we find Roman furiously beating his sides to keep some warmth in his arms. We reach the summit (south) and come right into the teeth of an opponent whose assaults in their inconceivable might and power are irresistable! The wind, which occasionally on the way up had, when it could get at us through the crevices of the ridge, given us sharp foretastes of what we might expect on the summit, now struck upon us as the concentrated blast of a thousand tempests! Of its incomprehensible velocity, its intense cold, its roaring and thunderous sound, as with lightning speed it tore through the clefts and crags on the edge of the cliff; of the arrowy, and stinging, and blinding force with which it struck our faces and eyes; of our own inability to take more than a momentary glance in the direction from which it blew (in its sweep it seemed to take the whole range of country clean from Utah to where we stood); of the extreme difficulty we had to keep our feet in it, (it blew us about and made us totter and reel as drunken men, and occasionally threw us down with relentless fury); of all these things "'twere vain to tell!" Aelous reigned supreme—all the furies of his cave were here let loose at once upon us. "Look at the thermometer," cries Roman. Twelve degrees below zero! [Probably Centigrade, or ten degrees above zero Fahrenheit] Look at ourselves! Faces purple, and looking as if we had just been suffocated!—eyes almost closed up!—lips scarcely movable!—limbs stiffening with the cold! Shall we go on? We are now on a level with the hot spring, and but two to three hundred feet below the highest peak! Shall we not try to make headway thereto? It is but a mile and a half along this ridge on which we stand, and then we are at it! Alas! The vital force could never maintain itself against the frightful power of this unutterably awful tempest. Long ere we could traverse the comparatively level region between us and the spring, the temperature of our bodies, and consequently our vital force, would be so lowered by the heat-abstracting power of this desolating tornado that nothing, in all probability, would be left us but quietly to sink down and die! Let us quit, therefore, while we can. . . .

Julia Archibald Holmes Climbs Pikes Peak, 1858

J ULIA ARCHIBALD HOLMES was well cast to become the first woman to climb a high peak in America. Her mother had been one of the first to campaign for the right of women to vote, and she and Julia gave speeches at the first national woman's suffrage convention. In 1858 she set out with her husband on a prospecting expedition to Colorado, a financial bust but a stimulating adventure for the young couple. Later they traveled south into New Mexico Territory, where, during the Civil War, James Holmes became territorial secretary and Julia, who was fluent in Spanish, served as a correspondent for the *New York Herald Tribune*. Later she and James divorced, and she lived more or less permanently in Washington, D.C., where she made a career working for the Department of the Interior and later the Bureau of Education.

During the expedition of 1858, the prospecting party stopped at what is today Colorado Springs, in the shadow of Pikes Peak. By this time, thirty-eight years after the pioneering ascent by Edwin James, the 14,110-foot mountain had been climbed several times, but never by a woman. Anyone who expected Holmes to be defeated by the mountain was disappointed; she and her husband completed the climb with little trouble, sensibly allowing several days for the round trip. That leisurely pace undoubtedly contributed to the literary quality and the positive, romantic tone of the selection below. It made the climb more enjoyable in a number of ways, not only allowing the couple time to become accustomed to the altitude of the peak, but also to feel at home there. They had time to explore the mountain, to appreciate it and to write about it on the scene.

The letters Julia wrote on the mountain were first published in *The Sybil*, an obscure journal dedicated, as one contemporary put it, "to reforms in every department of life, but principally to a reform in dress for women." Her feat became a little better known when the letters were reprinted in *The Whig Press* in 1859, but she has never been as widely recognized as she deserves to be, not only as an early and influential feminist, but also as a talented writer and pioneering climber.

Aug. 1st, 1858 — After an early breakfast this morning, my husband and I adjusted our packs to our backs and started for the ascent of Pike's Peak. My own pack weighed 17 pounds; nine of which were bread, the remainder a quilt and clothing. James' pack weighed 35 pounds, and was composed as follows — ten pounds bread, one pound hog meat, three fourths pound coffee, one pound sugar, a tin plate, knife and fork, half gallon canteen, half gallon tin pail and a tin pint cup, five quilts, clothing, a volume of Emerson's *Essays,* and writing materials made up the remainder. We calculate on this amount of food to subsist six days. A walk of a mile brought us to the crossing of Boiling spring river. It is an impetuous, ice-cold stream at this point, about twelve feet wide, knee deep, with a cobble stone bottom. Undressing our feet we attempted it several times before we could cross, the water was so intensely cold we were ready to drop down with pain on reaching the opposite bank. Three miles further we reached the wonderful Boiling Springs, which Fremont has made known to the world in his expeditions. There are but three which we noticed. The strong carbonated waters mingled with bubbles of carbonic acid gas, boil continually in the rocky fountains within which they are set by nature better than they could be by art. In the center of broad solid rocks somewhat elevated above the ground around them, composed by the deposition of their own waters, these springs ceaselessly boil. We speculated on the limestone cave which may somewhere exist above the spring in the heart of the mountains, since they are constantly bringing away limestone in solution. We drank deep from these Saratogas of the wilderness, and leaving them, in another mile were vigorously attacking the mountain. The first mile or so was sandy and extremely steep, over which we toiled slowly, as we frequently lost all we gained. But by persevering and every rod laying, or rather falling on our backs to rest, we at last reached the timber where we could obtain better footing. We neglected to fill our canteens and now began to feel the want of water. We toiled on and up in hope of soon finding a spring. At one time we went too far to the left — not knowing the route — and got among some huge boulders which we soon saw the necessity of getting out of the best way we could. After finding the right track we continued, but we had lost so much time in getting among the rocks, and become so hungry, that after proceeding a couple of miles farther, and catching a glimpse of water in a deep canyon, we halted and considered the state of our case. The question was, should we descend that terrible canyon only to ascend again, or proceed on our journey not knowing when we should reach water? Our longing for water triumphed and down we rushed with such eagerness as is only inspired by suffering. We are camped here until tomorrow. It is now ten o'clock in the evening, and I am reclining before some blazing pine logs beside a torrent in a mountain canyon several hundred feet deep. The straight, slender, tapering pines that stand around so beautiful in their death, smooth, white and sound, having been stripped of their bark by fire, calmly point to a sky more serene, and to stars far brighter than usual. The trees and the sky almost seem to strive together in preserving a deeper silence. But there is music from the foaming stream, sounds from a dozen little cascades near and far blend together—a thundering sound, a rushing sound, a rippling sound, and tinkling sounds there are; and a thousand shades of sound to fill up between them. The burning pine crackles and snaps, showering sparks, cinders and even coals around and all over the sheet I am writing on, as if to mock the tame thoughts they light me to write.

Snowdell, Aug. 4th—We have given this name to a little nook we are making our home in for a few days. It is situated about four or five rods above the highest spring which gushes from the side of the Peak. On the cold moss overhung by two huge rocks, forming a right angle, we have made a nest of spruce twigs. Some smaller rocks form, with the larger ones just mentioned, a trough about three feet wide, and ten feet long. At the outlet of this narrow space we have built a chimney. When we lie down the fire is burning but a yard from our feet, while we can stretch our hands over the smaller rocks into a large bank of snow. This we call our home. Eastward, we can look on a landscape of Kansas plains, our view hemmed only by the blue haze of the atmosphere, and extending perhaps two hundred miles. The beauty of this great picture is beyond my powers of description. Down at the base of the mountain the corral of fifteen wagons, and as many tents scattered around it, form a white speck, which we can occasionally distinguish. We think our location grandly romantic. We are on the east side of the Peak, whose summit looming above our head at an angle of forty five degrees, is yet two miles away—towards the sky. We arrived here day before yesterday about one o'clock P.M. during a little squall of snow. Yesterday we went in search of a supposed cave about three-fourths of a mile along the side of the mountain. We penetrated the canyon with much difficulty, being once obliged to take off our moccasins that we might use the toes and balls of our feet in clinging to the asperities of the sidling rock. We found no cave but a tremendous amphitheater-shaped space, whose perpendicular walls rose seven or eight hundred feet high. Piled around this vast circle at the foot of the walls, were granite boulders of all sizes and shapes rising against the walls like the terraced seats of a circus or theater. Deep in the center is a circular spot of green grass, with flowers, and a silvery stream winding through it. We called the place Amphitheater Canyon.

Today we remain at home resting, writing, and admiring the mocking landscape. For with beauty and deep truth does Emerson remark "the landscape must always appear mocking until it has human figures as good as itself."

These whole mountains are a feldsparic formation, with an occasional sample of quartz, soil that is covered with vegetation which does not occupy one fourth of the mountain where we are. Granite boulders and stones of every size and shape, with granite gravel occupy over three fourths. Beautiful flowers delicate in texture and aroma, grow everywhere, except on the bare rocks, and even within reach of the snow.

Aug. 5 — We left Snowdell early this morning for the summit, taking with us nothing but our writing materials and Emerson. We deviated somewhat from our course in order to pass the rim of Amphitheater Canyon. Here on the edge of the perpendicular walls, were poised stones and boulders of all sizes ready to be rolled, with a slight effort, into the yawning abyss. Starting these stones had been a favorite amusement with those who ascended before us, and it savored somewhat of the terrible. When a stone was started it seemed first to leap into the air, and passing from sight nothing would be heard of it for several seconds. Then would come a crashing, thundering sound from the hidden depths below, which seemed to continue until lost in the distant lower region. From these hollow distant sounds some of the men had supposed the existence of an inaccessable cave below. As we proved yesterday, however, nothing but a tremendous circular chasm exists. After enjoying this sport a short time we proceeded directly up towards the summit. Arriving within a few hundred yards of the top the surface changed into a huge pile of loose angular stones, so steep we found much difficulty in clambering up them. Passing to the right of a drift of snow some three or four hundred yards long, which sun and wind had turned into coarse ice, we stood upon a platform of near one hundred acres of feldspathic granite rock and boulders. Occasionally a little cranny among the rocks might be found in which had collected some coarse soil from the disintegration of the granite, where in one or two instances we found a green tuft about the size of a teacup from which sprung dozens of tiny blue flowers most bewitchingly beautiful. The little ultra-marine colored leaves of the flower seemed covered with an infinitude of minute sparkling crystals — they seemed children of the sky and snow. It was cold and rather cloudy, with squalls of snow, consequently our view was not so extensive as we had antici-pated. A portion only of the whitened back-bone ridge of the Rocky Moun-tains which forms the boundary line of so many territories could be seen, fifty miles to the west. We were now nearly fourteen thousand feet above the sea level. But we could not spend long in contemplating the grandeur of the scene for it was exceedingly cold, and leaving our names on a large rock, we com-menced letters to some of our friends, using a broad flat rock for a writing desk. When we were ready to return I read aloud the lines from Emerson.

> "A ruddy drop of manly blood,
>   The surging sea outweighs;
>   The world uncertain comes and goes,
>   The looser rooted stays."

Leaving this cloud capped bleak region, we were soon in Snowdell, where we remained only long enough to make up our packs. Before we were ready to say 'good bye' the snow was falling quite fast, and we left our pretty home as we first saw it, in a snowstorm. We pursued our journey in all possible haste, anxious to find a good camp for the night before dark. At last when I thought I could not go a rod further, we found a capital place, a real bears den it seemed, though large enough for half dozen. And here we are, enclosed on every side by huge boulders, with two or three large spruce trees stretching their protecting arms over our heads.

William Brewer Climbs Lassen Peak and Mount Brewer, and Attempts Mount Goddard, 1863-64

W ILLIAM HENRY BREWER was one of the most versatile and productive scientists associated with America's western surveys. After graduating in 1852 from the newly formed school of science at Yale, he put in two more years of study in Germany. From 1860 to 1864, before beginning a thirty-year tenure as agriculture professor at Yale, he served as field director for the California Geological Survey. In that capacity, he wrote in his journal, he traveled more than 2,000 miles on foot, almost 4,000 miles on mule-back, and 3,000 miles via other means. When his journal was finally published in 1930, it was under the appropriate title of *Up and Down California in 1860–1864.*

Brewer and his assistants were the first whites to visit many of California's mountain areas, and they made a number of notable ascents, including climbs of 10,457-foot Lassen Peak and 13,570-foot Mount Brewer, as well as a marathon attempt on remote, 13,568-foot Mount Goddard. Brewer's accounts of these three climbs, reprinted here from *Up and Down California,* are both sensitive and highly descriptive, giving us a clear view not only of the peaks but also of his companions. Particularly noteworthy is the portrait he paints of Clarence King and the "*very* tough" Richard Cotter – the two principals of the ascent of Mount Tyndall, the highest peak climbed by the survey and the core of King's classic book, *Mountaineering in the Sierra Nevada. Mountaineering,* excerpted in the selection after this one, has been called the greatest tale in American mountaineering literature, and the following account is thus worth reading not only for its own considerable merits, but also for the light it sheds on King's classic.

Fort Crook.
October 5.

SEPTEMBER 26 we made our first ascent of Lassen's Peak – King and I and the three friends who had come with us from their camp. We were up and off early, were on the summit before ten o'clock, and spent five hours there.

We had anticipated a grand view, the finest in the state, and it fully equaled our expectations, but the peak is not so high as we estimated, being only about 11,000 feet. The day was not entirely favorable – a fierce wind, raw and chilly, swept over the summit, making our very bones shiver. Clouds hung over a part of the landscape. Mount Shasta, eighty miles distant, rose clear and sharp against a blue sky, the top for six thousand feet rising above a stratum of clouds that hid the base. It was grand. Most of the clouds lay below us at the north. The great valley was very indistinct in the haze at the south, but the northern part was very clear.

We were back early, and had a hearty dinner of hot coffee, venison and trout, pork and beans — the former for a change, but the latter as a stand-by for fatigues and climbing. All were delighted with their trip.

We had a cold, windy, and cloudy night, and the next day, Sunday, September 27, a snowstorm set in, and our friends left us for the warmer climate of a lower altitude. During the forenoon we had fierce snow squalls, which whitened the ground. Without tent or other shelter than the trees, it was cold and cheerless. But in the afternoon it cleared up, and we had the freshest of air and the bluest of sky. The firs above us were silvered with snow, and the rugged peak whitened. It was too cold to write, so I read *Bleak House,* and finished it by the camp fire at evening.

September 28 the thermometer stood at 17° in the morning; it was cold and nearly clear. I had lain awake half the night to get up early and climb the peak again, but clouds deterred us; so King went down the valley to sketch the mountain, while I took a long tramp around the east side of the peak. We made our preparations for an ascent the next morning, should it be clear.

Tuesday, September 29, we were up at half-past one, had an early breakfast by the light of the bright moon, now two days past its full, and at 2.45 were on our way.

The description that follows I wrote on top of the mountain. It has the merit of rigid truthfulness in every particular.

First up a canyon for a thousand feet, then among rocks and over snow, crisp in the cold air, glittering in the bright moonlight. At four we are on the last slope, a steep ridge, now on loose bowlders and sliding gravel, now on firmer footing. We avoid the snow slopes — they are too steep to climb without cutting our way by steps. We are on the south side of the peak, and the vast region in the southeast lies dim in the soft light of the moon — valleys asleep in beds of vapor, mountains dark and shadowy.

At 4.30 appears the first faint line of red in the east, which gradually widens and becomes a livid arch as we toil up the last steep slope.

We reach the first summit, and the northern scene comes in view. The snows of Mount Shasta are still indistinct in the dusky dawn. We cross a snowfield, climb up bowlders, and are soon on the highest pinnacle of rock. It is still, cold, and intensely clear. The temperature rises to 25° — it has been 18°.

The arch of dawn rises and spreads along the distant eastern horizon. Its rosy light gilds the cone of red cinders across the crater from where we are. Mount Shasta comes out clear and well defined; the gray twilight bathing the dark mountains below grows warmer and lighter, the moon and stars fade, the shadowy mountain forms rapidly assume distinct shapes, and day comes on apace.

As we gaze in rapture, the sun comes on the scene, and as it rises, its disk flattened by atmospheric refraction, it gilds the peaks one after another, and at this moment the field of view is wider than at any time later in the day. The Marysville Buttes rise from the vapory plain, islands in a distant ocean of smoke, while far beyond appear the dim outlines of Mount Diablo and Mount Hamilton, the latter 240 miles distant.

North of the Bay of San Francisco the Coast Range is clear and distinct, from Napa north to the Salmon Mountains near the Klamath River. Mount St. Helena, Mount St. John, Yalloballey, Bullet Chup, and all its other prominent peaks are in distinct view, rising in altitude as we look north.

But rising high above all is the conical shadow of the peak we are on, projected in the air, a distinct form of cobalt blue on a ground of lighter haze, its top as sharp and its outlines as well defined as are those of the peak itself—a gigantic spectral mountain, projected so high in the air that it seems far higher than the original mountain itself—but, as the sun rises, the mountain sinks into the valley, and, like a ghost, fades away at the sight of the sun.

In the camp on the south fork of Kings River.
July 7.

It is a pleasant, clear day. For three days the sky has been of the intensest blue, not a cloud in sight day or night. I am alone in a beautiful camp and I will write.

We have come down into a deep valley, where it is warmer and there is good grass. We are still camped high, however—about 7,500 feet. A fine breeze plays up the valley, very pleasant, but it makes it hard to write—it flutters the paper and gives much trouble. The desolate granite peaks lie in sight—bare granite and glistening snow. It freezes every night.

Tuesday, June 28, we had a fine clear morning, and four of us started to visit a peak a few miles distant. We had a rough trail, over sharp ridges, and finally up a very steep pile of granite rocks, perhaps a thousand feet high, to the peak, which is over eleven thousand feet high, and which we called Mount Silliman, in honor of Professor Silliman, Junior.

In crossing a ridge we came on fresh bear tracks, and soon saw the animal himself, a fine black bear. We all shouted, and he went galloping away over the rocks and into a canyon. We had gone but a short distance farther when we saw a very large female grizzly with two cubs. She was enormous—would weigh as much as a small ox. After we looked at her a few minutes we all set up a shout. She rose on her hind legs, but did not see us, as we sat perfectly still. We continued to shout. She became frightened at the unseen noise, which echoed from the cliffs so that she could not tell where it came from, so she galloped away with the cubs. These would weigh perhaps 150 pounds each; she would weigh perhaps 900 pounds or more. We also saw a fine buck during the trip.

We reached the summit after a hard climb, and had a grand view of the rough landscape. Great rocky amphitheaters surrounded by rocky ridges, very sharp, their upper parts bare or streaked with snow, constituted a wild, rough, and desolate landscape. Clouds suddenly came on, and a snowstorm, which was a heavy rain in camp. We got back tired enough.

─────────── ▲ ───────────

July 1 we came on by a still rougher way, about eleven miles. We crossed the south fork of Kings River, down over tremendous rocks and up again by as rough a way. We struck a ridge which is a gigantic moraine left by a former glacier, the largest I have ever seen or heard of. It is several miles long and a thousand feet high.

We were working back toward high peaks, where we hoped to discover the sources of Kings, Kaweah, and Kern rivers, geographical problems of some considerable interest and importance. We got back as far as we could and camped at an altitude of 9,750 feet, by a rushing stream, but with poor feed. Wood was plenty, dry, from trees broken by avalanches in winter. A beautiful little lake was near us. About five miles east lay the high granite cone we hoped to reach—high and sharp, its sides bristling with sharp pinnacles.

Saturday, July 2, we were up at dawn, and Hoffmann and I climbed this cone, which I had believed to be the highest of this part of the Sierra. We had a rough time, made two unsuccessful attempts to reach the summit, climbing up terribly steep rocks, and at last, after eight hours of very hard climbing, reached the top. The view was yet wilder than we have ever seen before. We were not on the highest peak, although we were a thousand feet higher than we anticipated any peaks were. We had not supposed there were any over 12,000 or 12,500 feet, while we were actually up over 13,600, and there were a dozen peaks in sight beyond as high or higher!

Such a landscape! A hundred peaks in sight over thirteen thousand feet— many very sharp—deep canyons, cliffs in every direction almost rivaling Yosemite, sharp ridges almost inaccessible to man, on which human foot has never trod—all combined to produce a view the sublimity of which is rarely equaled, one which few are privileged to behold.

There is not so much snow as in the mountains farther north, not so much falls in winter, the whole region is drier, but all the higher points, above 12,000 feet are streaked with it, and patches occur as low as 10,500 feet. The last trees disappear at 11,500 feet—above this desolate bare rocks and snow. Several small lakes were in sight, some of them frozen over.

The view extended north eighty to ninety miles, south nearly as far—east we caught glimpses of the desert mountains east of Owens Valley—west to the Coast Range, 130 or more miles distant.

On our return we slid down a slope of snow perhaps eight hundred feet. We came down in two minutes the height that we had been over three hours in climbing. We got back very tired, but a cup of good tea and a fine venison soup restored us.

Sunday, July 3, we lay until late. On calculating the height of the peak, finding it so much higher than we expected, and knowing there were still higher peaks back, we were, of course, excited. Here there is the highest and grandest group of the Sierra—in fact, the grandest in the United States—not so high as Mount Shasta, but a great assemblage of high peaks.

King is enthusiastic, is wonderfully tough, has the greatest endurance I have ever seen, and is withal very muscular. He is a most perfect specimen of health. He begged me to let him and Dick try to reach them on foot. I feared them inaccessible, but at last gave in to their importunities, and gave my consent. They made their preparations that day, anxious for a trip fraught with so much interest, hardship, and danger.

July 4 all were up at dawn. We got breakfast, and King and Dick packed their packs—six days' provisions, blankets, and instruments made packs of thirty five or forty pounds each, to be packed into such a region! Gardner and I resolved to climb the cone again, as I had left instruments on the top, expecting someone would go up. Our way lay together for five miles, and up to thirteen thousand feet. I packed Dick's heavy pack to that point to give him a good start. I could never pack it as far as they hope to. Here we left them, and as we scaled the peak they disappeared over a steep granite ridge, the last seen of them. . . .

Camp 180, on the ridge north of Kings River.
July 21.

King and Dick got back in five days, and had a tremendous trip. They got on a peak nearly as high as Mount Shasta, or some 14,360 feet, and saw five more peaks still higher. They slept among the rocks and snow one night at an altitude of twelve thousand feet, crossed canyons, and climbed tremendous precipices, where they had to let each other down with a rope that they carried along. It was by far the greatest feat of strength and endurance that has yet been performed on the Survey. The climbing of Mount Shasta was not equal to it. Dick got his boots torn off and came back with an old flour sack tied around his feet. . . .

Middle fork of the San Joaquin.
August 14.

We are again back here, stopping over a day, and I will go on with my story. And yet I have a mind to pass it over, it is so like the rest. Rides over almost impassable ways, cold nights, clear skies, rocks, high summits, grand views, laborious days, and finally, short provisions—the same old story.

Yet one item is worth relating. A very high peak, over thirteen thousand feet, rises between the San Joaquin and Kings rivers, which we call Mount Goddard, after an old surveyor in this state. It was very desirable to get on this, as it commands a wide view, and from it we could get the topography of a large region. Toward it we worked, over rocks and ridges, through canyons, and by hard ways. We got as far as horses could go on the ninth, and thought that we were within about seven miles of the peak.

We camped at about ten thousand feet, and the next day four of us started for it—Hoffmann, Dick, Spratt (a soldier), and I. We anticipated a very heavy day's work, so we started at dawn. We crossed six high granite ridges, all rough, sharp, and rocky, and rising to over eleven thousand feet. We surmounted the seventh, a ridge very sharp and about twelve thousand feet, only to find the mountain still at least six miles farther, and two more deep canyons to cross. We had walked and climbed hard for nine hours incessantly, and had come perhaps twelve or fourteen miles. It was two o'clock in the afternoon. Hoffman and I resigned the intention of reaching it, for it was too far and we were too tired.

Dick and Spratt resolved to try it. We did not think they could accomplish it. Dick took the barometer and I took their baggage, a field glass, canteen, and Spratt's carbine, which he had brought along for bears. Hoffmann and I got on a higher ridge for bearings, and then started back and walked until long after sunset—but the moon was light—over rocks. We got down to about eleven thousand feet, where stunted pines begin to grow in the scanty soil and crevices of the rocks. We found a dry stump that had been moved by some avalanche on a smooth slope of naked granite. We stopped there and fired it, and camped for the night.

We had brought along a lunch, expecting to be gone but the day. It consisted of dry bread and drier jerked beef, the latter as dry and hard as a chip, literally. This we had divided into three portions, for three meals, a mere morsel for each. This scanty supper we ate, then went to sleep. The stump burned all night and kept us partially warm, yet the night was not a comfortable one. Excessive fatigue, the hard naked rock to lie on—not a luxurious bed—hunger, no blankets—although it froze all about us—the anxieties for the others who had gone on and were now out, formed the hard side of the picture.

But it was a picturesque scene after all. Around us, in the immediate vicinity, were rough bowlders and naked rock, with here and there a stunted bushy pine. A few rods below us lay two clear, placid lakes, reflecting the stars. The intensely clear sky, dark blue, *very* dark at this height; the light stars that lose part of their twinkle at this height; the deep stillness that reigned; the barren granite cliffs that rose sharp against the night sky, far above us, rugged, ill-defined; the brilliant shooting stars, of which we saw many; the solitude of the scene — all joined to produce a deep impression of the mind, which rose above the discomforts.

Early in the evening, at times, I shouted with all my strength, that Dick and Spratt might hear us and not get lost. The echoes were grand, from the cliffs on either side, softening and coming back fainter as well as softer from the distance and finally dying away after a comparatively long time. At length, even here, sleep, "tired nature's sweet restorer," came on. Notwithstanding the hard conditions, we were more refreshed than you would believe. After months of this rough life, sleeping only on the ground, in the open air, the rocky bed is not so hard in reality as it sounds when told. We actually lay "in bed" until after sunrise, waiting for Dick. They did not come; so, after our meager breakfast we started and reached camp in about nine hours. This was the hardest part. Still tired from yesterday's exertions, weak for want of food, in this light air, it was a hard walk.

At three in the afternoon we reached camp, tired, footsore, weak, hungry. Dick had been back already over an hour, but Spratt had given out. Gardner and two soldiers, supposing that Hoffmann and I also had given out, had started with some bread to look for us. We shot off guns, and near night they came in, and at the same time Spratt straggled into camp, looking as if he had had a hard time. Dick and he did not reach the top, but got within three hundred feet of it. They traveled all night and had no food — they had eaten their lunch all up at once. Dick is *very* tough. He had walked thirty two hours and had been twenty six entirely without food; yet, on the return, he had walked in four hours what had taken Hoffmann and me eight to do.

Clarence King and Richard Cotter Climb Mount Tyndall, 1864

CLARENCE KING, AUTHOR of what many readers feel is *the* classic of American mountaineering literature, was born in 1842 in Newport, Rhode Island. At age seventeen he entered Yale, where he studied the natural sciences, including geology under the influential J. D. Dana. In the spring of 1863, just a year after graduating, he joined the geologist James Gardiner on a horseback trip across the continent, a trip that was interrupted when a fire at the Comstock Lode mine in Nevada destroyed most of their gear. After working awhile to recoup their outfit, King and Gardiner walked across the Sierra Nevada into California, where they met William H. Brewer, then in charge of field operations for the geological survey of that state. King volunteered for the survey and stayed on for three years, helping to make the first systematic explorations of the Sierra. Later King organized a survey of his own, running a line eastward along the fortieth parallel from Colorado to California and setting new standards of excellence, both for the fieldwork itself and for the many scientific publications that resulted from it.

At the same time that the Brewer Survey was literally mapping the wild fastnesses of the Sierra Nevada, King was gathering materials for the book that, in the words of William Howarth, "put the Sierras on the map of the American imagination." That book was *Mountaineering in the Sierra Nevada*, first published in 1872. The two chapters within *Mountaineering* that describe the ascent of 14,018-foot Mount Tyndall – a difficult undertaking that entailed crossing two high divides just to reach the base of the peak – are a marvelously crafted climbing yarn, a mountaineering story that, it could be argued, both initiated the genre in this country and remains its finest example.

Some might say the same of John Muir's "A Near View of the High Sierra," which appears later in this collection, but there is unarguably much to praise in *Mountaineering*. King was a fine storyteller, and his account of the Tyndall climb moves quickly and easily from one thrilling episode to the next. He exaggerated the climb's dangers, but today's mountaineers still find that the details of his book ring true, as when he complains of his heavy pack, chafing at his shoulders and throwing him off balance, or when he loses track of time as he becomes involved in the exigencies of the climb. King sounds quite modern when, during a particularly airy passage in which he is literally hanging by his rope "between heaven and earth," he finds it "a deep satisfaction to look down at the wild gulf of desolation beneath, and up to unknown dangers ahead, and feel my nerves cool and unshaken." Like the modern climber, he is just as interested in savoring the challenge as he is in reaching the objective. At one point he even admits that a particular passage could be made easier if only he could anchor the rope to a spike of rock, but that being impossible, he proudly informs us of his intention to make the climb using "as little aid as possible" – a sportsmanlike resolve that has a decidedly modern ring to it.

While King's story overall has the ring of truth, in its particulars it is frequently exaggerated and occasionally downright false. Much of the exaggeration may be excused as part of King's rather bombastic style, a style typified by his description, early in the narrative, of the preparations for the ascent: he is not simply packing his pack to climb a mountain, but "overhauling campaign materials for a grand assault upon the summits." That was in camp; once King is actually high among the peaks the writing grows even more florid, frequently leaving the reader to wonder how he ever got anywhere, since so frequently it was "utterly impossible" to proceed.

King can also be accused of outright prevarication. The crossing of the Kings-Kern Divide can be as rough as King described it, but his route on Mount Tyndall is a straightforward scramble. Such details as the "precarious ice-ladder" are completely fictional, perhaps fabricated to enliven the narrative as it approached its climax. More serious is the way King never admits that he failed to accomplish his objective. At the beginning of the narrative, he resolves to reach "the top of California," that is, Mount Whitney, the high peak seen from atop Mount Brewer. Instead, he and Cotter climb Mount Tyndall, five hundred feet lower than Whitney. King must have been aware fairly early that he was not headed toward Whitney, for the two peaks are miles apart and clearly visible from the Kern River headwaters over which he made his final approach. Yet upon reaching the top, he feigns surprise at seeing the higher summit still many miles away.

Fortunately, none of this detracts from the story's many strengths: its smooth narration, careful structure, wealth of vivid description, and keen portrayal of character, particularly of Richard Cotter, King's partner on the climb. King was something of an eastern elitist, not completely comfortable with rough-cut westerners such as Cotter, the survey's packer. But the mountains proved to be an equalizing force, an environment in which social status had little meaning and in which, through the shared dangers of climbing, King could come to accept Cotter as something of an equal. King and Cotter are in fact the classic climbing partners, the Hillary and Tenzing of American mountaineering, and it is their partnership that gives the account below much of its force and charm. John Muir, the other great American climber of the nineteenth century, may have made harder climbs, but he generally did so alone; Cotter and King were a team, the first in American climbing literature. It thus seems appropriate that the story's true climax occurs, not when they reach the summit, but much later, when the tattered and exhausted climbers struggle up the last difficult slopes between them and the camp. Cotter, having gone ahead to climb a stretch King was unable to negotiate, finds himself perched on a narrow, sloping ledge from which the slightest pull of the rope will dislodge him. Having forged a strong bond with his partner in the crucible of their earlier climbing, Cotter makes no mention of the precariousness of his stance, instead calling confidently down to King, "Don't be afraid to bear your weight." Cotter had come to know his partner quite well, and this oblique appeal to King's pride proves to be just the trick to allow King to climb the stretch unaided.

In one sense, this beautifully handled episode is typical of King's entire narrative, because it remains genuinely moving even for those who sense its exaggeration. It captures the essence of mountaineering the way no American had before King, and, some would say, as none has done after.

Morning dawned brightly upon our bivouac among a cluster of dark firs in the mountain corridor opened by an ancient glacier of King's River into the heart of the Sierras. It dawned a trifle sooner than we could have wished, but Professor Brewer and Hoffman had breakfasted before sunrise, and were off with barometer and theodolite upon their shoulders, purposing to ascend our amphitheatre to its head and climb a great pyramidal peak which swelled up against the eastern sky, closing the view in that direction.

We who remained in camp spent the day in overhauling campaign materials and preparing for a grand assault upon the summits. For a couple of hours we could descry our friends through the field glasses, their minute, black forms moving slowly on among piles of giant *débris;* now and then lost, again coming to view, and at last disappearing altogether.

It was twilight of evening, and almost eight o'clock, when they came back to camp, Brewer leading the way, Hoffman following; and as they sat down by our fire without uttering a word, we read upon their faces terrible fatigue. So we hastened to give them supper of coffee and soup, bread and venison, which resulted, after a time, in our getting in return the story of the day. For eight whole hours they had worked up over granite and snow, mounting ridge after ridge, till the summit was made about two o'clock.

These snowy crests bounding our view at the eastward we had all along taken to be the summits of the Sierra, and Brewer had supposed himself to be

climbing a dominant peak, from which he might look eastward over Owens Valley and out upon leagues of desert. Instead of this, a vast wall of mountains, lifted still higher than his peak, rose beyond a tremendous cañon which lay like a trough between the two parallel ranks of peaks. Hoffmann showed us on his sketch-book the profile of this new range, and I instantly recognized the peaks which I had seen from Mariposa, whose great white pile had led me to believe them the highest points of California.

For a couple of months my friends had made me the target of plenty of pleasant banter about my "highest land," which they lost faith in as we climbed from Thomas's Mill, — I, too, becoming a trifle anxious about it; but now that the truth had burst upon Brewer and Hoffman, they could not find words to describe the terribleness and grandeur of the deep cañon, or for picturing those huge crags towering in line at the east. Their peak, as indicated by the barometer, was in the region of thirteen thousand four hundred feet [Mount Brewer is actually 13,570 feet], and a level across to the farther range showed its crests to be at least fifteen hundred feet higher [Mount Whitney, at 14,495 feet, is actually about 900 feet higher than Brewer]. They had spent hours upon the summit scanning the eastern horizon, and ranging downward into the labyrinth of gulfs below, and had come at last with reluctance to the belief that to cross this gorge and ascend the eastern wall of peaks was utterly impossible.

Brewer and Hoffman were old climbers, and their verdict of impossible oppressed me as I lay awake thinking of it; but early next morning I had made up my mind, and, taking Cotter aside, I asked him in an easy manner whether he would like to penetrate the Terra Incognita with me at the risk of our necks, provided Brewer should consent. In a frank, courageous tone he answered after his usual mode, "Why not?" Stout of limb, stronger yet in heart, of iron endurance, and a quiet, unexcited temperament, and, better yet, deeply devoted to me, I felt that Cotter was the one comrade I would choose to face death with, for I believed there was in his manhood no room for fear or shirk.

It was a trying moment for Brewer when we found him and volunteered to attempt a campaign for the top of California, because he felt a certain fatherly responsibility over our youth, a natural desire that we should not deposit our triturated remains in some undiscoverable hole among the feldspathic granites; but, like a true disciple of science, this was at last overbalanced by his intense desire to know more of the unexplored region. He freely confessed that he believed the plan madness, and Hoffman, too, told us we might as well attempt to get on a cloud as to try the peak. As Brewer gradually yielded his consent, I saw by his conversation that there was a possibility of success; so we spent the rest of the day in making preparations.

Our walking-shoes were in excellent condition, the hobnails firm and new. We laid out a barometer, a compass, a pocket-level, a set of wet and dry thermometers, note-books, with bread, cooked beans, and venison enough to last a week, rolled them all in blankets, making two knapsack-shaped packs strapped firmly together, with loops for the arms, which, by Brewer's estimate, weighed forty pounds apiece.

Gardiner declared he would accompany us to the summit of the first range to look over into the gulf we were to cross, and at last Brewer and Hoffman also concluded to go up with us.

Quite too early for our profit we all betook ourselves to bed, vainly hoping to get a long, refreshing sleep from which we should arise ready for our tramp.

Never a man welcomed those first gray streaks in the east gladder than I did, unless it may be Cotter, who has in later years confessed that he did not go to sleep that night. Long before sunrise we had finished our breakfast and were under way, Hoffman kindly bearing my pack, and Brewer Cotter's.

Our way led due east up the amphitheatre and toward Mount Brewer, as we had named the great pyramidal peak. Awhile after leaving camp, slant sunlight streamed in among gilded pinnacles along the slope of Mount Brewer, touching here and there, in broad dashes of yellow, the gray walls, which rose sweeping up on either hand like the sides of a ship.

——————— ▲ ———————

Climbing became exceedingly difficult, light air—for we had already reached twelve thousand five hundred feet—beginning to tell upon our lungs to such an extent that my friend, who had taken turns with me in carrying my pack, was unable to do so any longer, and I adjusted it to my shoulder for the rest of the day.

After four hours of slow, laborious work, we made the base of the *débris* slope which rose about a thousand feet to a saddle-pass in the western mountain-wall, that range upon which Mount Brewer is so prominent a point. We were nearly an hour in toiling up this slope, over an uncertain footing which gave way at almost every step. At last, when almost at the top, we paused to take breath, and then all walked out upon the crest, laid off our packs, and sat down together upon the summit of the ridge, and for a few moments not a word was spoken.

The Sierras are here two parallel summit ranges. We were upon the crest of the western ridge, and looked down into the gulf five thousand feet deep, sinking from our feet in abrupt cliffs nearly or quite two thousand feet, whose base plunged into a broad field of snow lying steep and smooth for a great distance, but broken near its foot by craggy steps often a thousand feet high.

Vague blue haze obscured the lost depths, hiding details, giving a bottomless distance, out of which, like the breath of wind, floated up a faint tremble, vibrating upon the senses, yet never clearly heard. Rising on the other side, cliff above cliff, precipice piled upon precipice, rock over rock, up against sky, towered the most gigantic mountain-wall in America, culminating in a noble pile of Gothic-finished granite and enamel-like snow. How grand and inviting looked its white form, its untrodden, unknown crest, so high and pure in the clear, strong blue! I looked at it as one contemplating the purpose of his life; and for just one moment I would have rather liked to dodge that purpose, or to have waited, or have found some excellent reason why I might not go; but all this quickly vanished, leaving a cheerful resolve to go ahead.

From the two opposing mountain-walls singular, thin, knife-blade ridges of stone jutted out, dividing the sides of the gulf into a series of amphitheatres, each one a labyrinth of ice and rock. Piercing thick beds of snow, sprang up knobs and straight, isolated spires of rock, mere obelisks curiously carved by frost, their rigid, slender forms casting a blue, sharp shadow upon the snow. Embosomed in depressions of ice, or resting on broken ledges, were azure lakes, deeper in tone than the sky, which at this altitude, even at midday, has a violet duskiness.

To the south, not more than eight miles, a wall of peaks stood across the gulf, dividing the King's, which flowed north at our feet, from the Kern River, that flowed down the trough in the opposite direction.

I did not wonder that Brewer and Hoffman pronounced our undertaking impossible; but when I looked at Cotter there was such complete bravery in his eye that I asked him if he was ready to start. His old answer, "Why not?" left the initiative with me; so I told Professor Brewer that we would bid him good-by. Our friends helped us on with our packs in silence, and as we shook hands there was not a dry eye in the party. Before he let go of my hand Professor Brewer asked me for my plan, and I had to own that I had but one, which was to reach the highest peak in the range.

After looking in every direction I was obliged to confess that I saw as yet no practicable way. We bade them a "good-by," receiving their "God bless you" in return, and started southward along the range to look for some possible cliff to descend. Brewer, Gardiner, and Hoffman turned north to push upward to the summit of Mount Brewer, and complete their observations. We saw them whenever we halted, until at last, on the very summit, their microscopic forms were for the last time discernible. With very great difficulty we climbed a peak which surmounted our wall just to the south of the pass, and, looking over the eastern brink, found that the precipice was still sheer and unbroken. In one place, where the snow lay against it to the very top, we went to its edge and contemplated the slide. About three thousand feet of unbroken white, at a fearfully steep angle, lay below us. We threw a stone over and watched it bound until it was lost in the distance; after fearful leaps we could only detect it by the flashings of snow where it struck, and as these were, in some instances, three hundred feet apart, we decided not to launch our own valuable bodies, and the still more precious barometer, after it.

There seemed but one possible way to reach our goal: that was to make our way along the summit of the cross ridge which projected between the two ranges. This divide sprang out from our Mount Brewer wall, about four miles to the south of us. To reach it we must climb up and down over the indented edge of the Mount Brewer wall. In attempting to do this we had a rather lively time scaling a sharp granite needle, where we found our course completely stopped by precipices four and five hundred feet in height. Ahead of us the summit continued to be broken into fantastic pinnacles, leaving us no hope of making our way along it; so we sought the most broken part of the eastern descent, and began to climb down. The heavy knapsacks, besides wearing our shoulders gradually into a black-and-blue state, overbalanced us terribly, and kept us in constant danger of pitching headlong. At last, taking them off, Cotter climbed down until he had found a resting-place upon a cleft of rock, then I lowered them to him with our lasso, afterward descending cautiously to his side, taking my turn in pioneering downward, receiving the freight of knapsacks by lasso as before. In this manner we consumed more than half the afternoon in descending a thousand feet of broken, precipitous slope; and it was almost sunset when we found ourselves upon the fields of level snow which lay white and thick over the whole interior slope of the amphitheatre.

The gorge below us seemed utterly impassable. At our backs the Mount Brewer wall rose either in sheer cliffs or in broken, rugged stairways, such as had offered us our descent. From this cruel dilemma the cross divide furnished the only hope, and the sole chance of scaling that was at its junction with the Mount Brewer wall. Toward this point we directed our course, marching wearily over stretches of dense, frozen snow, and regions of débris, reaching about sunset the last alcove of the amphitheatre, just at the foot of the Mount Brewer wall.

It was evidently impossible for us to attempt to climb it that evening, and we looked about the desolate recesses for a sheltered camping-spot. A high granite wall surrounded us upon three sides, recurring to the southward in long, elliptical curves; no part of the summit being less than two thousand feet above us, the higher crags not infrequently reaching three thousand feet. A single field of snow swept around the base of the rock, and covered the whole amphitheatre, except where a few spikes and rounded masses of granite rose through it, and where two frozen lakes, with their blue ice-disks, broke the monotonous surface. Through the white snow-gate of our amphitheatre, as through a frame, we looked eastward upon the summit group; not a tree, not a vestige of vegetation in sight, — sky, snow, and granite the only elements in this wild picture.

After searching for a shelter we at last found a granite crevice near the margin of one of the frozen lakes, — a sort of shelf just large enough for Cotter and me, — where we hastened to make our bed, having first filled the canteen from a small stream that trickled over the ice, knowing that in a few moments the rapid chill would freeze it. We ate our supper of cold venison and bread, and whittled from the sides of the wooden barometer-case shavings enough to warm water for a cup of miserably tepid tea, and then, packing our provisions and instruments away at the head of the shelf, rolled ourselves in our blankets and lay down to enjoy the view.

After such fatiguing exercises the mind has an almost abnormal clearness: whether this is wholly from within, or due to the intensely vitalizing mountain air, I am not sure; probably both contribute to the state of exaltation in which all alpine climbers find themselves. The solid granite gave me a luxurious repose, and I lay on the edge of our little rock niche and watched the strange yet brilliant scene.

All the snow of our recess lay in the shadow of the high granite wall to the west, but the Kern divide which curved around us from the southeast was in full light; its broken skyline, battlemented and adorned with innumerable rough-hewn spires and pinnacles, was a mass of glowing orange intensely defined against the deep violet sky. At the open end of our horseshoe amphitheatre, to the east, its floor of snow rounded over in a smooth brink, overhanging precipices which sank two thousand feet into the King's Cañon. Across the gulf rose the whole procession of summit peaks, their lower halves rooted in a deep, sombre shadow cast by the western wall, the heights bathed in a warm purple haze, in which the irregular marbling of snow burned with a pure crimson light. A few fleecy clouds, dyed fiery orange, drifted slowly eastward across the narrow zone of sky which stretched from summit to summit like a roof. At times the sound of waterfalls, faint and mingled with echoes, floated up through the still air. The snow near by lay in cold, ghastly shade, warmed here and there in strange flashes by light reflected downward from drifting clouds. The sombre waste about us; the deep violet vault overhead; those far summits, glowing with reflected rose; the deep, impenetrable gloom which filled the gorge, and slowly and with vapor-like stealth climbed the mountain wall, extinguishing the red light, combined to produce an effect which may not be described; nor can I more than hint at the contrast between the brilliancy of the scene under full light, and the cold, death-like repose which followed when the wan cliffs and pallid snow were all overshadowed with ghostly gray.

A sudden chill enveloped us. Stars in a moment crowded through the dark heaven, flashing with a frosty splendor. The snow congealed, the brooks ceased to flow, and, under the powerful sudden leverage of frost, immense blocks were dislodged all along the mountain summits and came thundering down the slopes, booming upon the ice, dashing wildly upon rocks. Under the lee of our shelf we felt quite safe, but neither Cotter nor I could help being startled, and jumping just a little, as these missiles, weighing often many tons, struck the ledge over our heads and whizzed down the gorge, their stroke resounding fainter and fainter, until at last only a confused echo reached us.

The thermometer at nine o'clock marked twenty degrees above zero. We set the "minimum" and rolled ourselves together for the night. The longer I lay the less I liked that shelf of granite; it grew hard in time, and cold also, my bones seeming to approach actual contact with the chilled rock; moreover, I found that even so vigorous a circulation as mine was not enough to warm up the ledge to anything like a comfortable temperature. A single thickness of blanket is a better mattress than none, but the larger crystals of orthoclase, protruding plentifully, punched my back and caused me to revolve on a horizontal axis with precision and frequency. How I loved Cotter! How I hugged him and got warm, while our backs gradually petrified, till we whirled over and thawed them out together! The slant of that bed was diagonal and excessive; down it we slid till the ice chilled us awake, and we crawled back and chocked ourselves up with bits of granite inserted under my ribs and shoulders. In this pleasant position we got dozing again, and there stole over me a most comfortable ease. The granite softened perceptibly. I was delightfully warm, and sank into an industrious slumber which lasted with great soundness till four, when we rose and ate our breakfast of frozen venison.

The thermometer stood at two above zero; everything was frozen tight except the canteen, which we had prudently kept between us all night. Stars still blazed brightly, and the moon, hidden from us by western cliffs, shone in pale reflection upon the rocky heights to the east, which rose, dimly white, up from the impenetrable shadow of the cañon. Silence, — cold, ghastly dimness, in which loomed huge forms, — the biting frostiness of the air, wrought upon our feelings as we shouldered our packs and started with slow pace to climb toward the "divide."

Soon, to our dismay, we found the straps had so chafed our shoulders that the weight gave us great pain, and obliged us to pad them with our handkerchiefs and extra socks, which remedy did not wholly relieve us from the constant wearing pain of the heavy load.

Directing our steps southward toward a niche in the wall which bounded us only half a mile distant, we travelled over a continuous snow-field frozen so densely as scarcely to yield at all to our tread, at the same time compressing enough to make that crisp, frosty sound which we all used to enjoy even before we knew from the books that it had something to do with the severe name of regelation.

As we advanced, the snow sloped more and more steeply up toward the crags, till by and by it became quite dangerous, causing us to cut steps with Cotter's large bowie-knife, — a slow, tedious operation, requiring patience of a pretty permanent kind. In this way we spent a quiet social hour or so. The sun had not yet reached us, being shut out by the high amphitheatre wall; but its cheerful light reflected downward from a number of higher crags, filling the recess with the brightness of day, and putting out of existence those shadows which so sombrely darkened the earlier hours. To look back when we stopped to rest was to realize our danger, — that smooth, swift slope of ice carrying the eye down a thousand feet to the margin of a frozen mirror of ice; ribs and needles of rock piercing up through the snow, so closely grouped that, had we fallen, a miracle only might save us from being dashed. This led to rather deeper steps, and greater care that our burdens should be held more nearly over the centre of gravity, and a pleasant relief when we got to the top of the snow and sat down on a block of granite to breathe and look up in search of a way up the thousand-foot cliff of broken surface, among the lines of fracture and the galleries winding along the face.

It would have disheartened us to gaze up the hard, sheer front of precipices, and search among splintered projections, crevices, shelves, and snow-patches for an inviting route, had we not been animated by a faith that the mountains could not defy us.

Choosing what looked like the least impossible way, we started; but, finding it unsafe to work with packs on, resumed the yesterday's plan, — Cotter taking the lead, climbing about fifty feet ahead, and hoisting up the knapsacks and barometer as I tied them to the end of the lasso. Constantly closing up in hopeless difficulty before us, the way opened again and again to our gymnastics, until we stood together upon a mere shelf, not more than two feet wide, which led diagonally up the smooth cliff. Edging along in careful steps, our backs flattened upon the granite, we moved slowly to a broad platform, where we stopped for breath.

There was no foothold above us. Looking down over the course we had come, it seemed, and I really believe it was, an impossible descent; for one can climb upward with safety where he cannot downward. To turn back was to give up in defeat; and we sat at least half an hour, suggesting all possible routes to the summit, accepting none, and feeling disheartened. About thirty feet directly over our heads was another shelf, which, if we could reach, seemed to offer at least a temporary way upward. On its edge were two or three spikes of granite; whether firmly connected with the cliff, or merely blocks of *débris,* we could not tell from below. I said to Cotter, I thought of but one possible plan: it was to lasso one of these blocks, and to climb, sailor-fashion, hand over hand, up the rope. In the lasso I had perfect confidence, for I had seen more than one Spanish bull throw his whole weight against it without parting a strand. The shelf was so narrow that throwing the coil of rope was a very difficult undertaking. I tried three times, and Cotter spent five minutes vainly whirling the loop up at the granite spikes. At last I made a lucky throw, and it tightened upon one of the protuberances. I drew the noose close, and very gradually threw my hundred and fifty pounds upon the rope; then Cotter joined me, and for a moment we both hung our united weight upon it. Whether the rock moved slightly, or whether the lasso stretched a little, we were unable to decide; but the trial must be made, and I began to climb slowly. The smooth precipice-face against which my body swung offered no foothold, and the whole climb had therefore to be done by the arms, an effort requiring all one's determination. When about half way up I was obliged to rest, and curling my feet in the rope managed to relieve my arms for a moment. In this position I could not resist the fascinating temptation of a survey downward.

Straight down, nearly a thousand feet below, at the foot of the rocks, began the snow, whose steep, roof-like slope, exaggerated into an almost vertical angle, curved down in a long, white field, broken far away by rocks and polished, round lakes of ice.

Cotter looked up cheerfully, and asked how I was making it; to which I answered that I had plenty of wind left. At that moment, when hanging between heaven and earth, it was a deep satisfaction to look down at the wild gulf of desolation beneath, and up to unknown dangers ahead, and feel my nerves cool and unshaken.

A few pulls hand over hand brought me to the edge of the shelf, when, throwing an arm around the granite spike, I swung my body upon the shelf, and lay down to rest, shouting to Cotter that I was all right, and that the prospects upward were capital. After a few moments' breathing I looked over the brink, and directed my comrade to tie the barometer to the lower end of the lasso, which he did, and that precious instrument was hoisted to my station, and the lasso sent down twice for the knapsacks, after which Cotter came up the rope in his very muscular way, without once stopping to rest. We took our loads in our hands, swinging the barometer over my shoulder, and climbed up a shelf which led in a zigzag direction upward and to the south, bringing us out at last upon the thin blade of a ridge which connected a short distance above with the summit. It was formed of huge blocks, shattered, and ready, at a touch, to fall.

So narrow and sharp was the upper slope that we dared not walk, but got astride, and worked slowly along with our hands, pushing the knapsacks in advance, now and then holding our breath when loose masses rocked under our weight.

Once upon the summit, a grand view burst upon us. Hastening to step upon the crest of the divide, which was never more than ten feet wide, frequently sharpened to a mere blade, we looked down the other side, and were astonished to find we had ascended the gentler slope, and that the rocks fell from our feet in almost vertical precipices for a thousand feet or more. A glance along the summit toward the highest group showed us that any advance in that direction was impossible, for the thin ridge was gashed down in notches three or four hundred feet deep, forming a procession of pillars, obelisks, and blocks piled upon each other, and looking terribly insecure.

We then deposited our knapsacks in a safe place, and, finding that it was already noon, determined to rest a little while and take a lunch, at over thirteen thousand feet above the sea.

West of us stretched the Mount Brewer wall, with its succession of smooth precipices and amphitheatre ridges. To the north the great gorge of the King's River yawned down five thousand feet. To the south the valley of the Kern, opening in the opposite direction, was broader, less deep, but more filled with broken masses of granite. Clustered about the foot of the divide were a dozen alpine lakes; the higher ones blue sheets of ice, the lowest completely melted. Still lower in the depths of the two cañons we could see groups of forest trees; but they were so dim and so distant as never to relieve the prevalent masses of rock and snow. Our divide cast its shadow for a mile down King's Cañon, in dark blue profile upon the broad sheets of sunny snow, from whose brightness the hard, splintered cliffs caught reflections and wore an aspect of joy. Thou-

sands of rills poured from the melting snow, filling the air with a musical tinkle as of many accordant bells. The Kern Valley opened below us with its smooth, oval outline, the work of extinct glaciers, whose form and extent were evident from worn cliff-surface and rounded wall; snow-fields, relics of the former *névé*, hung in white tapestries around its ancient birthplace; and as far as we could see, the broad, corrugated valley, for a breadth of fully ten miles, shone with burnishings wherever its granite surface was not covered with lakelets or thickets of alpine vegetation.

Through a deep cut in the Mount Brewer wall we gained our first view to the westward, and saw in the distance the wall of the South King's Cañon, and the granite point which Cotter and I had climbed a fortnight before. But for the haze we might have seen the plain; for above its farther limit were several points of the Coast Ranges, isolated like islands in the sea.

The view was so grand, the mountain colors so brilliant, immense snowfields and blue alpine lakes so charming, that we almost forgot we were ever to move, and it was only after a swift hour of this delight that we began to consider our future course.

The King's Cañon, which headed against our wall, seemed untraversable—no human being could climb along the divide; we had, then, but one hope of reaching the peak, and our greatest difficulty lay at the start. If we could climb down to the Kern side of the divide, and succeed in reaching the base of the precipices which fell from our feet, it really looked as if we might travel without difficulty among the *roches moutonnées* to the other side of the Kern Valley, and make our attempt upon the southward flank of the great peak. One look at the sublime white giant decided us. We looked down over the precipice, and at first could see no method of descent. Then we went back and looked at the road we had come up, to see if that were not possibly as bad; but the broken surface of the rocks was evidently much better climbing-ground than anything ahead of us. Cotter, with danger, edged his way along the wall to the east and I to the west, to see if there might not be some favorable point; but we both returned with the belief that the precipice in front of us was as passable as any of it. Down it we must.

After lying on our faces, looking over the brink, ten or twenty minutes, I suggested that by lowering ourselves on the rope we might climb from crevice to crevice; but we saw no shelf large enough for ourselves and the knapsacks too. However, we were not going to give it up without a trial; and I made the rope fast around my breast, and looping the noose over a firm point of rock, let myself slide gradually down to a notch forty feet below. There was only room beside me for Cotter, so I made him send down the knapsacks first. I then tied these together by the straps with my silk handkerchiefs, and hung them off as far to the left as I could reach without losing my balance, looping the handkerchiefs over a point of rock. Cotter then slid down the rope, and, with considerable difficulty, we whipped the noose off its resting-place above, and cut off our connection with the upper world.

"We're in for it now, King," remarked my comrade, as he looked aloft, and then down; but our blood was up, and danger added only an exhilarating thrill to the nerves.

The shelf was hardly more than two feet wide, and the granite so smooth that we could find no place to fasten the lasso for the next descent; so I determined to try the climb with only as little aid as possible. Tying it around my breast again, I gave the other end into Cotter's hands, and he, bracing his back against the cliff, found for himself as firm a foothold as he could, and promised to give me all the help in his power. I made up my mind to bear no weight unless it was absolutely necessary; and for the first ten feet I found cracks and protuberances enough to support me, making every square inch of surface do friction duty, and hugging myself against the rocks as tightly as I could. When within about eight feet of the next shelf, I twisted myself round upon the face, hanging by two rough blocks of protruding feldspar, and looked vainly for some further hand-hold; but the rock, besides being perfectly smooth, overhung slightly, and my legs dangled in the air. I saw that the next cleft was over three feet broad, and I thought possibly I might, by a quick slide, reach it in safety without endangering Cotter. I shouted to him to be very careful and let go in case I fell, loosened my hold upon the rope and slid quickly down. My shoulder struck against the rock and threw me out of balance; for an instant I reeled over upon the verge, in danger of falling, but, in the excitement, I thrust out my hand and seized a small alpine gooseberry-bush, the first piece of vegetation we had seen. Its roots were so firmly fixed in the crevice that it held my weight and saved me.

I could no longer see Cotter, but I talked to him, and heard the two knapsacks come bumping along till they slid over the eaves above me, and swung down to my station, when I seized the lasso's end and braced myself as well as possible, intending, if he slipped, to haul in slack and help him as best I might. As he came slowly down from crack to crack, I heard his hobnailed shoes grating on the granite; presently they appeared dangling from the eaves above my head. I had gathered in the rope until it was taut, and then hurriedly told him to drop. He hesitated a moment, and let go. Before he struck the rock I had him by the shoulder, and whirled him down upon his side, thus preventing his rolling overboard, which friendly action he took quite coolly.

The third descent was not a difficult one, nor the fourth; but when we had climbed down about two hundred and fifty feet, the rocks were so glacially polished and water-worn that it seemed impossible to get any farther. To our right was a crack penetrating the rock, perhaps a foot deep, widening at the surface to three or four inches, which proved to be the only possible ladder. As the chances seemed rather desperate, we concluded to tie ourselves together, in order to share a common fate; and with a slack of thirty feet between us, and our knapsacks upon our backs, we climbed into the crevice, and began descending with our faces to the cliff. This had to be done with unusual caution, for the foothold was about as good as none, and our fingers slipped annoyingly on the smooth stone; besides, the knapsacks and instruments kept a steady backward pull, tending to overbalance us. But we took pains to descend one at a time, and rest wherever the niches gave our feet a safe support. In this way we got down about eighty feet of smooth, nearly vertical wall, reaching the top of a rude granite stairway, which led to the snow; and here we sat down to rest, and found to our astonishment that we had been three hours from the summit.

After breathing a half-minute we continued down, jumping from rock to rock, and having, by practice, become very expert in balancing ourselves, sprang on, never resting long enough to lose the *aplomb*; and in this manner made a quick descent over rugged *débris* to the crest of a snow-field, which, for seven or eight hundred feet more, swept down in a smooth, even slope, of very high angle, to the borders of a frozen lake.

Without untying the lasso which bound us together, we sprang upon the snow with a shout, and glissaded down splendidly, turning now and then a somersault, and shooting out like cannon-balls almost to the middle of the frozen lake; I upon my back, and Cotter feet first, in a swimming position. The ice cracked in all directions. It was only a thin, transparent film, through which we could see deep into the lake. Untying ourselves, we hurried ashore in different directions, lest our combined weight should be too great a strain upon any point.

With curiosity and wonder we scanned every shelf and niche of the last descent. It seemed quite impossible we could have come down there, and now it actually was beyond human power to get back again. But what cared we? "Sufficient unto the day—" We were bound for that still distant, though gradually nearing, summit; and we had come from a cold, shadowed cliff into deliciously warm sunshine, and were jolly, shouting, singing songs, and calling out the companionship of a hundred echoes. Six miles away, with no grave danger, no great difficulty, between us, lay the base of our grand mountain. Upon its skirts we saw a little grove of pines, an ideal bivouac, and toward this we bent our course.

After the continued climbing of the day walking was a delicious rest, and forward we pressed with considerable speed, our hobnails giving us firm footing on the glittering, glacial surface. Every fluting of the great valley was in itself a considerable cañon, into which we descended, climbing down the scored rocks, and swinging from block to block, until we reached the level of the pines. Here, sheltered among *roches moutonnées,* began to appear little fields of alpine grass, pale yet sunny, soft under our feet, fragrantly jewelled with flowers of fairy delicacy, holding up amid thickly clustered blades chalices of turquoise and amethyst, white stars, and fiery little globes of red. Lakelets, small but innumerable, were held in glacial basins, the striae and grooves of that old dragon's track ornamenting their smooth bottoms.

One of these, a sheet of pure beryl hue, gave us much pleasure from its lovely transparency, and because we lay down in the necklace of grass about it and smelled flowers, while tired muscles relaxed upon warm beds of verdure, and the pain in our burdened shoulders went away, leaving us delightfully comfortable.

After the stern grandeur of granite and ice, and with the peaks and walls still in view, it was relief to find ourselves again in the region of life. I never felt for trees and flowers such a sense of intimate relationship and sympathy. When we had no longer excuse for resting, I invented the palpable subterfuge of measuring the altitude of the spot, since the few clumps of low, wide-boughed pines near by were the highest living trees. So we lay longer with less and less will to rise, and when resolution called us to our feet, the getting-up was sorely like Rip Van Winkle's in the third act.

The deep, glacial cañon-flutings across which our march then lay proved to be great consumers of time: indeed, it was sunset when we reached the eastern ascent, and began to toil up through scattered pines, and over trains of moraine rocks, toward the great peak. Stars were already flashing brilliantly in the sky, and the low, glowing arch in the west had almost vanished when we came to the upper trees, and threw down our knapsacks to camp. The forest grew on a sort of plateau-shelf with a precipitous front to the west—a level surface which stretched eastward and back to the foot of our mountain, whose lower spurs reached within a mile of camp. Within the shelter lay a huge, fallen log, like all these alpine woods one mass of resin, which flared up when we applied a match, illuminating the whole grove. By contrast with the darkness outside, we seemed to be in a vast, many-pillared hall. The stream close by afforded water for our blessed teapot; venison frizzled with a mild, appetizing sound upon the ends of pine sticks; matchless beans allowed themselves to become seductively crisp upon our tin plates. That supper seemed to me then the quintessence of gastronomy, and I am sure Cotter and I must have said some very good *aprés-dîner* things, though I long ago forgot them all. Within the ring of warmth, on elastic beds of pine-needles, we curled up, and fell swiftly into a sound sleep.

I woke up once in the night to look at my watch, and observed that the sky was overcast with a thin film of cirrus cloud to which the reflected moonlight lent the appearance of a glimmering tent, stretched from mountain to mountain over cañons filled with impenetrable darkness, only the vaguely lighted peaks and white snow-fields distinctly seen. I closed my eyes and slept soundly until Cotter woke me at half-past three, when we arose, breakfasted by the light of our fire, which still blazed brilliantly, and, leaving our knapsacks, started for the mountain with only instruments, canteens, and luncheon.

In the indistinct moonlight climbing was very difficult at first, for we had to thread our way along a plain which was literally covered with glacier bowlders, and the innumerable brooks which we crossed were frozen solid. However, our march brought us to the base of the great mountain, which, rising high against the east, shut out the coming daylight, and kept us in profound shadow. From base to summit rose a series of broken crags, lifting themselves from a general slope of *débris*. Toward the left the angle seemed to be rather gentler, and the surface less ragged; and we hoped, by a long *détour* round the base, to make an easy climb up this gentler face. So we toiled on for an hour over the rocks, reaching at last the bottom of the north slope. Here our work began in good earnest. The blocks were of enormous size, and in every stage of unstable equilibrium, frequently rolling over as we jumped upon them, making it necessary for us to take a second leap and land where we best could. To our relief we soon surmounted the largest blocks, reaching a smaller size, which served us as a sort of stairway.

The advancing daylight revealed to us a very long, comparatively even snow-slope, whose surface was pierced by many knobs and granite heads, giving it the aspect of an ice-roofing fastened on with bolts of stone. It stretched in far perspective to the summit, where already the rose of sunrise reflected gloriously, kindling a fresh enthusiasm within us.

Immense bowlders were partly embedded in the ice just above us, whose constant melting left them trembling on the edge of a fall. It communicated no very pleasant sensation to see above you these immense missiles hanging by a mere band, knowing that, as soon as the sun rose, you would be exposed to a constant cannonade.

The east side of the peak, which we could now partially see, was too precipitous to think of climbing. The slope toward our camp was too much broken into pinnacles and crags to offer us any hope, or to divert us from the single way, dead ahead, up slopes of ice and among fragments of granite. The sun rose upon us while we were climbing the lower part of this snow, and in less than half an hour, melting, began to liberate huge blocks, which thundered down past us, gathering and growing into small avalanches below.

We did not dare climb one above another, according to our ordinary mode, but kept about an equal level, a hundred feet apart, lest, dislodging the blocks, one should hurl them down upon the other.

We climbed up smooth faces of granite, clinging simply by the cracks and protruding crystals of feldspar, and then hewed steps up fearfully steep slopes of ice, zigzagging to the right and left, to avoid the flying bowlders. When midway up this slope we reached a place where the granite rose in perfectly smooth bluffs on either side of a gorge, — a narrow cut or walled way leading up to the flat summit of the cliff. This we scaled by cutting ice steps, only to find ourselves fronted again by a still higher wall. Ice sloped from its front at too steep an angle for us to follow, but had melted in contact with it, leaving a space three feet wide between the ice and the rock. We entered this crevice and climbed along its bottom, with a wall of rock rising a hundred feet above us on one side, and a thirty-foot face of ice on the other, through which light of an intense cobalt-blue penetrated.

Reaching the upper end, we had to cut our footsteps upon the ice again, and, having braced our backs against the granite, climbed up to the surface. We were now in a dangerous position: to fall into the crevice upon one side was to be wedged to death between rock and ice; to make a slip was to be shot down five hundred feet, and then hurled over the brink of the precipice. In the friendly seat which this wedge gave me, I stopped to take wet and dry observations with the thermometer, — this being an absolute preventive of a scare, — and to enjoy the view.

The wall of our mountain sank abruptly to the left, opening for the first time an outlook to the eastward. Deep — it seemed almost vertically — beneath us we could see the blue water of Owens Lake, ten thousand feet down. The summit peaks to the north were piled in Titanic confusion, their ridges overhanging the eastern slope with terrible abruptness. Clustered upon the shelves and plateaus below were several frozen lakes, and in all directions swept magnificent fields of snow. The summit was now not over five hundred feet distant, and we started on again with the exhilarating hope of success. But if nature had intended to secure the summit from all assailants, she could not have planned her defences better; for the smooth granite wall which rose above the snow slope continued, apparently, quite around the peak, and we looked in great anxiety to see if there was not one place where it might be climbed. It was all blank except in one spot; quite near us the snow bridged across the crevice and rose in a long point to the summit of the wall, — a great icicle-column frozen in a niche of the bluff, — its base about ten feet wide, narrowing to two feet at the top. We climbed to the base of this spire of ice, and, with the utmost care, began to cut our stairway. The material was an exceedingly compacted snow, passing into clear ice as it neared the rock. We climbed the first half of it with comparative ease; after that it was almost vertical, and so thin that we did not dare to cut the footsteps deep enough to make them absolutely safe. There was a constant dread lest our ladder should break off, and we be thrown either down the snow-slope or into the bottom of the crevasse. At last, in order to prevent myself from falling over backward, I was obliged to thrust my hand into the crack between the ice and the wall, and the spire became so narrow that I could do this on both sides, so that the climb was made as upon a tree, cutting mere toe-holes and embracing the whole column of ice in my arms. At last I reached the top, and, with the greatest caution, wormed my body over the brink, and, rolling out upon the smooth surface of the granite, looked over and watched Cotter make his climb. He came steadily up, with no sense of nervousness, until he got to the narrow part of the ice, and here he stopped and looked up with a forlorn face to me; but as he climbed up over the edge the broad smile came back to his face, and he asked me if it had occurred to me that we had, by and by, to go down again.

We had now an easy slope to the summit, and hurried up over rocks and ice, reaching the crest at exactly twelve o'clock. I rang my hammer upon the topmost rock; we grasped hands, and I reverently named the grand peak MOUNT TYNDALL.

To our surprise, upon sweeping the horizon with my level, there appeared two peaks equal in height with us, and two rising even higher. That which looked highest of all was a cleanly cut helmet of granite upon the same ridge with Mount Tyndall, lying about six miles south, and fronting the desert with a bold, square bluff which rises to the crest of the peak, where a white fold of snow trims it gracefully. Mount Whitney, as we afterward called it, in honor of our chief, is probably the highest land within the United States. Its summit looked glorious, but inaccessible.

The general topography overlooked by us may be thus simply outlined. Two parallel chains, enclosing an intermediate trough, face each other. Across this deep, enclosed gulf, from wall to wall, juts the thin but lofty and craggy ridge, or "divide," before described, which forms an important water-shed sending those streams which enter the chasm north of it into King's River, those south forming the most important sources of the Kern, whose straight, rapidly deepening valley stretches south, carved profoundly in granite, while the King's, after flowing longitudinally in the opposite course for eight or ten miles, turns abruptly west round the base of Mount Brewer, cuts across the western ridge, opening a gate of its own, and carves a rock channel transversely down the Sierra to the California plain.

————————— ▲ —————————

Having completed our observations, we packed up the instruments, glanced once again round the whole field of view, and descended to the top of our icicle ladder. Upon looking over, I saw to my consternation that during the day the upper half had broken off. Scars traced down upon the snowfield below it indicated the manner of its fall, and far below, upon the shattered *débris*, were strewn its white relics. I saw that nothing but the sudden gift of wings could possibly take us down to the snow-ridge. We held council, and concluded to climb quite round the peak in search of the best mode of descent.

As we crept about the east face, we could look straight down upon Owen's Valley, and into the vast glacier gorges, and over piles of moraines and fluted rocks, and the frozen lakes of the eastern slope. When we reached the south-west front of the mountain we found that its general form was that of an immense horseshoe, the great eastern ridge forming one side, and the spur which descended to our camp the other, we having climbed up the outer part of the toe. Within the curve of the horseshoe was a gorge, cut almost perpendicularly down two thousand feet, its side rough-hewn walls of rocks and snow, its narrow bottom almost a continuous chain of deep blue lakes with loads of ice and *débris* piles. The stream which flowed through them joined the waters from our home grove, a couple of miles below the camp. If we could reach the level of the lakes, I believed we might easily climb round them and out of the upper end of the horseshoe, and walk upon the Kern plateau round to our bivouac.

It required a couple of hours of very painstaking, deliberate climbing to get down the first descent, which we did, however, without hurting our barometer, and fortunately without the fatiguing use of the lasso, reaching finally the uppermost lake, a granite bowlful of cobalt-blue water, transparent and unrippled. So high and enclosing were the tall walls about us, so narrow and shut in the cañon, so flattened seemed the cover of sky, we felt oppressed after the expanse and freedom of our hours on the summit.

The snow-field we followed, descending farther, was irregularly honeycombed in deep pits, circular or irregular in form, and melted to a greater or less depth, holding each a large stone embedded in the bottom. It seems they must have fallen from the overhanging heights with sufficient force to plunge into the snow.

Brilliant light and strong color met our eyes at every glance — the rocks of a deep purple-red tint, the pure alpine lakes of a cheerful sapphire blue, the snow glitteringly white. The walls on either side for half their height were planed and polished by glaciers, and from the smoothly glazed sides the sun was reflected as from a mirror.

Mile after mile we walked cautiously over the snow and climbed round the margins of lakes, and over piles of *débris* which marked the ancient terminal moraines. At length we reached the end of the horseshoe, where the walls contracted to a gateway, rising on either side in immense, vertical pillars a thousand feet high. Through this gateway we could look down the valley of the Kern, and beyond to the gentler ridges where a smooth growth of forest darkened the rolling plateau. Passing the last snow, we walked through this gateway and turned westward round the spur toward our camp. The three miles which closed our walk were alternately through groves of *Pinus flexilis* and upon plains of granite.

The glacier sculpture and planing are here very beautiful, the large crystals of orthoclase with which the granite is studded being cut down to the common level, their rosy tint making with the white base a beautiful, burnished porphyry.

The sun was still an hour high when we reached camp, and with a feeling of relaxation and repose we threw ourselves down to rest by the log, which still continued blazing. We had accomplished our purpose.

During the last hour or two of our tramp Cotter had complained of his shoes, which were rapidly going to pieces. Upon examination we found to our dismay that there was not over half a day's wear left in them, a calamity which gave to our difficult homeward climb a new element of danger. The last nail had been worn from my own shoes, and the soles were scratched to the quick, but I believed them stout enough to hold together till we should reach the main camp.

We planned a pair of moccasins for Cotter, and then spent a pleasant evening by the campfire, rehearsing our climb to the detail, sleep finally overtaking us and holding us fast bound until broad daylight next morning, when we woke with a sense of having slept for a week, quite bright and perfectly refreshed for our homeward journey.

After a frugal breakfast, in which we limited ourselves to a few cubic inches of venison, and a couple of stingy slices of bread, with a single meagre cup of diluted tea, we shouldered our knapsacks, which now sat lightly upon toughened shoulders, and marched out upon the granite plateau.

We had concluded that it was impossible to retrace our former way, knowing well that the precipitous divide could not be climbed from this side; then, too, we had gained such confidence in our climbing powers, from constant victory, that we concluded to attempt the passage of the great King's Cañon, mainly because this was the only mode of reaching camp, and since the geological section of the granite it exposed would afford us an exceedingly instructive study.

The broad granite plateau which forms the upper region of the Kern Valley slopes in general inclination up to the great divide. This remarkably pinnacled ridge, where it approaches the Mount Tyndall wall, breaks down into a broad depression where the Kern Valley sweeps northward, until it suddenly breaks off in precipices three thousand feet down into the King's Cañon.

The morning was wholly consumed in walking up this gently inclined plane of granite, our way leading over the glacier-polished foldings and along graded undulations among labyrinths of alpine garden and wildernesses of erratic bowlders, little lake-basins, and scattered clusters of dwarfed and sombre pine.

About noon we came suddenly upon the brink of a precipice which sank sharply from our feet into the gulf of the King's Cañon. Directly opposite us rose Mount Brewer, and up out of the depths of those vast sheets of frozen snow swept spiry buttress-ridges, dividing the upper heights into those amphitheatres over which we had struggled on our outward journey. Straight across from our point of view was the chamber of rock and ice where we had camped on the first night. The wall at our feet fell sharp and rugged, its lower two-thirds hidden from our view by the projections of a thousand feet of crags. Here and there, as we looked down, small patches of ice, held in rough hollows, rested upon the steep surface, but it was too abrupt for any great fields of snow. I dislodged a boulder upon the edge and watched it bound down the rocky precipice, dash over eaves a thousand feet below us, and disappear, the crash of its fall coming up to us from the unseen depths fainter and fainter, until the air only trembled with confused echoes.

A long look at the pass to the south of Mount Brewer, where we had parted from our friends, animated us with courage to begin the descent, which we did with utmost care, for the rocks, becoming more and more glacier-smoothed, afforded us hardly any firm footholds. When down about eight hundred feet we again rolled rocks ahead of us, and saw them disappear over the eaves, and only heard the sound of their stroke after many seconds, which convinced us that directly below lay a great precipice.

At this juncture the soles came entirely off Cotter's shoes, and we stopped upon a little cliff of granite to make him moccasins of our provision bags and slips of blanket, tying them on as firmly as we could with the extra straps and buckskin thongs. Climbing with these proved so insecure that I made Cotter go behind me, knowing that under ordinary circumstances I could stop him if he fell.

Here and there in the clefts of the rocks grew stunted pine bushes, their roots twisted so firmly into the crevices that we laid hold of them with the utmost confidence whenever they came within our reach. In this way we descended to within fifty feet of the brink, having as yet no knowledge of the cliffs below, except our general memory of their aspect from the Mount Brewer wall.

The rock was so steep that we descended in a sitting posture, clinging with our hands and heels. I heard Cotter say, "I think I must take off these moccasins and try it barefooted, for I don't believe I can make it." These words were instantly followed by a startled cry, and I looked round to see him slide quickly toward me, struggling and clutching at the smooth granite. As he slid by I made a grab for him with my right hand, catching him by the shirt, and, throwing myself as far in the other direction as I could, seized with my left hand a little pine tuft, which held us. I asked Cotter to edge along a little to the left, where he could get a brace with his feet and relieve me of his weight, which he cautiously did. I then threw a couple of turns with the lasso round the roots of the pine bush, and we were safe, though hardly more than twenty feet from the brink. The pressure of curiosity to get a look over that edge was so strong within me that I lengthened out sufficient lasso to reach the end, and slid slowly to the edge, where, leaning over, I looked down, getting a full view of the wall for miles. Directly beneath, a sheer cliff of three or four hundred feet stretched down to a pile of *débris* which rose to unequal heights along its face, reaching the very crest not more than a hundred feet south of us. From that point to the bottom of the cañon, broken rocks, ridges rising through vast sweeps of *débris,* tufts of pine and frozen bodies of ice covered the further slope.

**View of Mount King
from Arrow Peak
showing King and Cotter's
ascent route. The
cross marks their first camp.**

I returned to Cotter, and, having loosened ourselves from the pine bush, inch by inch we crept along the granite until we supposed ourselves to be just over the top of the *débris* pile, where I found a firm brace for my feet, and lowered Cotter to the edge. He sang out, "All right!" and climbed over on the uppermost *débris,* his head only remaining in sight of me; then I lay down upon my back, making knapsack and body do friction duty, and, letting myself move, followed Cotter and reached his side.

From that point the descent required two hours of severe, constant labor, which was monotonous of itself, and would have proved excessively tiresome but for the constant interest of glacial geology beneath us. When at last we reached the bottom and found ourselves upon a velvety green meadow, beneath the shadow of wide-armed pines, we realized the amount of muscular force we had used up, and threw ourselves down for a rest of half an hour, when we rose, not quite renewed, but fresh enough to finish the day's climb.

In a few minutes we stood upon the rocks just above King's River—a broad, white torrent fretting its way along the bottom of an impassable gorge. Looking down the stream, we saw that our right bank was a continued precipice, affording, so far as we could see, no possible descent to the river's margin, and indeed, had we gotten down, the torrent rushed with such fury that we could not possibly have crossed it. To the south of us, a little way up stream, the river flowed out from a broad, oval lake, three quarters of a mile in length, which occupied the bottom of the granite basin. Unable to cross the torrent, we must either swim the lake or climb round its head. Upon our side the walls of the basin curved to the head of the lake in sharp, smooth precipices, or broken slopes of *débris,* while on the opposite side its margin was a beautiful shore of emerald meadow, edged with a continuous grove of coniferous trees. Once upon this other side, we should have completed the severe part of our journey, crossed the gulf, and have left all danger behind us; for the long slope of granite and ice which rose upon the west side of the cañon and the Mount Brewer wall opposed to us no trials save those of simple fatigue.

Around the head of the lake were crags and precipices in singularly forbidding arrangement. As we turned thither we saw no possible way of overcoming them. At its head the lake lay in an angle of the vertical wall, sharp and straight like the corner of a room; about three hundred feet in height, and for two hundred and fifty feet of this a pyramidal pile of blue ice rose from the lake, rested against the corner, and reached within forty feet of the top. Looking into the deep blue water of the lake, I concluded that in our exhausted state it was madness to attempt to swim it. The only alternative was to scale that slender pyramid of ice and find some way to climb the forty feet of smooth wall above it; a plan we chose perforce, and started at once to put into execution, determined that if we were unsuccessful we would fire a dead log that lay near, warm ourselves thoroughly, and attempt the swim. At its base the ice mass overhung the lake like a roof, under which the water had melted its way for a distance of not less than a hundred feet, a thin eave overhanging the water. To the very edge of this I cautiously went, and, looking down into the lake, saw through its beryl depths the white granite blocks strewn upon the bottom at least one hundred feet below me. It was exceedingly transparent, and, under ordinary circumstances, would have been a most tempting place for a dive; but at the end of our long fatigue, and with the still unknown tasks ahead, I shrank from a swim in such a chilly temperature.

We found the ice-angle difficultly steep, but made our way successfully along its edge, clambering up the crevices melted between its body and the smooth granite to a point not far from the top, where the ice had considerably narrowed, and rocks overhanging it encroached so closely that we were obliged to change our course and make our way with cut steps out upon its front. Streams of water, dropping from the overhanging rock-eaves at many points, had worn circular shafts into the ice, three feet in diameter and twenty feet in depth. Their edges offered us our only foothold, and we climbed from one to another, equally careful of slipping upon the slope itself, or falling into the wells. Upon the top of the ice we found a narrow, level platform, upon which we stood together, resting our backs in the granite corner, and looked down the awful pathway of King's Cañon, until the rest nerved us up enough to turn our eyes upward at the forty feet of smooth granite which lay between us and safety. Here and there were small projections from its surface, little, protruding knobs of feldspar, and crevices riven into its face for a few inches.

As we tied ourselves together, I told Cotter to hold himself in readiness to jump down into one of these in case I fell, and started to climb up the wall, succeeding quite well for about twenty feet. About two feet above my hands was a crack, which, if my arms had been long enough to reach, would probably have led me to the very top; but I judged it beyond my powers, and, with great care, descended to the side of Cotter, who believed that his superior length of arm would enable him to make the reach.

I planted myself against the rock, and he started cautiously up the wall. Looking down the glare front of ice, it was not pleasant to consider at what velocity a slip would send me to the bottom, or at what angle, and to what probable depth, I should be projected into the ice-water. Indeed, the idea of such a sudden bath was so annoying that I lifted my eyes toward my companion. He reached my farthest point without great difficulty, and made a bold spring for the crack, reaching it without an inch to spare, and holding on wholly by his fingers. He thus worked himself along the crack toward the top, at last getting his arms over the brink, and gradually drawing his body up and out of sight. It was the most splendid piece of slow gymnastics I ever witnessed.

For a moment he said nothing; but when I asked if he was all right, cheerfully repeated, "All right."

It was only a moment's work to send up the two knapsacks and barometer, and receive again my end of the lasso. As I tied it round my breast, Cotter said to me, in an easy, confident tone, "Don't be afraid to bear your weight." I made up my mind, however, to make that climb without his aid, and husbanded my strength as I climbed from crack to crack. I got up without difficulty to my former point, rested there a moment, hanging solely by my hands, gathered every pound of strength and atom of will for the reach, then jerked myself upward with a swing, just getting the tips of my fingers into the crack. In an instant I had grasped it with my right hand also. I felt the sinews of my fingers relax a little, but the picture of the slope of ice and the blue lake affected me so strongly that I redoubled my grip, and climbed slowly along the crack until I reached the angle and got one arm over the edge, as Cotter had done. As I rested my body upon the edge and looked up at Cotter, I saw that, instead of a level top, he was sitting on a smooth, roof-like slope, where the least pull would have dragged him over the brink. He had no brace for his feet, nor hold for his hands, but had seated himself calmly, with the rope tied around his breast, knowing that my only safety lay in being able to make the climb entirely unaided; certain that the least waver in his tone would have disheartened me, and perhaps made it impossible. The shock I received on seeing this affected me for a moment, but not enough to throw me off my guard, and I climbed quickly over the edge. When we had walked back out of danger we sat down upon the granite for a rest.

In all my experience of mountaineering I have never known an act of such real, profound courage as this of Cotter's. It is one thing, in a moment of excitement, to make a gallant leap, or hold one's nerves in the iron grasp of will, but to coolly seat one's self in the door of death, and silently listen for the fatal summons, and this all for a friend, — for he might easily have cast loose the lasso and saved himself, — requires as sublime a type of courage as I know.

But a few steps back we found a thicket of pine overlooking our lake, by which there flowed a clear rill of snow-water. Here, in the bottom of the great gulf, we made our bivouac; for we were already in the deep evening shadows, although the mountaintops to the east of us still burned in the reflected light. It was the luxury of repose which kept me awake half an hour or so, in spite of my vain attempts at sleep. To listen to the pulsating sound of waterfalls and arrowy rushing of the brook by our beds was too deep a pleasure to quickly yield up.

Under the later moonlight I rose and went out upon the open rocks, allowing myself to be deeply impressed by the weird Dantesque surroundings — darkness, out of which to the sky towered stern, shaggy bodies of rock;

snow, uncertainly moonlit with cold pallor; and at my feet the basin of the lake, still, black, and gemmed with reflected stars, like the void into which Dante looked through the bottomless gulf of Dis. A little way off there appeared upon the brink of a projecting granite cornice two dimly seen forms; pines I knew them to be, yet their motionless figures seemed bent forward, gazing down the cañon; I allowed myself to name them Mantuan and Florentine, thinking at the same time how grand and spacious the scenery, how powerful their attitude, and how infinitely more profound the mystery of light and shade, than any of those hard, theatrical conceptions with which Doré has sought to shut in our imagination. That artist, as I believe, has reached a conspicuous failure from an overbalancing love of solid, impenetrable darkness. There is in all his Inferno landscape a certain sharp boundary between the real and unreal, and never the infinite suggestiveness of great regions of half-light, in which everything may be seen, nothing recognized. Without waking Cotter, I crept back to my blankets, and to sleep.

The morning of our fifth and last day's tramp must have dawned cheerfully; at least, so I suppose from its aspect when we first came back to consciousness, surprised to find the sun risen from the eastern mountain-wall, and the whole gorge flooded with its direct light. Rising as good as new from our mattress of pine twigs, we hastened to take breakfast, and started up the long, broken slope of the Mount Brewer wall. To reach the pass where we had parted from our friends required seven hours of slow, laborious climbing, in which we took advantage of every outcropping spine of granite and every level expanse of ice to hasten at the top of our speed. Cotter's feet were severely cut; his tracks upon the snow were marked by stains of blood, yet he kept on with undiminished spirit, never once complaining. The perfect success of our journey so inspired us with happiness that we forgot danger and fatigue, and chatted in liveliest strain.

It was about two o'clock when we reached the summit, and rested a moment to look back over our new Alps, which were hard and distinct under direct, unpoetic light; yet with all their dense gray and white reality, their long, sculptured ranks, and cold, still summits, we gave them a lingering, farewell look, which was not without its deep fulness of emotion, then turned our backs and hurried down the *débris* slope into the rocky amphitheatre at the foot of Mount Brewer, and by five o'clock had reached our old camp-ground. We found here a note pinned to a tree, informing us that the party had gone down into the lower cañon, five miles below, that they might camp in better pasturage.

The wind had scattered the ashes of our old camp-fire, and banished from it the last sentiment of home. We hurried on, climbing among the rocks which reached down to the crest of the great lateral moraine, and then on in rapid stride along its smooth crest, riveting our eyes upon the valley below, where we knew the party must be camped.

At last, faintly curling above the sea of green tree-tops, a few faint clouds of smoke wafted upward into the air. We saw them with a burst of strong emotion, and ran down the steep flank of the moraine at the top of our speed. Our shouts were instantly answered by the three voices of our friends, who welcomed us to their campfire with tremendous hugs.

After we had outlined for them the experience of our days, and as we lay outstretched at our ease, warm in the blaze of the glorious camp-fire, Brewer said to me: "King, you have relieved me of a dreadful task. For the last three days I have been composing a letter to your family, but somehow I did not get beyond, 'It becomes my painful duty to inform you.'"

George Davidson
Climbs Makushin, 1867

B ORN IN ENGLAND in 1825, George Davidson was seven years old when he moved to the United States with his parents. He graduated at the head of his class from a Philadelphia high school and then did scientific work at Girard College, where, apparently, he never took a degree – a fact that did not stop him from becoming one of the nineteenth century's most productive scientists. In 1845 he joined the U.S. Coast Survey, and five years later was placed in charge of a survey of the coast of California. In 1866 he was ordered to map the southern coast of Alaska, the largely uncharted territory that would shortly be added to the nation as "Seward's Folly." Davidson later made astronomical observations that for the first time established the precise longitude of points on the West Coast. For several years he was president of the California Academy of Sciences, was a regent of the University of California, and served on the Irrigation Commission of California, on whose behalf he traveled to Egypt, India, and China to study methods of dryland reclamation.

It was during the 1866–67 coast survey that Davidson made the first known ascent of an Alaskan peak. Though the volcano Makushin is only 5,691 feet high, its ascent was in many ways the most difficult yet accomplished in the United States. Makushin was as heavily glaciated as Mount Rainier, which had not yet seen a complete ascent, and in addition was far more remote and suffered worse weather. Understandably, Davidson took a cautious approach to the climb, moving methodically up the mountain with a large party, in the style of virtually every subsequent Alaskan ascent for the next hundred years.

The diary Davidson kept during the climb was not published until December of 1884, when it appeared in *Appalachia,* from which the selection below is reprinted.

Sept. 7, 1867. — Having yesterday organized a party for the ascent of the active volcano of Makushin, laid down on the imperfect charts as six and a half miles in a straight line from the opening of the glacier valley of the western part of Captain's Harbor, with an elevation of 5,474 feet, they started this morning from the ship at 9.30 o'clock. The party consisted of Theodore Blake, geologist; Dr. Albert Kellogg, botanist; Lieutenant Hodgson; Engineer Ball; and two seamen, Welsh and Penny. The party, with the outfit and provisions, was rowed to the village of Illiouliouk, where a guide and three packers were obtained. These natives accompanied the party, but the guide had never ascended the mountain. They were landed at the entrance of the valley opening upon the northwest side of Captain's Harbor in Unalaska Bay, about seven miles from Illiouliouk and twelve miles from our vessel.

This valley is a full mile wide at the entrance, quite flat, swampy, covered with very high, coarse grass and bushes, drained very poorly by a stream flowing from the base of the volcano, and receiving numerous rivulets from the transverse valleys and gullies that border and hem it in with their steep slopes of nearly half a mile in height. This valley rises very gradually, not over one hundred feet in the first four miles, but contracts rapidly. The walking through it was very tiring, as the wet, soft, yielding nature of the turfy bottom of *Sphagnum* and heavy grass made it a dragging matter, especially to the leader. Dr. Kellogg was at once open to the botany, and seized every new plant or beautiful specimen of old acquaintance, while the others urged him to wait until they came back; but as he had his own load to pack, he felt equal to a few additional plants, and wisely secured the treasures, shrewdly guessing that the return home would be hurried, even with five days' provisions. The three aneroid barometers, which had been compared with the mercurial standard, and the three thermometers were read every hour. This afforded all a welcome breathing-spell.

At 5.30 P.M., after ascending a small slope at the head of the valley, they entered a ravine where the eight-foot Δ tent was pitched for camping. Close by it was a beautiful little crystal stream, fed by the melting ice above. A fire was started from the roots of bushes, as not a tree exists on the whole island; small willows had been passed in the valley, but they were only from one to three feet high.

The hot coffee, hard-tack, and broiled salt pork were enjoyed with that keen relish obtained only by such a party, intent upon pleasure when it is spiced by labor and the consciousness that no human foot has trod the summit of the volcano before them. The natives luxuriated in dried salmon and whale blubber. Some of our party tried these luxuries, but had not been reduced by hunger to appreciate their fine points. A matting of fern leaves eight inches deep was laid in the bottom of the tent, and made it really comfortable. The observations of the barometer made this station 472 feet above the sea. The day had been pleasant, with sunshine and high, fleecy clouds; but at half past seven the rains came down, and our tired travellers, who had been cramped for months on shipboard, wrapped themselves in their blankets and gladly sought sleep.

No less than nine persons were crowded into this small tent, including the four natives, about whose parasitical friends many grave suspicions were aroused. Sardines well packed were nothing compared to the "eternal fitness" of this crowd. It rained hard throughout the night, with strong gusts of wind; and the unnatural positions and discomfort of the party allowed little chance for sleep or fresh air. So they turned out at daylight, prepared and despatched a hasty breakfast, packed up their bundles and tent, and at seven o'clock commenced the ascent of the hill immediately over their tent. The ascent was sharp, for at eight o'clock they had risen to 1,278 feet above the sea. The hardest part of the route had been crawled along the sharp edge of a ridge formed by two ravines. When once this hill was gained, the view beneath and around was grand. Eternal snow covered Makushin; extinct volcanoes showed their red tops and furrowed lava-sides on either hand; and the valley the party had ascended was marked by the silver thread bearing icy water to the Bering Sea. Thence the ascent was over alternating small peaks and valleys, gaining an additional elevation of only 180 feet by nine o'clock, at which level snow was found in patches. At 9.30 A.M. they reached the base of a very steep mountain, which we afterwards saw from the vessel, — its almost perpendicular, black, scarred front looking like a great fortress on the outer flank of the snow-covered mountains. At its base the herbage was removed, and the earth at six inches below the surface was so hot that no one could bear his hands in it. The surface was cool; but, curiously enough, no one thought of observing the temperatures.

This extinct volcano is shaped liked the frustum of a cone; it is composed wholly of volcanic matter, and within recent years was in active eruption. The area of the top, which is composed of lava, scoria, and ashes, is about two acres.

At ten o'clock its summit was reached, and the elevation determined to be 1,927 feet above the sea. The station of 8 A.M. was seen about one and a half miles distant, and bore N. by E., magnetic.

After lunching, the party made a small descent of 172 feet, being the farthest point the guide had ever reached; so from here our people had to rely upon their own resources and judgment for success. The course now lay along the sides of steep mountains and steeper ravines, into whose deep chasms the loosened rocks would bound and rebound until lost with a dull, ominous sound that warned them of their fate if a misstep should befall them. Here they had evidence of the violence of Nature in rifting mountains; the mighty forces from beneath having upheaved, split, and torn them into every conceivable distortion, — with tops broken to fragments, sides marked by the lodgment of detached masses, and the deeps below filled with the *débris* of a thousand years.

Several plateaus were passed over, between which were deep ravines cut by the snow and ice. Down one of these the party managed to descend, and then travelled on the perfectly hard snow that lay in it, until at noon they reaced about the level of the lowest ice limit, being the foot of the glacier of Makushin, lying open to the Eastward (or Lincoln) Harbor, where the vessel was anchored. This was at an elevation of 1,969 feet. Here extensive moraines of lava and ashes were exhibited in furrows and ridges from six to thirty feet high, with side moraines. The width of this glacier was here about two thousand feet, and thirty feet thick, crossed by immense fissures, which we could see on a clear day from the ship, twelve miles distant. Along the north side of this glacier the party travelled, frequently impeded by fissures in the lava from three to five feet across, and from thirty to fifty feet deep.

At one o'clock, P.M., they were ascending along the glacier; and no vegetation was found to exist above the height they had reached, which was 2,528 feet above the sea. At two o'clock they had been travelling on the hard snow for two hundred yards, when the angle of inclination of the glacier surface was found to be by measurement at ten to twelve degrees, and the elevation 3,105 feet. At three o'clock the height was 3,287 feet, and at four they agreed to camp for the night, when after some search they found a small space of level lava protruding three feet above the snow. Clearing the ground of the débris, they pitched tent, and supped with gusto upon hard-tack and raw pork, devouring it with the whetted appetites of hungry but scientific wolves. No water was to be had; so each ate as much snow as he desired. The observed elevation of this camping station was 3,385 feet.

The day had been pleasant, but cloudy, with little wind. Makushin had been enveloped in clouds; and no one yet knew, from personal observation, whether it was an active volcano. It was agreed, before settling to their hard beds of lava, that in the morning all the *impedimenta* of the party should be left at this camp except life lines and provisions, and a push made for the crater. The night was very cold, the weather squally and accompanied by a fall of rain and snow; so that after a most uncomfortable night's rest, made somewhat solemn by the subterranean rumblings and an occasional rush, roar, and thunder of a bounding avalanche detached by rain and wind, at five o'clock in the morning (September 9) the party was ready to move, after a light, uncooked, and hurried breakfast. The top of the mountain was plainly in sight, but over two thousand feet above them, with smoke issuing from the crater, which lies to the northwest of the main peak, while the smell of sulphurous vapors was very strong. At this point the native guide and packers protested against advancing; but they were compelled to accompany the party, not only as packers, but to render assistance in case of accident, — a not at all improbable incident, as the travelling was now along the snow ridge at the inclination of fifteen to seventeen degrees, where it was necessary to stamp a foot-hole, and feel secure before advancing another step. At six o'clock an elevation of

3,532 feet was reached, and the weather became squally with rain and snow. The hard work of climbing made the party unheedful of the cold, which was now nearly down to freezing. At seven o'clock the elevation attained was 4,379 feet, and one barometer had reached its limit of action. Up to this time all of them had agreed remarkably well. At 8 A.M. the party were ascending at an angle of inclination of twenty-five degrees, had reached an elevation of 4,955 feet, and were in the clouds. Soon after eight o'clock the second barometer failed to record.

At one point below a projecting mass of lava some of the party were hauled up by ropes. Here was the most dangerous part of the ascent; for, had any one lost his foothold, he would have been precipitated down the sharp incline into some profound chasms to the eastward. From this standpoint of lava the party enjoyed a grand spectacle. In the far distance, on the sea horizon (which was eighty miles away), lay an island, and at their feet were the tops of extinct volcanoes that had loomed up as great mountains before reaching the levels of their summits, but were now relatively dwarfed to hills. Into many craters their eyes were the first to look. Whence had shot forth flame and stream and ashes and scoriae, now were beautiful lakes; where the mountain-sides had been covered with liquid lava and furrowed by molten torrents, now reposed broad lines of perpetual snow. To their vision all was sublime; to their minds it was food for deep and wondering reflection.

At nine o'clock the crater was discovered, shaped like an immense bowl, and about three hundred yards in diameter, with inner sloping sides composed of snow. The clouds rifted and opened for a few moments, and the smoke and vapors were seen issuing from an opening in the further side of the crater, directly in front of the party.

The elevation of the crater is 5,590 feet. Bordering it on the southern side is a steep cliff, up which the party ascended to catch a better glimpse of it; this was the summit of the mountain, and it is 5,691 feet above the ocean. For a few minutes the clouds broke away, and almost beneath the feet of the party lay the crater, rolling out volumes of smoke and yellow sulphurous vapors. It was bordered by treacherously overhanging snow, which some of the party proposed to reach and thus descend into it; but the clouds suddenly formed and shut out the spectacle. The opening in the crater whence the smoke and vapors were ejected was estimated to be one hundred yards in diameter, round, and sloping in like a cylindrical ring.

The party now rested for the clouds to dissipate, and employed their time in writing their names, the date of the ascent, the circumstances of their visit, etc.; this was placed in a bottle, and left upon the summit. The flag was secured to a staff carried up for that purpose, and left there. Lunch reconciled them to the clouds; but when that had been despatched, and the latter not only showed signs of persistence but changed to snow, they commenced the return. At this time the barometer stood at 23.68 inches, and the thermometer recorded 30°.5 Fahr.; and the distance in a direct line to the point of debarkation was estimated at eight miles.

So thick were the cloud and snow that it was impossible to see over ten feet ahead, and the descent became imperative while yet their tracks remained uncovered. In descending, a small detour was made to the right, passing close along the verge of the precipice, to obtain if possible a glimpse of the terrific chasms. But the dense cloud hid everything; and after some narrow escapes the party reached the snow limit (3,105 feet elevation) at three quarters past eleven, A.M., having stopped at their lava camp, made another meal off raw pork and hard-tack, and packed their tent and bedding. On the return the two barometers that had ceased their actions at certain elevations recommenced their record at the same elevations, and all three worked smoothly together. When the party reached the glacier, the driving snow and clouds were so dense that they could see nothing. On the glacier it was raining without the fog. They attempted to reach the valley by a rapid descent through one of the ravines, but it was found impracticable on account of the numerous cascades and their great heights; so they had to reclimb its steep side, and make a circuit around the ravines. At half past twelve, P.M., the ice-limit was reached (2,229 feet); this was firm, solid ice, and not in patches. At ten minutes past three the descent had been made to 1,589 feet, and at seven o'clock they reached the camping-ground of the first night. The thermometer stood at 46° Fahr. With the usual improvidence of the natives, the guide and packers had started with about half a supply of provisions; and the party, having generously shared with them, had now run short of bread. So, soon after seven o'clock, all hands turned in, tired out, and their hunger half appeased with uncooked "prog." It rained hard all night, but no one complained of sleeplessness.

William N. Byers
Climbs Longs Peak, 1868

W ILLIAM NEWTON BYERS, remembered today as the founder of the
Rocky Mountain News, was born in Ohio in 1831. By age nineteen
he had become a competent surveyor, and during the 1850s he
worked on various government surveys throughout the West. In 1859 he
bought a printing press and moved with it to Denver, and for the next two
decades he edited and published the *News*, that city's first newspaper. As was
often the case with frontier newspapermen, Byers was an enthusiastic booster
for the region. He promoted Denver relentlessly, served as a delegate to
Colorado's first constitutional convention, and agitated noisily for Congress to
do something about the territory's "Indian problem," helping whip up the
hysteria that led to the Sand Creek Massacre of 1864.

When Byers climbed Longs Peak in 1868, the prominent mountain had
long been considered "inaccessible." There is no trivial way up the peak; a
trail reaches the top today, but even the trail route involves an airy passage
that has been known to stop inexperienced climbers. The difficulty occurs at
the steep slab girdling the final summit, which, as Byers wrote, "presents the
appearance, in every direction, of being a great block of granite, perfectly
smooth and unbroken." Others had tried the ascent but failed to find a way
past this obstacle, and Byers was probably fortunate to have in his party a man
quite capable of facing the unknown: the explorer John Wesley Powell, who in
1869 would lead the first party to descend the length of the Grand Canyon.

The account below, sandwiched between notices of "Indian depra-
dations" and appeals to elect U. S. Grant president, appeared in the September 1, 1868, edition of *The Rocky Mountain News*.

August 20. The party destined for the ascent of Long's Peak, consisting of
Major J. W. Powell, W. H. Powell, I. W. Keplinger, Sam'l Garman, Ned E.
Farrell, John C. Sumner, and the writer, left camp at the west side of Grand
Lake, each mounted, and with one pack mule for the party. The mule was
laden with ten days' rations, though we expected to make the trip in much less
time. Each man carried his bedding under or behind his saddle, a pistol at his

Major John Wesley Powell

belt, and those not encumbered with instruments, took their guns. We had two barometers and two sets of thermometers.

Crossing the Grand where it leaves the lake, we made one half its circuit, around the northern shore, through a dense mass of brush and fallen timber, and at a point directly opposite our camp on the eastern shore, began the ascent of the mountain.

The lake is fed by two principal streams; one coming from the northeast and the other from the southeast. The first is about thirty feet wide and a foot deep, and the latter nearly double that size. The southeasterly branch has a roaring cascade a short distance from the mouth, which presents the curious phenomenon of quite as often sounding at the northeast side of the lake as in its true position. The stream is formed by two branches which unite a little way from the lake. They are all very rapid, and, as we learned, frequently interrupted by unbroken ledges or masses of rock which occasion the formation of deep lakes of greater or less extent.

Turning away from the lake at right angles, we followed up a sharp, narrow ridge, very steep, rocky and almost impassable on account of the fallen timber. Progress was necessarily slow, and we were full three hours making the first four miles. Then we entered green timber and got along much faster. In about seven miles from the starting point we reached the limit of timber growth and wound around the crest of the sharp, rocky ridge which forms the divide between the two streams before mentioned. The route is very rough and tortuous. On either side, thousands of feet below, are chains of little lakes, dark and solitary-looking in their inaccessibility. About five miles from the timber line we camped for the night, turning down, for that purpose, to the edge of the timber on our right. The barometer showed an altitude of about 11,500 feet, and the frost was quite sharp.

August 21. Our start was over much the same kind of country traversed in the afternoon yesterday; skirting around the side of a very lofty mountain; clambering over broken rocks, or climbing up or down to get around impassable ledges. In some places we pass over great snow banks, which are really the best travelling we find. At the end of a mile we came to an impassable precipice, which subsequent exploration proved to extend from the summit of the mountain on the left down to the stream on our right, and thence down parallel with it. We spent the day in searching for a place to get down or around it, but without success, and were compelled to go into camp, like the night before, at the timber line. We had proved one thing, that horses and mules could go no further, and we made preparations for proceeding on foot. The animals were turned loose to feed on the short, young grass of the mountain side; the trail by which we came down being barricaded by a few loose stones and a pole or two to prevent their going back. Escape in any other direction was impossible.

August 22. We were off at seven o'clock; each man with biscuit and bacon in his pockets for two days' rations. One or two carried blankets, but most preferred doing without to carrying them. Arms were also left behind. After some search a place was found where we descended the precipice — not without risk — then crossed a little valley, just at the timber line, and began the ascent of the range directly over a huge mountain which had the appearance of extending quite to Long's Peak. Gaining its summit, we found ourselves still further from our destination than we supposed we were the day before. Descending its precipitous northern face — which upon looking back appeared utterly impassable — we followed for a mile along a very low ridge, which is the real dividing range — then turned eastward along a similar ridge, which connects Long's Peak with the range. It has been generally supposed that the great mountain was a part of the range, though occupying an acute angle in it, but such is not the case. It is not less than two miles from the range, and all its waters flow toward the Atlantic. Following up this ridge, it soon culminated in a very lofty mountain, only a few hundred feet lower than Long's, but with a crest so narrow that some of the party became dizzy in traveling along it. This, we supposed, would lead us to the great mountain, but found the route cut off by impassable chasms when yet more than a mile distant. There remained but one route — to descend to the valley and climb again all that we had already twice made. Turning to the right, we clambered down with infinite labor to the valley of a branch of St. Vrain, where we went into camp at the extreme timber line. Some explorations were made, however, preparatory to tomorrow's labor; the most important by Mr. Keplinger, who ascended to within about eight hundred feet of the summit, and did not return until after dark. We became very uneasy about him, [f]earing that he would be unable to make his way down in safety. A man was sent to meet him, and bonfires kindled on some high rocks near us. An hour after dark they came in; Mr. K. with the report that the ascent might be possible, but he was not very sanguine. The night was a most cheerless one, with gusts of wind and sprinkles of rain; our only shelter under the sides of an immense boulder, where we shivered the long hours through.

August 23. Unexpectedly the day dawned fair, and at six o'clock we were facing the mountain. Approaching from the south our course was over a great rockslide and then up a steep gorge down which the broken stone had come. In many places it required the assistance of hands as well as feet to get along, and the ascent at best was very laborious. There was no extraordinary obstacle until within seven or eight hundred feet of the summit. Above that point the mountain presents the appearance, in every direction, of being a great block of granite, perfectly smooth and unbroken. Close examination, however, removed this delusion in some degree, and we were most agreeably surprised to find a passable way, though it required great caution, coolness, and infinite labor to make headway; life often depending upon a grasp of the fingers in a crevice that would hardly admit them. Before ten o'clock the entire party stood upon the extreme summit without accident or mishap of any kind.

The Peak is a nearly level surface, paved with irregular blocks of granite, and without vegetation of any kind, except a little gray lichen. The outline is nearly a parallelogram — east and west — widening a little toward the western extremity, and five or six acres in extent. On the eastern end are some large boulders, giving it an apparent altitude of ten or fifteen feet above the remainder of the surface. Along the northern edge, and especially at the northwest corner, the surface rounds off considerably, though the general appearance is almost that of a perfect level.

The view is very extensive in all directions; including Pike's Peak, south, the Sahwatch ranges southwest, Gore's range and the Elkhorn Mountains west, the Medicine Bow and Sweetwater ranges north, and a vast extent of the plains east. Denver is plainly distinguishable to the naked eye; also the Hot Springs in the Middle Park.

Barometric and thermometric observations were taken to determine altitude, and a monument erected to commemorate our visit. A record of the event with notes of the instrumental readings was deposited, along with other mementoes, in a tin case in the monument, and from a flag-staff on its summit a flag was unfurled and left floating in the breeze. After nearly three hours' stay on the Peak we began the descent, which occupied two hours. A snow squall enveloped us on the way down, but it lasted for only a few minutes. Over thirty Alpine lakes were counted from the summit.

Our way back down was by the head waters of St. Vrain; three considerable branches of which were crossed. The valley of each is filled with lakes alternated with great fields of snow. The latter is strewn with grasshoppers, which could be gathered by wagonloads. Upon these the bears were feasting, and the country seems to be literally infested with them. We saw two, and the tracks of others in every snow bank and soft spot of ground. We stopped for the night on the most westerly branch of the St. Vrain, and spent a second night without blankets around a camp fire, yet more cheerless because we were out of "grub."

August 24. — Without breakfast to eat or baggage to pack we had no impediment to an early start, and had almost reached the summit of the range before old Sol's greeting. Our path was up a great gorge, over a snowfield, then a frozen lake — a small part clear of ice — and then more snow to the summit. Then down an easier slope with grass, and boulders, and great, black ledges to the head of the Grand, and our old camp, where our stock had been left. A hasty but a hearty breakfast, and then we saddled up and retraced our trail along the mountain ridge, through the tangled, fallen timber, and around the lake to our old and pleasant camp. We had been gone only five days; had been eminently successful, and of course were satisfied; the more so because the mountain had always before been pronounced inaccessible, and ours was the first party that had ever set foot upon its summit.

Messrs. Keplinger and Garman were left at our mountain camp to make a series of barometrical observations on the summit of a very high mountain near by, extending through eight or ten days, to aid in calculating the altitude of other neighboring points where less frequent readings were made.

August 25. — Returned to the Springs, finding there a camp of near one hundred visitors who had come in during our nine days' absence. The Indians have all left; pulling down their lodges and going off very suddenly this morning. It is said they have gone toward the South Park.

John Muir Climbs
Mount Ritter, 1871

N O ONE KNEW America's mountains as well, or did as much for them, as John Muir. Born in 1838 in Dunbar, Scotland, Muir was schooled early in Latin and French and compelled as a boy to memorize long passages from the King James version of the Bible, an experience painful at the time but probably responsible for much of the rhythm and clarity of his prose. When Muir was eleven the family emigrated to the United States, settling eventually in the Wisconsin outback. There Muir worked long, hard hours on the farm, developing the physical endurance that later would serve him so well in the mountains.

After a stint at college, where he studied geology and chemistry, Muir gained a reputation as a sort of mechanical genius. He might have gone on to a career as an inventor had it not been for the famous accident that so profoundly changed his life. In 1867 a file slipped from his hand and temporarily blinded him; the experience convinced him to give up mechanics and devote himself instead to understanding the workings of the natural world, which he thought of as the inventions of God. Soon afterward, Muir set out on his "thousand-mile walk to the Gulf," a journey that took him across the Appalachian Mountains and south to Florida. He had originally planned to continue on to the Caribbean and South America, but instead, after a bout with malaria, he sailed via the Isthmus of Panama to California, then spent the pivotal summer of 1869 in the Yosemite region. This proved to be the first of many years spent climbing peaks and studying the remarkable glacial geology of the Sierra Nevada. As both climber and scientist, Muir proved to be ahead of his time. Several of his ascents were notably harder than any previously done in America, and his geological observations – which included the discovery of living glaciers in the Sierra and led him to conclude that Yosemite Valley had been carved by glaciation into its final striking form – were eventually confirmed as accurate, even though they had escaped the notice of the government-sponsored geologists of the Brewer Survey.

The Sierra Nevada affected Muir deeply. When, after years of solitary exploring, he finally left his beloved mountains and rejoined society, it was to awaken the nation to the wonders he had seen. He began writing about his experiences, and soon had been published on both coasts. He became a lecturer and a leader in the forest conservation movement. In 1889 he camped in Yosemite with Robert Underwood Johnson, his editor at *The Century*; Johnson was so impressed with the Sierra, and so dismayed by the commercial interests already destroying it, that he joined with Muir to help establish Yosemite National Park. Later Muir helped found the Sierra Club, and with it, some say, the environmental movement.

In his many conservation campaigns, Muir's primary weapon was his pen. He had an engaging prose style, rooted in the Bible and the work of poets such as Milton and Burns, whose books he carried in his knapsack when the weight might more sensibly have been reserved for bread or blankets. He took copious notes in the field, using them later as the basis for his ten books and numerous magazine articles. The essay below, one of his most polished, was first published as "A Near View of the High Sierra" in *The Overland Monthly* in 1872 and then included in *The Mountains of California*, which, in 1894, was the first of his books to be published.

Muir was the most skilled American climber of his day. Many of his routes are steep and exposed enough that those following in his footsteps have been glad of a rope, yet Muir climbed them alone. His spartan style has become legendary, and is plainly evident in the story below, in which Muir bivouacs without tent or blanket – in mid-October, at eleven thousand feet – and then sets off casually in the morning, without so much as an ice axe or a coat, for the top of a 13,157-foot peak. The ascent proves difficult enough that Muir must draw repeatedly on his route-finding skill. Even so, he finds himself trapped on the crucial passage of the climb, gripped with fear and unable to move either up or down – until the "stifling smoke" clears from his mind and he finds himself possessed of that mysterious power that has fascinated so many mountaineers since. Muir's description of that power, so central to the climbing experience, is one of the most moving passages in the literature, and makes this essay a classic of the genre.

Early one bright morning in the middle of Indian summer, while the glacier meadows were still crisp with frost crystals, I set out from the foot of Mount Lyell, on my way down to Yosemite Valley, to replenish my exhausted store of bread and tea. I had spent the past summer, as many preceding ones, exploring the glaciers that lie on the head waters of the San Joaquin, Tuolumne, Merced, and Owen's rivers, measuring and studying their movements, trends, crevasses, moraines, etc., and the part they had played during the period of their greater extension in the creation and development of the landscapes of this alpine wonderland. The time for this kind of work was nearly over for the year, and I began to look forward with delight to the approaching winter with its wondrous storms, when I would be warmly snow-bound in my Yosemite cabin with plenty of bread and books; but a tinge of regret came on when I considered that possibly I might not see this favorite region again until the next summer, excepting distant views from the heights about the Yosemite walls.

To artists, few portions of the High Sierra are, strictly speaking, pictur-esque. The whole massive uplift of the range is one great picture, not clearly divisible into smaller ones, differing much in this respect from the older, and what may be called, riper mountains of the Coast Range. All the landscapes of the Sierra, as we have seen, were born again, remodeled from base to summit by the developing ice-floods of the last glacial winter. But all these new land-scapes were not brought forth simultaneously; some of the highest, where the ice lingered longest, are tens of centuries younger than those of the warmer regions below them. In general, the younger the mountain-landscapes, — younger, I mean, with reference to the time of their emergence from the ice of the glacial period, — the less separable are they into artistic bits capable of being made into warm, sympathetic, lovable pictures with appreciable human-ity in them.

Here, however, on the head waters of the Tuolumne, is a group of wild peaks on which the geologist may say that the sun has but just begun to shine, which is yet in a high degree picturesque, and in its main features so regular and evenly balanced as almost to appear conventional — one somber cluster of snow-laden peaks with gray pine-fringed granite bosses braided around its base, the whole surging free into the sky from the head of a magnificent valley, whose lofty walls are beveled away on both sides so as to embrace it all without admitting anything not strictly belonging to it. The foreground was now aflame with autumn colors, brown and purple and gold, ripe in the mellow sunshine; contrasting brightly with the deep, cobalt blue of the sky, and the black and gray, and pure, spiritual white of the rocks and glaciers. Down through the midst, the young Tuolumne was seen pouring from its crystal fountains, now resting in glassy pools as if changing back again into ice, now leaping in white cascades as if turning to snow; gliding right and left between granite bosses, then sweeping on through the smooth, meadowy levels of the valley, swaying pensively from side to side with calm, stately gestures past dipping willows and sedges, and around groves of arrowy pine; and through-out its whole eventful course, whether flowing fast or slow, singing loud or low, ever filling the landscape with spiritual animation, and manifesting the gran-deur of its sources in every movement and tone.

Pursuing my lonely way down the valley, I turned again and again to gaze on the glorious picture, throwing up my arms to inclose it as in a frame. After long ages of growth in the darkness beneath the glaciers, through sunshine and storms, it seemed now to be ready and waiting for the elected artist, like yellow wheat for the reaper; and I could not help wishing that I might carry colors and brushes with me on my travels, and learn to paint. In the mean time I had to be content with photographs on my mind and sketches in my note-books. At length, after I had rounded a precipitous headland that puts out from the west wall of the valley, every peak vanished from sight, and I pushed rapidly along the frozen meadows, over the divide between the waters of the Merced and Tuolumne, and down through the forests that clothe the slopes of Cloud's Rest, arriving in Yosemite in due time — which, with me, is *any* time. And, strange to say, among the first people I met here were two artists who, with letters of introduction, were awaiting my return. They inquired whether in the course of my explorations in the adjacent mountains I had ever come upon a landscape suitable for a large painting; whereupon I began a description of the one that had so lately excited my admiration. Then, as I went on further and further

into details, their faces began to glow, and I offered to guide them to it, while they declared that they would gladly follow, far or near, whithersoever I could spare the time to lead them.

Since storms might come breaking down through the fine weather at any time, burying the colors in snow, and cutting off the artists' retreat, I advised getting ready at once.

I led them out of the valley by the Vernal and Nevada Falls, thence over the main dividing ridge to the Big Tuolumne Meadows, by the old Mono trail, and thence along the upper Tuolumne River to its head. This was my companions' first excursion into the High Sierra, and as I was almost always alone in my mountaineering, the way that the fresh beauty was reflected in their faces made for me a novel and interesting study. They naturally were affected most of all by the colors—the intense azure of the sky, the purplish grays of the granite, the red and browns of dry meadows, and the translucent purple and crimson of huckleberry bogs; the flaming yellow of aspen groves, the silvery flashing of the streams, and the bright green and blue of the glacier lakes. But the general expression of the scenery — rocky and savage — seemed sadly disappointing; and as they threaded the forest from ridge to ridge, eagerly scanning the landscapes as they were unfolded, they said: "All this is huge and sublime, but we see nothing as yet at all available for effective pictures. Art is long, and art is limited, you know; and here are foregrounds, middle-grounds, backgrounds, all alike; bare rock-waves, woods, groves, diminutive flecks of meadow, and strips of glittering water." "Never mind," I replied, "only bide a wee, and I will show you something you will like."

At length, toward the end of the second day, the Sierra Crown began to come into view, and when we had fairly rounded the projecting headland before mentioned, the whole picture stood revealed in the flush of the alpenglow. Their enthusiasm was excited beyond bounds, and the more impulsive of the two, a young Scotchman, dashed ahead, shouting and gesticulating and tossing his arms in the air like a madman. Here, at last, was a typical alpine landscape.

After feasting awhile on the view, I proceeded to make camp in a sheltered grove a little way back from the meadow, where pine-boughs could be obtained for beds, and where there was plenty of dry wood for fires, while the artists ran here and there, along the river-bends and up the sides of the cañon, choosing foregrounds for sketches. After dark, when our tea was made and a rousing fire had been built, we began to make our plans. They decided to remain several days, at the least, while I concluded to make an excursion in the mean time to the untouched summit of Ritter.

It was now about the middle of October, the springtime of snow-flowers. The first winter-clouds had already bloomed, and the peaks were strewn with fresh crystals, without, however, affecting the climbing to any dangerous extent. And as the weather was still profoundly calm, and the distance to the foot of the mountain only a little more than a day, I felt that I was running no great risk of being storm-bound.

Mount Ritter is king of the mountains of the middle portion of the High Sierra, as Shasta of the north and Whitney of the south sections. Moreover, as far as I know, it had never been climbed. I had explored the adjacent wilderness summer after summer, but my studies thus far had never drawn me to the top of it. Its height above sea level is about 13,300 feet [actually 13,157 feet], and it is fenced round by steeply inclined glaciers, and cañons of tremendous depth and ruggedness, which render it almost inaccessible. But difficulties of this kind only exhilarate the mountaineer.

Next morning, the artists went heartily to their work and I to mine. Former experiences had given good reason to know that passionate storms, invisible as yet, might be brooding in the calm sun-gold; therefore, before bidding farewell, I warned the artists not to be alarmed should I fail to appear before a week or ten days, and advised them, in case a snow-storm should set in, to keep up big fires and shelter themselves as best they could, and on no account to become frightened and attempt to seek their way back to Yosemite alone through the drifts.

My general plan was simply this: to scale the cañon wall, cross over to the eastern flank of the range, and then make my way southward to the northern spurs of Mount Ritter in compliance with the intervening topography; for to push on directly southward from camp through the innumerable peaks and pinnacles that adorn this portion of the axis of the range, however interesting, would take too much time, besides being extremely difficult and dangerous at this time of year.

All my first day was pure pleasure, simply mountaineering indulgence, crossing the dry pathways of the ancient glaciers, tracing happy streams, and learning the habits of the birds and marmots in the groves and rocks. Before I had gone a mile from camp, I came to the foot of a white cascade that beats its way down a rugged gorge in the cañon wall, from a height of about nine hundred feet, and pours its throbbing waters into the Tuolumne. I was acquainted with its fountains, which, fortunately, lay in my course. What a fine traveling companion it proved to be, what songs it sang, and how passionately it told the mountains' own joy! Gladly I climbed along its dashing border, absorbing its divine music, and bathing from time to time in waftings of irised spray. Climbing higher, higher, new beauty came streaming on the sight: painted meadows, late-blooming gardens, peaks of rare architecture, lakes here and there, shining like silver, and glimpses of the forested middle region and the yellow lowlands far in the west. Beyond the range I saw the so-called Mono Desert, lying dreamily silent in thick purple light — a desert of heavy sun-glare beheld from a desert of ice-burnished granite. Here the waters divide, shouting in glorious enthusiasm, and falling eastward to vanish in the volcanic sands and dry sky of the Great Basin, or westward to the Great Valley of California, and thence through the Bay of San Francisco and the Golden Gate to the sea.

Passing a little way down over the summit until I had reached an elevation of about 10,000 feet, I pushed on southward toward a group of savage peaks that stand guard about Ritter on the north and west, groping my way, and dealing instinctively with every obstacle as it presented itself. Here a huge gorge would be found cutting across my path, along the dizzy edge of which I scrambled until some less precipitous point was discovered where I might safely venture to the bottom and then, selecting some feasible portion of the opposite wall, reascend with the same slow caution. Massive, flat-topped spurs alternate with the gorges, plunging abruptly from the shoulders of the snowy peaks, and planting their feet in the warm desert. These were everywhere marked and adorned with characteristic sculptures of the ancient glaciers that swept over this entire region like one vast ice-wind, and the polished surfaces produced by the ponderous flood are still so perfectly preserved that in many places the sunlight reflected from them is about as trying to the eyes as sheets of snow.

God's glacial mills grind slowly, but they have been kept in motion long enough in California to grind sufficient soil for a glorious abundance of life, though most of the grist has been carried to the lowlands, leaving these high regions comparatively lean and bare; while the post-glacial agents of erosion have not yet furnished sufficient available food over the general surface for more than a few tufts of the hardiest plants, chiefly carices and eriogonae. And it is interesting to learn in this connection that the sparseness and repressed character of the vegetation at this height is caused more by want of soil than by harshness of climate; for, here and there, in sheltered hollows (countersunk beneath the general surface) into which a few rods of well-ground moraine chips have been dumped, we find groves of spruce and pine thirty to forty feet high, trimmed around the edges with willow and huckleberry bushes, and oftentimes still further by an outer ring of tall grasses, bright with lupines, larkspurs, and showy columbines, suggesting a climate by no means repressingly severe. All the streams, too, and the pools at this elevation are furnished with little gardens wherever soil can be made to lie, which, though making scarce any show at a distance, constitute charming surprises to the appreciative observer. In these bits of leafiness a few birds find grateful homes. Having no acquaintance with man, they fear no ill, and flock curiously about the stranger, almost allowing themselves to be taken in the hand. In so wild and so beautiful a region was spent my first day, every sight and sound inspiring, leading one far out of himself, yet feeding and building up his individuality.

Now came the solemn, silent evening. Long, blue, spiky shadows crept out across the snow-fields, while a rosy glow, at first scarce discernible, gradually deepened and suffused every mountain-top, flushing the glaciers and the harsh crags above them. This was the alpenglow, to me one of the most impressive of all the terrestrial manifestations of God. At the touch of this divine light, the mountains seemed to kindle to a rapt, religious consciousness, and stood hushed and waiting like devout worshipers. Just before the alpenglow began to fade, two crimson clouds came streaming across the summit like wings of flame, rendering the sublime scene yet more impressive; then came darkness and the stars.

Icy Ritter was still miles away, but I could proceed no farther that night. I found a good camp-ground on the rim of a glacier basin about 11,000 feet above the sea. A small lake nestles in the bottom of it, from which I got water for my tea, and a stormbeaten thicket nearby furnished abundance of resiny fire-wood. Somber peaks, hacked and shattered, circled half-way around the horizon, wearing a savage aspect in the gloaming, and a waterfall chanted solemnly across the lake on its way down from the foot of a glacier. The fall and the lake and the glacier were almost equally bare; while the scraggy pines anchored in the rock-fissures were so dwarfed and shorn by storm-winds that you might walk over their tops. In tone and aspect the scene was one of the most desolate I ever beheld. But the darkest scriptures of the mountains are illumined with bright passages of love that never fail to make themselves felt when one is alone.

I made my bed in a nook of the pine-thicket, where the branches were pressed and crinkled overhead like a roof, and bent down around the sides. These are the best bedchambers the high mountains afford—snug as squirrel-nests, well ventilated, full of spicy odors, and with plenty of wind-played needles to sing one asleep. I little expected company, but, creeping in through a low side-door, I found five or six birds nestling among the tassels. The night-wind began to blow soon after dark; at first only a gentle breathing, but increasing toward midnight to a rough gale that fell upon my leafy roof in ragged surges like a cascade, bearing wild sounds from the crags overhead. The waterfall sang in chorus, filling the old ice-fountain with its solemn roar, and seeming to increase in power as the night advanced—fit voice for such a landscape. I had to creep out many times to the fire during the night, for it was biting cold and I had no blankets. Gladly I welcomed the morning star.

The dawn in the dry, wavering air of the desert was glorious. Everything encouraged my undertaking and betokened success. There was no cloud in the sky, no storm-tone in the wind. Breakfast of bread and tea was soon made. I fastened a hard, durable crust to my belt by way of provision, in case I should be compelled to pass a night on the mountain-top; then, securing the remainder of my little stock against wolves and wood-rats, I set forth free and hopeful.

How glorious a greeting the sun gives the mountains! To behold this alone is worth the pains of any excursion a thousand time over. The highest peaks burned like islands in a sea of liquid shade. Then the lower peaks and spires caught the glow, and long lances of light, streaming through many a notch and pass, fell thick on the frozen meadows. The majestic form of Ritter was full in sight, and I pushed rapidly on over rounded rock-bosses and pavements, my iron-shod shoes making a clanking sound, suddenly hushed now and then in rugs of bryanthus, and sedgy lake-margins soft as moss. Here, too, in this so-called "land of desolation," I met cassiope, growing in fringes among the battered rocks. Her blossoms had faded long ago, but they were still clinging with happy memories to the evergreen sprays, and still so beautiful as to thrill every fiber of one's being. Winter and summer, you may hear her voice, the low, sweet melody of her purple bells. No evangel among all the mountain plants speaks Nature's love more plainly than cassiope. Where she dwells, the re-demption of the coldest solitude is complete. The very rocks and glaciers seem to feel her presence, and become imbued with her fountain sweetness. All things were warming and awakening. Frozen rills began to flow, the marmots came out of their nests in boulder-piles and climbed sunny rocks to bask, and the dun-headed sparrows were flitting about seeking their breakfasts. The lakes seen from every ridge-top were brilliantly rippled and spangled, shim-mering like the thickets of the low Dwarf Pines. The rocks, too, seemed responsive to the vital heat — rock-crystals and snow-crystals thrilling alike. I strode on exhilarated, as if never more to feel fatigue, limbs moving of them-selves, every sense unfolding like the thawing flowers, to take part in the new day harmony.

All along my course thus far, excepting when down in the cañons, the landscapes were mostly open to me, and expansive, at least on one side. On the left were the purple plains of Mono, reposing dreamily and warm; on the right, the near peaks springing keenly into the thin sky with more and more impressive sublimity. But these larger views were at length lost. Rugged spurs, and moraines, and huge, projecting buttresses began to shut me in. Every feature became more rigidly alpine, without, however, producing any chilling effect; for going to the mountains is like going home. We always find that the strangest objects in these fountain wilds are in some degree familiar, and we look upon them with a vague sense of having seen them before.

On the southern shore of a frozen lake, I encountered an extensive field of hard, granular snow, up which I scampered in fine tone, intending to follow it to its head, and cross the rocky spur against which it leans, hoping thus to come direct upon the base of the main Ritter peak. The surface was pitted with oval hollows, made by stones and drifted pine needles that had melted them-selves into the mass by the radiation of absorbed sun-heat. These afforded good footholds, but the surface curved more and more steeply at the head, and the pits became shallower and less abundant, until I found myself in danger of being shed off like avalanching snow. I persisted, however, creeping on all fours, and shuffling up the smoothest places on my back, as I had often done on burnished granite, until after slipping several times, I was compelled to retrace my course to the bottom, and make my way around the west end of the lake, and thence up to the summit of the divide between the headwaters of Rush Creek and the northernmost tributaries of the San Joaquin.

Arriving on the summit of this dividing crest, one of the most exciting pieces of pure wilderness was disclosed that I ever discovered in all my moun-taineering. There, immediately in front, loomed the majestic mass of Mount Ritter, with a glacier swooping down its face nearly to my feet, then curving westward and pouring its frozen flood into a dark blue lake, whose shores were bound with precipices of crystalline snow; while a deep chasm drawn between the divide and the glacier separated the massive picture from everything else. I could see only the one sublime mountain, the one glacier, the one lake; the whole veiled with one blue shadow — rock, ice, and water close together without a single leaf or sign of life. After gazing spellbound, I began instinctively to scrutinize every notch and gorge and weathered buttress of the mountain, with reference to making the ascent. The entire front above the glacier appeared as one tremendous precipice, slightly receding at the top, and bristling with spires and pinnacles set above one another in formidable array. Massive lichen-stained battlements stood forward here and there, hacked at the top with angular notches, and separated by frosty gullies and recesses that have been veiled in shadow ever since their creation; while to right and left, as far as I could see, were huge, crumbling buttresses, offering no hope to the climber. The head of the glacier sends up a few finger-like branches through narrow *couloirs*; but these seemed too steep and short to be available, especially as I had no ax with which to cut steps, and the numerous narrow-throated gullies down which stones and snow are avalanched seemed hopelessly steep, besides being interrupted by vertical cliffs; while the whole front was rendered still more terribly forbidding by the chill shadow and the gloomy blackness of the rocks.

Descending the divide in a hesitating mood, I picked my way across the yawning chasm at the foot, and climbed out upon the glacier. There were no meadows now to cheer with their brave colors, nor could I hear the dun-headed sparrows, whose cheery notes so often relieve the silence of our highest mountains. The only sounds were the gurgling of small rills down in the veins and crevasses of the glacier, and now and then the rattling report of falling stones, with the echoes they shot out into the crisp air.

I could not distinctly hope to reach the summit from this side, yet I moved on across the glacier as if driven by fate. Contending with myself, the season is too far spent, I said, and even should I be successful, I might be storm-bound on the mountain; and in the cloud-darkness, with the cliffs and crevasses covered with snow, how could I escape? No; I must wait till next summer. I would only approach the mountain now, and inspect it, creep about its flanks, learn what I could of its history, holding myself ready to flee on the approach of the first storm-cloud. But we little know until tried how much of the uncontrollable there is in us, urging across glaciers and torrents, and up dangerous heights, let the judgment forbid as it may.

I succeeded in gaining the foot of the cliff on the eastern extremity of the glacier, and there discovered the mouth of a narrow avalanche gully, through which I began to climb, intending to follow it as far as possible, and at least obtain some fine wild views for my pains. Its general course is oblique to the plane of the mountain-face, and the metamorphic slates of which the mountain is built are cut by cleavage planes in such a way that they weather off in angular blocks, giving rise to irregular steps that greatly facilitate climbing on the sheer places. I thus made my way into a wilderness of crumbling spires and battlements, built together in bewildering combinations, and glazed in many places with a thin coating of ice, which I had to hammer off with stones. The situation was becoming gradually more perilous; but, having passed several dangerous spots, I dared not think of descending; for, so steep was the entire ascent, one would inevitably fall to the glacier in case a single misstep were made. Knowing, therefore, the tried danger beneath, I became all the more anxious concerning the developments to be made above, and began to be conscious of a vague foreboding of what actually befell; not that I was given to fear, but rather because my instincts, usually so positive and true, seemed vitiated in some way, and were leading me astray. At length, after attaining an elevation of about 12,800 feet, I found myself at the foot of a sheer drop in the bed of the avalanche channel I was tracing, which seemed absolutely to bar further progress. It was only about forty-five or fifty feet high, and somewhat roughened by fissures and projections; but these seemed so slight and insecure, as footholds, that I tried hard to avoid the precipice altogether, by scaling the wall of the channel on either side. But, though less steep, the walls were smoother than the obstructing rock, and repeated efforts only showed that I must either go right ahead or turn back. The tried dangers beneath seemed even greater than that of the cliff in front; therefore, after scanning its face again and again, I began to scale it, picking my holds with intense caution. After gaining a point about halfway to the top, I was suddenly brought to a dead stop, with arms outspread, clinging close to the face of the rock, unable to move hand or foot either up or down. My doom appeared fixed. I *must* fall. There would be a moment of bewilderment, and then a lifeless rumble down the one general precipice to the glacier below.

When this final danger flashed upon me, I became nerve-shaken for the first time since setting foot on the mountains, and my mind seemed to fill with a stifling smoke. But this terrible eclipse lasted only a moment, when life blazed forth again with preternatural clearness. I seemed suddenly to become possessed of a new sense. The other self, bygone experiences, Instinct, or Guardian Angel, — call it what you will, — came forward and assumed control. Then my trembling muscles became firm again, every rift and flaw in the rock was seen as through a microscope, and my limbs moved with a positiveness and precision with which I seemed to have nothing at all to do. Had I been borne aloft upon wings, my deliverance could not have been more complete.

Above this memorable spot, the face of the mountain is still more savagely hacked and torn. It is a maze of yawning chasms and gullies, in the angles of which rise beetling crags and piles of detached boulders that seem to have been gotten ready to be launched below. But the strange influx of strength I received seemed inexhaustible. I found a way without effort, and soon stood upon the topmost crag in the blessed light.

How truly glorious the landscape circled around this noble summit! — giant mountains, valleys innumerable, glaciers and meadows, rivers and lakes, with the wide blue sky bent tenderly over them all. But in my first hour of freedom from that terrible shadow, the sunlight in which I was laving seemed all in all.

Looking southward along the axis of the range, the eye is first caught by a row of exceedingly sharp and slender spires, which rise openly to a height of about a thousand feet, above a series of short, residual glaciers that lean back against their bases; their fantastic sculpture and the unrelieved sharpness with which they spring out of the ice rendering them peculiarly wild and striking. These are "The Minarets." Beyond them you behold a sublime wilderness of mountains, their snowy summits towering together in crowded abundance, peak beyond peak, swelling higher, higher as they sweep on southward, until the culminating point of the range is reached on Mount Whitney, near the head of the Kern River, at an elevation of nearly 14,700 feet above the level of the sea.

Westward, the general flank of the range is seen flowing sublimely away from the sharp summits, in smooth undulations; a sea of huge gray granite waves dotted with lakes and meadows, and fluted with stupendous cañons that grow steadily deeper as they recede in the distance. Below this gray region lies the dark forest zone, broken here and there by upswelling ridges and domes; and yet beyond lies a yellow, hazy belt, marking the broad plain of the San Joaquin, bounded on its farther side by the blue mountains of the coast.

Turning now to the northward, there in the immediate foreground is the glorious Sierra Crown, with Cathedral Peak, a temple of marvelous architecture, a few degrees to the left of it; the gray, massive form of Mammoth Mountain to the right; while Mounts Ord, Gibbs, Dana, Conness, Tower Peak, Castle Peak, Silver Mountain, and a host of noble companions, as yet nameless, make a sublime show along the axis of the range.

Eastward, the whole region seems a land of desolation covered with beautiful light. The torrid volcanic basin of Mono, with its one bare lake fourteen miles long; Owen's Valley and the broad lava table-land at its head, dotted with craters, and the massive Inyo Range, rivaling even the Sierra in height; these are spread, map-like, beneath you, with countless ranges beyond, passing and overlapping one another and fading on the glowing horizon.

At a distance of less than 3,000 feet below the summit of Mount Ritter you may find tributaries of the San Joaquin and Owen's rivers, bursting forth from the ice and snow of the glaciers that load its flanks; while a little to the north of here are found the highest affluents of the Tuolumne and Merced.

Thus, the fountains of four of the principal rivers of California are within a radius of four or five miles.

Lakes are seen gleaming in all sorts of places, — round, or oval, or square, like very mirrors; others narrow and sinuous, drawn close around the peaks like silver zones, the highest reflecting only rocks, snow and the sky. But neither these nor the glaciers, nor the bits of brown meadow and moorland that occur here and there, are large enough to make any marked impression upon the mighty wilderness of mountains. The eye, rejoicing in its freedom, roves about the vast expanse, yet returns again and again to the fountain peaks. Perhaps some one of the multitude excites special attention, some gigantic castle with turret and battlement, or some Gothic cathedral more abundantly spired than Milan's. But, generally, when looking for the first time from an all-embracing standpoint like this, the inexperienced observer is oppressed by the incomprehensible grandeur, variety, and abundance of the mountains rising shoulder to shoulder beyond the reach of vision; and it is only after they have been studied one by one, long and lovingly, that their far-reaching harmonies become manifest. Then, penetrate the wilderness where you may, the main telling features, to which all the surrounding topography is subordinate, are quickly perceived, and the most complicated clusters of peaks stand revealed harmoniously correlated and fashioned like works of art— eloquent monuments of the ancient ice-rivers that brought them into relief from the general mass of the range. The cañons, too, some of them a mile deep, mazing wildly through the mighty host of mountains, however lawless and ungovernable at first sight they appear, are at length recognized as the necessary effects of causes which followed each other in harmonious sequence—Nature's poems carved on tables of stone—the simplest and most emphatic of her glacial compositions.

Could we have been here to observe during the glacial period, we should have overlooked a wrinkled ocean of ice as continuous as that now covering the landscapes of Greenland; filling every valley and cañon with only the tops of the fountain peaks rising darkly above the rock-encumbered ice-waves like islets in a stormy sea—those islets the only hints of the glorious landscapes now smiling in the sun. Standing here in the deep, brooding silence all the wilderness seems motionless, as if the work of creation were done. But in the midst of this outer steadfastness we know there is incessant motion and change. Ever and anon, avalanches are falling from yonder peaks. These cliff-bound glaciers, seemingly wedged and immovable, are flowing like water and grinding the rocks beneath them. The lakes are lapping their granite shores and wearing them away, and every one of these rills and young rivers is fretting the air into music, and carrying the mountains to the plains. Here are the roots of all the life of the valleys, and here more simply than elsewhere is the eternal flux of nature manifested. Ice changing to water, lakes to meadows, and mountains to plains. And while we thus contemplate Nature's methods of landscape creation, and, reading the records she has carved on the rocks, reconstruct, however imperfectly, the landscapes of the past, we also learn as these we now behold have succeeded those of the pre-glacial age, so they in turn are withering and vanishing to be succeeded by others yet unborn.

But in the midst of these fine lessons and landscapes, I had to remember that the sun was wheeling far to the west, while a new way down the mountain had to be discovered to some point on the timberline where I could have a fire; for I had not even burdened myself with a coat. I first scanned the western spurs, hoping some way might appear through which I might reach the northern glacier, and cross its snout; or pass around the lake into which it flows, and thus strike my morning track. This route was soon sufficiently unfolded to show that, if practicable at all, it would require so much time that reaching camp that night would be out of the question. I therefore scrambled back eastward, descending the southern slopes obliquely at the same time. Here the crags seemed less formidable, and the head of a glacier that flows northeast came in sight, which I determined to follow as far as possible, hoping thus to make my way to the foot of the peak on the east side, and thence across the intervening cañons and ridges to camp.

The inclination of the glacier is quite moderate at the head, and, as the sun had softened the *névé,* I made safe and rapid progress, running and sliding, and keeping up a sharp outlook for crevasses. About half a mile from the head, there is an ice-cascade, where the glacier pours over a sharp declivity and is shattered into massive blocks separated by deep, blue fissures. To thread my way through the slippery mazes of this crevassed portion seemed impossible, and I endeavored to avoid it by climbing off to the shoulder of the mountain. But the slopes rapidly steepened and at length fell away into sheer precipices, compelling a return to the ice. Fortunately, the day had been warm enough to loosen the ice-crystals so as to admit of hollows being dug in the rotten portions of the blocks, thus enabling me to pick my way with far less difficulty than I had anticipated. Continuing down over the snout, and along the left lateral moraine, was only a confident saunter, showing that the ascent of the mountain by way of this glacier is easy, provided one is armed with an ax to cut steps here and there.

The lower end of the glacier was beautifully waved and barred by the outcropping edges of the bedded ice-layers which represent the annual snowfalls, and to some extent the irregularities of structure caused by the weathering of the walls of crevasses, and by separate snowfalls which have been followed by rain, hail, thawing and freezing, etc. Small rills were gliding and swirling over the melting surface with a smooth, oily appearance, in channels of pure ice — their quick, compliant movements contrasting most impressively with the rigid, invisible flow of the glacier itself, on whose back they all were riding.

Night drew near before I reached the eastern base of the mountain, and my camp lay many a rugged mile to the north; but ultimate success was assured. It was now only a matter of endurance and ordinary mountain-craft. The sunset was, if possible, yet more beautiful than that of the day before. The Mono landscape seemed to be fairly saturated with warm, purple light. The peaks marshalled along the summit were in shadow, but through every notch and pass streamed vivid sunfire, soothing and irradiating their rough, black angles, while companies of small, luminous clouds hovered above them like very angels of light.

Darkness came on, but I found my way by the trends of the cañons and the peaks projected against the sky. All excitement died with the light, and then I was weary. But the joyful sound of the waterfall across the lake was heard at last, and soon the stars were seen reflected in the lake itself. Taking my bearings from these, I discovered the little pine thicket in which my nest was, and then I had a rest such as only a tired mountaineer may enjoy. After lying loose and lost for awhile, I made a sunrise fire, went down to the lake, dashed water on my head, and dipped a cupful for tea. The revival brought about by bread and tea was as complete as the exhaustion from excessive enjoyment and toil. Then I crept beneath the pine tassels to bed. The wind was frosty and the fire burned low, but my sleep was none the less sound, and the evening constellations had swept far to the west before I awoke.

After thawing and resting in the morning sunshine, I sauntered home, — that is, back to the Tuolumne camp, — bearing away toward a cluster of peaks that hold the fountain snows of one of the north tributaries of Rush Creek. Here I discovered a group of beautiful glacier lakes, nestled together in a grand amphitheater. Toward evening, I crossed the divide separating the Mono waters from those of the Tuolumne, and entered the glacier basin that now holds the fountain snows of the stream that forms the upper Tuolumne cascades. This stream I traced down through its many dells and gorges, meadows and bogs, reaching the brink of the main Tuolumne at dusk.

A loud whoop for the artists was answered again and again. Their camp-fire came in sight, and half an hour afterward I was with them. They seemed unreasonably glad to see me. I had been absent only three days; nevertheless, though the weather was fine, they had already been weighing chances as to whether I would ever return, and trying to decide whether they should wait longer or begin to seek their way back to the lowlands. Now their curious troubles were over. They packed their precious sketches, and next morning we set out homeward bound, and in two days entered the Yosemite Valley from the north by way of Indian Cañon.

John Muir in the Minarets
and on Matterhorn Peak, 1873

MUIR WROTE HIS highly polished account of his Mount Ritter climb in the comfort of a warm study, hundreds of miles and many years removed from the actual event. But the story was based on a journal (Muir's "journal" is actually an assortment of more than sixty notebooks of varying types and sizes) composed on the spot, often by the light of a remote campfire after a hard day of climbing or in the shelter of some overhanging boulder during a snowstorm. Understandably, the journal is not as carefully structured and refined as Muir's books and magazine articles. Nonetheless it makes excellent reading. Never intended for an audience, it is more spontaneous and revealing than the finished work, more vivid and energetic. The excerpts below are typical, being shot through with stunning imagery and giving the reader an unveiled view of John Muir, the half-wild mountaineer, in action.

The ascents described below were made during Muir's last year of carefree climbing. After leaving the mountains in 1873, he decided his field studies had been completed and it was time to begin the work of making his beloved Sierra known to the world. That decision carried a personal cost. As a mountaineer Muir had been, as he once put it, too insignificant to be missed in the outside world, but in his self-appointed role as evangelist for the wilderness he became famous, and was soon bound up in the world of clocks and calendars, the constricting society of which for so many years he'd been gloriously free. It was also a decision for which we can be profoundly grateful, for it led to the formation of Yosemite National Park and the founding of the modern conservation movement. Muir's loss was our gain, and the account below is all the more poignant for being the product of Muir's final days of freedom in the mountains.

Set out early for the glaciers of the Minarets, and whatsoever else they had to give me. The morning was bright and bracing. I walked fast, for I feared noon rains. Besides, the Minarets have been waited for a long time. . . .

I saw six woodchucks — high livers all of them, at an altitude of ten thousand, seven hundred feet — on a sloping moraine meadow. They were fine burly sufficient-looking fellows, in every way equal to the situation.

▲

I thought of ascending the highest Minaret, which is the one farthest south, but, after scanning it narrowly, discovered it was inaccessible.

There is one small glacier on the west side near the south which I set out to examine. On the way I had to ascend or cross many *névés* and old moraines and rock bosses, domish in form, with which the bottom of the wide canyon is filled. At the foot of a former moraine of this west glacier is a small lake not one hundred yards long, but grandly framed with a sheer wall of *névé* twenty feet high. . . .

Beautiful caves reached from the water's edge; in some places granite walls overleaned and big blocks broke off from the main *névé* wall, and, with angles sharp as those of ice, leaned into the lake. Undermined by the water, the fissures filled with blue light, and water dripped and trickled all along the white walls. The sun was shining. I never saw so grand a setting for a glacier lake. The sharp peaks of Ritter seen over the snow shone with splendid effect.

The ascent from this rare lakelet to the foot of the moraine of the present glacier is about one hundred feet. This glacier has the appearance of being cut in two by a belt of avalanche rock reaching from the first of the cliffs above the glacier to its terminal moraine. This avalanche is quite recent, probably sent down by the Inyo earthquake of a year ago last twenty-sixth of March. Slate is able to stand earthquake action in much slimmer forms than granite. . . . This is the first instance I have discovered of a large avalanche on a glacier.

I wished to reach the head of this glacier, and after asaending a short distance came to where the avalanche by which I was making the attempt was so loosened by the melting of snow and ice beneath that it constantly gave way in small slides that rattled past with some danger. I therefore tried the glacier itself, but the surface was bare of snow, and steps had to be cut. This soon became tedious, and I again attempted to thread my way cautiously among the ill-settled avalanche stones. . . . At length I reached the top, examined the wall above the glacier, and thought it possibly might be scaled where avalanches descended. I worked cautiously up the face of the cliff above the ice, wild-looking and wilder every step. Soon I was halted by a dangerous step, passed it with knit lips, again halted, made [a] little foothold, with my hatchet. Again stopped, made a horizontal movement and avoided this place. Again I was stopped by fine gravel covering the only possible foot- or hand-holds. This I cleared away with the hatchet, holding on with one hand the while. It is hard to turn back, especially when the danger is certain either way. But now the sky was black as the rocks, and I saw the rain falling on the peaks of the Merced group. Besides, the rocks in the shapes they took seemed to be determined to baffle me. I decided to attempt return. After most delicate caution in searching for and making steps, I reached the head of the glacier. Cut steps again, and began to work my way down. Now the first lightning shot was fired among the crags overhead. The wind hissed and surged among the spires. Ritter was capped with cloud, yet loomed aloft higher. Oh, grandly the black spires came out on the pale edges of the storm-cloud heavy behind them! . . . More and more lightning, but as yet no rain fell here, although I saw it falling about Lyell [Mount Lyell, 13,114 feet, the highest point in Yosemite National Park]. I ran down the avalanche excitedly, half enjoying, half fearing. Clad free as a Highlander, I cared not for a wetting, yet thought I should endeavor to reach camp at once. I started, but, on passing along the face of the grand spire, made a dash for the summit of a pass nearly in the middle of the group of Minarets. I reached the top by careful climbing. The pass is exceedingly narrow, some places only a few feet wide, made by water and snow acting on dissoluble seams in the slate. . . . Walls of the pass were vertical, and grand beyond all description. A glorious view broke from the top—another glacier, of which I could see a strip through a yet narrower gorge pass of the east side, volcanoes of Mono, a section of a fine lake, also a good portion of the Inyo Mountains. A splendid irised cloud sallied overhead, the black clouds disappeared, while the wind played wild music on the Minarets as on an instrument.

I began to descend the east side of the glacier, which reached to the top of the pass. I had to cut my steps very carefully in the hard, clear ice, as a slip of one step would ensure a glissade of half a mile at death speed. I wedged myself most of the way through the lane-like gorge between the ice and wall, all the time cutting steps. Came out at last after many a halt for consideration of the position of my steps, and to look back upward at the wild, wild cliffs, and the wild, wild clouds rushing over them. It was a weird unhuman pathway, and as I now look back from my campfire, it seems strange I should have dared its perils.

————————————— ▲ —————————————

Wildly came the wind all through the half-lighted night, clouds black and cold hanging about the summits. But will attempt the Matterhorn [Muir's "Matterhorn" is probably Rodgers Peak, 12,978 feet]. Coffee, and away freelegged as any Highlander. Arrived at the summit after a stiff climb over *névés* and glaciers and loose, rocky taluses, but alack!—the Matterhorn was yet miles away and fenced off from the shattered crest I was on, by a series of

jagged, unscalable crests and glaciers that seemed steeper and glassier than any I had seen. After studying the situation like a chessboard, narrowly scanning each spiky wall and its glacier-guarded base, I made up my mind to the unhappy opinion that it would be wrong to incur so many dangers in seeking a way from this direction to the peak of the Matterhorn. I concluded to spend the day with three glaciers to the left towards Ritter, and seek the Matterhorn again next day by ascending a canyon leading up from the north.

Yet, in order to make sure of the practicability of even that route, I scaled the peak next me on the left [possibly Mount Davis, 12,311 feet] to get a wider view of the jagged zigzag topography. On reaching the top (twelve thousand feet), I saw it was possible to descend to one of the glaciers which before seemed to threaten so much, and that at its top it was not only snow-covered but less steeply inclined, and that on its shattered, precipitous headwall there was a narrow slot, three or four feet wide, which I could reach from the head of the glacier, and possibly descend on the south side into what promised to be a canyon leading up the highest *névés* of Matterhorn, towards which I could see a long, easy spur coming down from the summit.

It is hard give up a brave mountain, like the Matterhorn, that you have counted on for years, and the upshot of this new view was that I began to scramble down towards the first glacier that lay beneath me, reached it, struck my ax into its snow, and found it in good condition — crisp, yet not too hard. There were some crevasses that threatened, and in some places the schrund yawned in what is called a cruel and infernal manner, but I escaped all these, passing the schrund by a snow-bridge, and reached the narrow gap (eleven thousand seven hundred feet altitude). There I found, to my delight, I could clamber down the south side, and that after I reached the edge of a little lake in which snowbergs were drifting, the rest of the way to the Matterhorn peak was nothing but simple scrambling over snow slopes, over the snout of the Matterhorn glacier, across moraines, down the faces of fissured precipices, up couloirs threatened with avalanches of loose stones, on up higher, higher, peaks in crowds rising all around — Dana, Hoffman, Ritter, pinnacles of the Minaret group — and I could see the Merced group clouded with ice and snow, and glaciers near and far, and a score of lake gems. With many a rest for breath and for gazing upon the sublimity of the ever-changing landscape, and without any fierce effort or very apparent danger, I reached the topmost stone.

Selected Bibliography

Sources Used in This Anthology

Anon. "A Ramble among the White Mountains." *Worcester Scientific and Historical Journal* 1 (October 1825), 1–7.

Anon. "A Visit to Mount Ranier." *The Columbian* (Olympia, Wash.), Vol. I, No. 2, September 18, 1852, p. 2.

Bartram, William. *Travels through North and South Carolina.* Philadelphia: James and Johnson, 1791.

Belknap, Jeremy. *The History of New Hampshire.* Dover, NH: O. Crosby and J. Varney, 1812.

Bradford, William. *Bradford's History "Of Plimoth Plantation."* Boston: Wright & Potter, 1901.

Brewer, William H. *Up and Down California in 1860–1864.* New Haven: Yale University Press, 1930.

Brickell, John. *The Natural History of North Carolina.* Dublin: James Carson, 1737.

Byers, William Newton. "The Powell Expedition. From Grand Lake to Longs Peak." *The Daily Rocky Mountain News* (Denver, Colo.). Vol. X, No. 6, September 1, 1868, p. 1.

Byrd, William. *William Byrd's Histories of the Dividing Line Betwixt Virginia and North Carolina.* ed. William K. Boyd. Raleigh: The North Carolina Historical Commission, 1929.

Caruthers, William Alexander. *The Knights of the Horse-Shoe.* Wetumpka, AL: Charles Yancey, 1845.

Catesby, Mark. *The Natural History of Carolina, Florida and the Bahama Islands.* London: B. White, 1771.

Davidson, George. "The First Ascent of the Volcano Makushin." *Appalachia* IV (1884–1886), pp. 1–11.

Dryer, Thomas Jefferson. "First Ascent of Mount Hood." *The Oregonian* (Portland, Ore.), August 19, 1854, p. 1.

———. Letter concerning an ascent of Mount Saint Helens. *The Oregonian* (Portland, Ore.), September 3, 1853, p. 1.

Fallam, Robert. "The Expedition of Batts and Fallam: John Clayton's Transcript of the Journal of Robert Fallam," in Clarence Walworth Alvord and

Lee Bidgood, *The First Explorations of the Trans-Alleghany Region by the Virginians 1650–1674* (Cleveland: Arthur H. Clark, 1912).

Frémont, John Charles. *The Exploring Expedition to the Rocky Mountains, Oregon and California.* Buffalo, NY: Geo. H. Derby and Co., 1851.

Holmes, Julia Archibald. Letters concerning an ascent of Pikes Peak. *The Whig Press* (Middletown, NY), March 16 and March 23, 1859. Reprinted in *A Bloomer Girl on Pikes Peak 1858* (Denver: Denver Public Library, 1949).

Irving, Washington. *The Adventures of Captain Bonneville U.S.A. in the Rocky Mountains and the Far West.* New York: G. P. Putnam, 1861.

Isaacs, A. C. Article concerning an attempt on Mount Shasta. *California Daily Chronicle* (San Francisco), April 9, 1856.

James, Edwin. *Account of an Expedition . . . Under the Command of Major Stephen H. Long.* Philadelphia: Carey and Lea, 1823.

Josselyn, John. *New Englands Rarities Discovered.* London: G. Widdowes, 1672.

King, Clarence. *Mountaineering in the Sierra Nevada.* Boston: J. R. Osgood, 1872.

Lederer, John. *The Discoveries of John Lederer.* London: Samuel Hayrick, 1672. Reprinted in Clarence Walworth Alvord and Lee Bidgood, *The First Explorations of the Trans-Alleghany Region by the Virginians 1650–1674* (Cleveland: Arthur H. Clark, 1912).

Leonard, Zenas. *Narrative of the Adventures of Zenas Leonard.* Clearfield, PA: D. W. Moore, 1839.

Michaux, Andre. "Journal of Travels into Kentucky, July 15, 1793–April 11, 1796," in Reuben Gold Thwaites, ed., *Early Western Travels, 1748–1846* (Cleveland: Arthur H. Clark, 1904).

Mitchell, Elisha. "Notice of the Heights of Mountains in North Carolina." *The American Journal of Science and Arts* (January 1839), pp. 377–380.

Muir, John. *John of the Mountains: The Unpublished Journals of John Muir.* ed. Linnie Marsh Wolfe. Boston: Houghton Mifflin, 1938.

———. "A Near View of the High Sierra," in *The Mountains of California* (New York: The Century Co., 1894).

Pike, Zebulon Montgomery. *Account of Expeditions to the Sources of the Mississippi and through the Western Parts of Louisiana to the Sources of the Arkansaw.* Philadelphia: C. and A. Conrad et al., 1810.

Preuss, Charles. *Exploring with Frémont.* ed. Erwin G. and Elisabeth K. Gudde. Norman, OK: University of Oklahoma Press, 1958.

Redfield, William C. "Some Account of Two Visits to the Mountains in Essex County." *The Family Magazine* V (1838), pp. 345–354.

Thoreau, Henry David. *The Maine Woods.* Boston: Houghton Mifflin, 1893.

———. "A Walk to Wachusett." *The Boston Miscellany of Literature* (January 1843).

——. *A Week on the Concord and Merrimack Rivers*. Boston: Houghton Mifflin, 1867.

Turner, Charles Jr. "A Description of Natardin or Catardin Mountain." *Collections of the Massachusetts Historical Society*, Second Series, Vol. 8 (1819), pp. 112–116.

Winthrop, John. *Winthrop's Journal, "History of New England," 1630–1649*. ed. James Kendall Hosmer. New York: Barnes & Noble, 1908.

Other Writings by Early American Mountain Climbers

Ball, Benjamin Lincoln. *Three Days on the White Mountains; Being the Perilous Adventures of Dr. B. L. Ball on Mount Washington*. Boston: Nathaniel Noyes, 1856. Ball nearly died after being trapped on the mountain by a severe snowstorm.

Bigelow, Jacob. "Some Account of the White Mountains of New Hampshire." *New England Journal of Medicine and Surgery* 5 (November 1816), pp. 321–338. Bigelow was part of the wave of botanists who visited the White Mountains in the early nineteenth century.

Bowles, Samuel. *Across the Continent: A Summer's Journey to the Rocky Mountains, the Mormons and the Pacific States*. Springfield, MA: Samuel Bowles & Company, 1866. Bowles made a number of climbs, some on horseback, of easy peaks in the Rockies.

——. *The Switzerland of America: A Summer Vacation in the Parks and Mountains of Colorado*. Springfield, MA: Samuel Bowles & Company, 1869.

Brewer, William H. *Rocky Mountain Letters*. Denver: Colorado Mountain Club, 1930. These letters, written by Brewer to his wife from Colorado, include descriptions of climbs in the central Rockies.

Cutler, William Parker and Julia Perkins Cutler. *Life, Journals and Correspondence of Rev. Manasseh Cutler, L.L.D.* Cincinnati: Robert Clark & Company, 1888. Includes Cutler's version of the 1784 Mount Washington climb with Jeremy Belknap.

Pierce, James. "Notice of an Excursion among the White Mountains of New Hampshire, and to the Summit of Mount Washington." *American Journal of Science and Arts* 8 (August 1824), pp. 172–181.

Shattuck, George. "Some Account of an Excursion to the White Mountains of New Hampshire in the Year 1807." *Philadelphia Medical and Physical Journal* Vol. 3, Part 1 (1808), pp. 26–35.

Shepard, Forrest. "Notice of an Ascent up Mt. Lafayette and of Irised Shadows." *American Journal of Science and Arts* 12 (June 1827), p. 172ff.

Starr King, Thomas. *The White Hills: Their Legends, Landscape, and Poetry.* Boston: Crosby and Nichols, 1862.

Tuckerman, Edward. "A Further Enumeration of Some Interesting Plants of New England." *Boston Journal of Natural History* 5 (January 1845), pp. 93–104. Tuckerman, for whom Tuckerman Ravine was named, did much of his pioneering work in the study of lichens on Mount Washington.

———. "Observations of Some Interesting Plants of New England." *American Journal of Science and Arts* 45 (October 1843), pp. 27–49.

Whitney, Josiah Dwight. *The Yosemite Guidebook: A Description of the Yosemite Valley and the Adjacent Region.* Sacramento, CA: Geological Survey of California, 1869. Whitney was head of the California Geological Survey and John Muir's chief nemesis in matters of Sierra geology.

Works About Early
American Climbing and Climbers

Badè, William Frederic. *The Life and Letters of John Muir.* Boston: Houghton Mifflin, 1924.

Bent, Allen H. "Early American Mountaineers." *Appalachia* XIII (1913–1915), pp. 45–67.

Blair, John G. and Augustus Trowbridge. "Thoreau on Katahdin." *American Quarterly* 12 (1960), pp. 508–517.

Bueler, William M. *Roof of the Rockies: A History of Mountaineering in Colorado.* Boulder, CO: Pruett Publishing, 1974.

Burt, Allen F. *The Story of Mount Washington.* Hanover, NH: Dartmouth Publications, 1960.

Carpenter, Delma R. "The Route Followed by Governor Spotswood in 1716 across the Blue Ridge Mountains." *Virginia Magazine of History and Biography* LXXIII (October 1965), pp. 405–412.

Carson, Russell M. L. *Peaks and People of the Adirondacks.* Glens Falls, NY: Adirondack Mountain Club, 1986.

Coleman, E. T. "Mountains and Mountaineering in the Far West." *The Alpine Journal* 8 (August 1877), p. 232ff.

Connelly, Thomas L. *Discovering the Appalachians.* Harrisburg, PA: Stackpole Books, 1968.

Dodson, Leonidas. *Alexander Spotswood: Governor of Colonial Virginia, 1710–1722.* Philadelphia: University of Pennsylvania Press, 1932.

Ekstrom, Fannie Hardy. "Thoreau's 'Maine Woods.'" *Atlantic Monthly* 102 (1908), pp. 242–250.

Fagin, Bryllion. *William Bartram: Interpreter of the American Landscape.* Baltimore: 1933.

Farquhar, Francis Peloubet. *First Ascents in the United States.* Berkeley: Grabhorn Press, 1948.

———. *History of the Sierra Nevada.* Berkeley: University of California Press, 1966.

Frome, Michael. *Strangers in High Places: The Story of the Great Smoky Mountains.* Garden City, NY: Doubleday, 1966.

Graustein, Jeanette E. "Early Scientists in the White Mountains." *Appalachia* (June 1964), pp. 44–63.

Hart, John L. Jerome. "Seventy Years of Climbing on Longs Peak." *American Alpine Journal* 1/2 (1929), pp. 182–185.

Howarth, William L., ed. *Thoreau in the Mountains: Writings by Henry David Thoreau.* New York: Farrar Straus Giroux, 1982.

Jones, Chris. *Climbing in North America.* Berkeley: University of California Press, 1976.

McIntosh, James Henry. *Thoreau's Shifting Stance Toward Nature: A Study in Romanticism.* Ph.D. dissertation, Yale University, 1967.

Meany, Edmond Stephen, ed. *Mount Rainier: A Record of Exploration.* New York: Macmillan, 1916.

Peattie, Roderick, ed. *The Great Smokies and the Blue Ridge: The Story of the Southern Appalachians.* New York: The Vanguard Press, 1943.

Singer, Armand, ed. *Essays on the Literature of Mountaineering.* Morgantown, WV: West Virginia University Press, 1982.

Terrie, Philip G. "The High Peak of Essex." *Adirondac* (August 1987), pp. 20–22.

Tuckerman, Edward. "History of the Exploration of the White Hills," in Thomas Starr King, *The White Hills: Their Legends, Landscape and Poetry* (Boston: Crosby & Nichols, 1862).

Tuckerman, Frederick. "Early Visits to the White Mountains." *Appalachia* XV (August 1921), pp. 122ff.

Waterman, Laura and Guy Waterman. "The Marcy Explorations: Sesquicentennial." *Adirondac* Vol. 50, No. 7, pp. 12–15.

———. "Reverends, Soldiers, Scientists: The Belknap-Cutler Ascent of Mount Washington, 1784." *Appalachia* 178 (Summer 1984), pp. 41–52.

Wilkins, Thurman. *Clarence King: A Biography.* New York: The Macmillan Company, 1958.

Bibliographies

Anon. *Bibliography of Southern Appalachia.* Boone, NC: Appalachian Consortium Press, 1976.

Banks, Mary and Eleanor Ruth Lockwood. *Bibliography of the Cascade Mountains.* Portland, OR: The Mazamas, 1905 and 1907.

Bent, Allen H. *A Bibliography of the White Mountains*. Boston: Houghton Mifflin, 1941.

Downes, William Howe. "Literature of the White Mountains." *New England Magazine* (July 1891).

Farquhar, Francis Peloubet. *The Literature of Mountaineering*. Boston: Appalachian Mountain Club, 1940.

Fisher, Joel E. *Bibliography of Alaskan and Pacific Coast States Mountain Ascents*. 1945.

———. *Bibliography of Eastern Seaboard Mountain Ascents*. 1945.

Mason, R. L. and Myron H. Avery. "A Bibliography for the Great Smokies." *Appalachia,* June 1931.

Smith, Edward S. C. and Myron H. Avery. *An Annotated Bibliography of Katahdin*. Washington, DC: The Appalachian Trail Conference, 1936. Supplement, 1937.

Wagner, Henry R. and Charles L. Camp. *The Plains and the Rockies: A Bibliography of Original Narratives of Travel and Adventure, 1800–1865*. San Francisco: 1953.

Key to Illustrations

Page 4 – View from "The Point," Lookout Mountain, Southern Appalachians, by Harry Fenn. From William Cullen Bryant, ed., *Picturesque America; Or, The Land We Live In* (New York: D. Appleton & Company, 1872), p. 55.

Page 14 – Mount Washington from the top of Thompson's Falls, Pinkham Pass, by Harry Fenn. *Picturesque America,* p. 164.

Page 17 – Mount Madison seen over Adams Ravine, artist unknown. From Thomas Starr King, *The White Hills, Their Legends, Landscape and Poetry* (Boston: Crosby and Nichols, 1862), p. 362.

Page 19 – Cumberland Gap in the Southern Appalachians, by Harry Fenn. *Picturesque America,* p. 233.

Page 28 – View of Chattanooga from Lookout Mountain, Southern Appalachians, by Harry Fenn. *Picturesque America,* p. 56.

Page 45 – Map of the "Enemy Mountains" in the Cherokee country of the Southern Appalachians, 1762, by Henry Timberlake. From *The Memoirs of Lieut. Henry Timberlake* (London: J. Ridley, W. Nicoll and C. Henderson, 1765).

Page 57 – Tuckerman Ravine from Hermit Lake, White Mountains, by Harry Fenn. *Picturesque America,* p. 160.

Page 63 – Cumberland Gap from Eagle Cliff, Southern Appalachians, by Harry Fenn. *Picturesque America,* p. 236.

Page 70 – Pike's map of "the internal part of Louisiana," 1808. From Elliott Coues, ed., *The Expeditions of Zebulon Montgomery Pike* (Minneapolis: Ross & Haines, 1965).

Page 75 – View of Pikes Peak from forty miles distant, artist unknown. From John Charles Frémont, *Report of the Exploring Expedition to the Rocky Mountains in the Year 1842* (Washington: Gales and Seaton, 1845), p. 114.

Page 82 – View from the Mount Washington Road, by Harry Fenn. *Picturesque America,* p. 151.

Page 89 – View of the Wind River Mountains, artist unknown. *Report,* p. 66.

Page 96—Pass in the Sierra Nevada of California, artist unknown. *Report,* p. 234.

Page 99—Yosemite Fall, by James D. Smillie. *Picturesque America,* p. 484.

Page 106—Great Trap Dyke at Avalanche Lake in the Adirondacks, artist unknown. From Ebenezer Emmons, *Geology of New-York, Part II* (Albany: A. White & J. Visscher, 1842).

Page 115—John Charles Frémont, artist unknown. From *The Expeditions of John Charles Frémont* (Chicago: University of Illinois Press, 1970), frontispiece.

Page 119—Central chain of the Wind River Mountains, artist unknown. *Report,* p. 70.

Page 138—White Mountains from Milan, artist unknown. *The White Hills,* frontispiece.

Page 151—Crawford Notch in the White Mountains, by Harry Fenn. *Picturesque America,* p. 157.

Page 157—Map of Oregon and Upper California (detail), by Charles Preuss. *Expeditions,* map portfolio.

Page 162—Cliffs on the Yellowstone, by Harry Fenn. *Picturesque America,* p. 301.

Page 167—Mount Hood from the Columbia River, by R. Swain Gifford. *Picturesque America,* p. 49.

Page 174—The Three Sisters, by R. Swain Gifford. *Picturesque America,* p. 424.

Page 177—Mount Shasta, by James D. Smillie. *Picturesque America,* p. 424.

Page 186—Lassen Peak, by R. Swain Gifford. *Picturesque America,* p. 412.

Page 195—View of the High Sierra, Kings River region, by Bolton Coit Brown. From *The Sierra Club Bulletin,* 1896.

Page 204—Arrow Peak from the North, Kings River Sierra, by Bolton Coit Brown. *Sierra Club Bulletin.*

Page 215—Mount King in the Kings River Sierra, by Bolton Coit Brown. *Sierra Club Bulletin.*

Page 228—Maj. John Wesley Powell, artist unknown. From F. V. Hayden, ed., *The Great West: Its Attractions and Resources* (Bloomington, IL: Charles R. Brodix, 1880), p. 1.

Page 235—View of Yosemite Valley from foot of the Sentinel Fall, by James D. Smillie. *Picturesque America,* p. 479.

Page 236—View of Yosemite Valley from Clouds Rest in the High Sierra, by James D. Smillie. *Picturesque America,* p. 491.

Page 249—Rock pinnacles in Northern California, by R. Swain Gifford. *Picturesque America,* p. 416.

Page 252—Tenaya Canyon from Glacier Point in the Sierra, by James D. Smillie. *Picturesque America,* p. 488.